AMERICAN PARTIES
IN DECLINE

AMERICAN PARTIES IN DECLINE

Second Edition

WILLIAM CROTTY
Northwestern University

LITTLE, BROWN AND COMPANY
Boston   Toronto

Library of Congress Cataloging in Publication Data

Crotty, William J.
American parties in decline.

Includes index.
1. Political parties—United States.   I. Title.
JK2261.C84   1984   324.273'09   84-930
ISBN 0-316-16224-8

Library of Congress Catalog Card No. 84–930

ISBN 0-316-16224-8

9 8 7 6 5 4 3 2 1

ALP
Published simultaneously in Canada
by Little, Brown & Company (Canada) Limited

Printed in the United States of America

Preface

This book is intended for students in introductory courses on American government and for students in courses on political parties. It is meant as an introduction to the current state and contemporary difficulties of the parties, to supplement the more standardized treatments found in textbooks on American government and on political parties concerning the operations and functioning of political parties in a democratic society.

We are witnessing a decline in the role and significance of political parties in the United States. The reasons for this decline are many: society is changing; a new technology of politics has arisen; an evolving electorate is placing new and unaccustomed demands on the party agencies. The political parties are responding as best they can. The overall result is a period of confusion and an evolving transformation in the party system. In this book we analyze these concerns. In the process, we will attempt to assess the current status and the continuing difficulties facing the political parties.

The book is divided into four parts. The first three carry the burden of the substantive argument. In Part I we review the changes of the last two decades in the mood and composition of the electorate as well as the implications these changes have for the political parties. Particularly significant are the rise in issue orientation and the accelerating trend toward independent voting. In

Part II we introduce the technology of the new politics. Emphasis is placed on the role of money in winning office, the rising significance of corporate and trade Political Action Committees (PACs), single-issue and ideological groups, and campaign consultants, the gurus of the new politics, and the services they offer. All have contributed significantly to the decline of political parties.

In Part III we analyze the problems of, and the transformations within, the party in the government, and, more specifically, the parties in Congress. Party loyalty is decreasing, and this fact is especially true in Congress. We trace the reasons for this decrease and explore the implications of this trend for presidential-congressional relations and for policy outcomes. The Epilogue is a brief conclusion that reviews some of the issues raised by the weakening of a once vital party system for a democratic form of governance.

We wish to extend our particular thanks to Don Palm, the political science editor, and to Susan McNally, Victoria Keirnan, Kimberley Rieck, Janice Friedman, Diana Scott, and Carolyn Ingalls, who oversaw the book's production at Little, Brown.

William Crotty

Contents

I
THE DECLINE OF THE
PARTY IN THE ELECTORATE

Introduction

The American electorate of the late twentieth century is a "turned-off" electorate. It is characterized by low levels of voter participation; a decline in party loyalty, with a concomitant increase in split-ticket voting and wild and unpredictable swings in outcomes and vote margins from one election to the next; an increasing emphasis on issue voting; and claims, at least, of a more ideological electorate. All have significance for the operations and continued vitality of the party system.

"Turn out is a turn off"

1
Participation in Elections: A "Turned-Off" Electorate

TURNOUT

The number of nonvoters in the United States is reaching critical proportions.[1] However, the problem of nonvoting is little understood and badly underresearched. It has received little public or political attention. The major voting studies have focused on voting and, more specifically, voter decision making in choosing between candidates and parties in an election year. Little attention has been, or is even now, given to the fact that nonvoting is increasing. Without being unduly alarmist, we may say that it is reaching epidemic proportions. As one commentator has noted,

[1] Among the available studies see: Sidney Verba and Norman H. Nie, *Participation in America: Political Democracy and Social Equality* (New York: Harper and Row, 1972); S. Verba, N. Nie, and J. Kim, *Participation and Political Equality: A Seven-Nation Comparison* (Cambridge: Cambridge University Press, 1978); Arthur T. Hadley, *The Empty Polling Booth* (Englewood Cliffs, N.J.: Prentice-Hall, 1978); Penn Kimble, *The Disconnected* (New York: Columbia University Press, 1972); W. Crotty, *Political Reform and the American Experiment* (New York: Thomas Y. Crowell, 1977); and Samuel A. Kirkpatrick, ed., "Voter Turnout," *American Politics Quarterly*, Vol. 9 (April 1981).

TABLE 1.1
Voter Turnout in Selected Democratic Nations

Country	Turnout	Country	Turnout
Malta	94.4%	New Zealand	82.7%
Australia	92.6	Israel	78.2
Austria	91.9	Ireland	75.7
Sweden	91.4	Canada	74.9
Italy	90.8	Great Britain	72.8
Iceland	90.3	Japan	72.6
West Germany	89.9	India	60.5
Belgium	88.3	United States	54.4
Denmark	88.2	(presidential)	
Holland	87.5	Switzerland	51.7
France	83.5	United States	37.0
Norway	82.8	(midterm)	

Source: Data compiled by the British journal *The Economist*. Used by permission.

voting is now a "minority habit."[2] By any standards, the problem is severe.

In contrast to that in other democratic nations, voter turnout in the United States is anemic. In fact, in comparisons with twenty-one other democratic countries, the United States ranks last (Table 1.1). Its position is challenged only by Switzerland, a country whose constant referenda on matters of public concern apparently overtax its citizenry's interest. It is claimed that American voting turnout exceeds that of only one other democracy — Botswana.

Curtis Gans of the Committee for the Study of the American Electorate, a bipartisan, nonprofit research group that concentrates on studying voter turnout, argues,

> The central and perhaps the greatest single problem of the American polity today is . . . the degree to which the vital underpinnings of American democracy are being eroded. The legitimacy of a democratic leadership and the health of the democratic process depend squarely on the informed and active participation of

[2] Martin F. Nolan, "The Off-Year Election Blues," *Boston Globe*, October 15, 1978, p. A1.

Is the decline irreversible?

the electorate. Yet the level of political participation is now sinking *and the decline seems irreversible.* [Italics added.][3]

These are somber words, but Gans's committee is prepared to back them up. The seriousness of the situation is fully apparent.

— During the last ten years, fully 15 million Americans who were once regular voters have dropped out of the political process.

— Nearly 70 million eligible Americans failed to vote in the 1976 presidential election; more than 100 million eschewed the ballot box in the congressional election of 1974.

Fewer than 28 percent of Jimmy Carter's fellow citizens voted for him in the presidential election of 1976; Brendan Byrne became governor of New Jersey with a mandate of less than 15 percent of New Jersey's eligible voters; Mayor Koch was the choice of less than 12 percent of New York City's electorate; Senator Henry Jackson won the 1976 New York presidential primary with less than 6 percent of the total vote.[4]

a minority selects leadership

Alarm appears justified. American voting turnout over time is decreasing, and it has reached unusual lows (Table 1.2). Moreover, it is not likely to improve significantly in the immediate future. About one-half or a little more of the American people vote in presidential contests, the most highly publicized of elections. Turnout in these elections has been consistently declining from highs of over 60 percent in the 1960s. By the 1970s it was in the mid-fiftieth percentiles. In terms of numbers, rather than percentages, the severity of the decline is more apparent. In a voting age population of 150 million in 1980, over 68 million Americans did not participate in even the most rudimentary form of political expression: casting their ballot for a presidential nominee.

Lance Tarrance has used governmental statistical sources to estimate the number of registered voters in each election since 1928 and the division of the vote among the parties. He has introduced the conception of the "Non-Voter" party, a term that covers the numbers of people not participating in presidential elections.[5]

[3] Curtis B. Gans, "The Empty Ballot Box: Reflections on Nonvoters in America," *Public Opinion,* September/October 1978, p. 54.

[4] *Ibid.*

[5] V. Lance Tarrance, "Suffrage and Voter Turnout in the United States: The Vanishing Voter," in Jeff Fishel (ed.), *Parties and Elections in an Anti-Party Age* (Bloomington: Indiana University Press, 1978), pp. 77–85.

TABLE 1.2
Turnout in Presidential and Congressional Elections, 1920–82

Year	Office President	Office U.S. House	Year	Office President	Office U.S. House
1920	43.5%	40.8%	1952	61.6%	57.6%
1922	—	32.1	1954	—	41.7
1924	43.9	40.6	1956	59.3	55.9
1926	—	29.8	1958	—	43.0
1928	51.8	47.7	1960	62.8	58.5
1930	—	33.7	1962	—	45.4
1932	52.4	49.7	1964	61.9	57.8
1934	—	41.4	1966	—	45.4
1936	56.0	53.5	1968	60.9	55.1
1938	—	44.0	1970	—	43.5
1940	58.9	55.4	1972	55.5	51.9
1942	—	32.5	1974	—	36.2
1944	56.0	52.7	1976	54.3	49.6
1946	—	37.1	1978	—	35.5
1948	51.1	48.1	1980	53.2	47.9
1950	—	41.1	1982	—	37.8

Source: U.S. Department of Commerce, Bureau of the Census, *Statistical Abstract of the United States* (Washington, D.C.: U.S. Government Printing Office, 1972 and 1981). The data for 1920–1930 are from the 1972 edition (Table 597, p. 373); the data for 1932–1980 are from the 1981 edition (Table 824, p. 496).

Richard Nixon won a landslide victory in 1972 with the greatest plurality in votes (19 million) ever recorded by a presidential candidate. Yet the "Non-Voter" party easily won the election with 62 million votes to Nixon's 47 million. In 1976, Jimmy Carter was elected president by 28 percent of the voters. Forty-five percent of the eligible electorate chose not to vote. In 1980, Ronald Reagan's "ideological revolution" was launched by 27 percent of the nation's electorate in an election in which 47 percent of the eligible voters did not participate.

The significance of these figures is manifold. The largest number of potential voters is not supporting one candidate or party or the other. Rather, these people are withdrawing from the electorate. The number of nonvoters has always been substantial; but there was solace in the belief that participation rates seemed to be climbing, slowly to be sure, but consistently. Unfortunately, this is no longer the case. The rates are falling, and the numbers of nonparticipants are increasing substantially. From the 1950s through 1968, the average percentage of eligible voters not turning out was 39 percent, and the average number of people not participating was under 43 million. These figures may be high in cross-national perspective, but they look good when compared to those of the 1970s and 1980s. An expanded electorate exacerbated the problem. Turnout rates in the 1970s and 1980s are a little over one-half of the eligible adult (18 years and older) population and, most importantly, the number of nonvoters *now averages more than 60 million*. And the figures are still climbing.[6]

The potential impact of these nonvoters (if they participated) in close elections, such as 1976 (or 1968 or 1960), would be decisive, of course. Even the pluralities in the lopsided contests (1980) pale in comparison to the numbers who simply do not vote. Any of the election outcomes in the modern era could have been reversed through the participation in sufficient numbers of those who have withdrawn from the electorate. No president in modern American history has been elected by a majority of the electorate. This includes, as indicated, the overwhelming victories of Lyndon Johnson and Richard Nixon.

The thought is sobering. Equally important are the problems caused for an otherwise stable and vigorous democratic order that fails to include sizable portions of its citizenry in its active electorate. It is reasonable to believe that people who consistently do not vote receive minimal representation (at best) of their views. Their ties to the political system are not likely to be strong, and they provide the potential — should the right candidate or combination of circumstances come along — for a major disruption of the American political scene. Nonvoting of this magnitude is not a healthy condition for a democratic society.

LOWER-LEVEL CONTESTS

We might expect presidential elections to have modest turn-outs because they are the farthest removed from the individual

[6] *Ibid.*

voter and his concerns. As contests become closer to home, voter interest and familiarity with the candidates and issues should rise, leading to corresponding increases in turnout. This is not the case. Presidential elections consistently excite the most interest and the highest levels of involvement. As one progresses from these contests to the congressional, state, and local races, voters' information about the contests, their enthusiasm for participating, and their rates of involvement drop substantially.[7] For example, as shown in Table 1.2, there is a fall off in voting for congressional offices during presidential years. In midterm contests, the voter turnout can drop ten to fifteen percentage points. At present, less than 40 percent of the electorate votes in off-year congressional races. In absolute terms, although the eligible voting-age population increased 5.4 million between 1976 and 1978, voting participation dropped 13 million. Better than 96 million adults did not bother to vote in the 1978 off-year election, and over 100 million did not in 1982.

These figures are troublesome, and they get no better as we examine state and local races. The Committee for the Study of the American Electorate, mentioned earlier, noted that the combined turnout (37.9 percent) for all races in the 1978 election year was the lowest since 1942.[8] An analysis of voter involvement in elections in New York, New Jersey, and Connecticut over several decades found that turnout had dropped perceptibly.[9] In presidential elections for 1952–76, turnout was down 11 percent in New York State and 9 percent in both New Jersey and Connecticut. The falloff was particularly noticeable in the largest cities such as New York, where the decline in voting participation reached 25 percent. In terms of numbers (rather than percentages), and despite the population growth, fewer people voted in New York State in 1976 (6.6 million) than in 1952 (7.2 million). In gubernatorial races in New York between 1958 and 1978, the proportion turning out fell twenty-nine percentage points (and forty points in New York City). The decline in participation rates for gubernatorial elections in New Jersey and Connecticut was fifteen and fourteen percentage points, respectively. The percentage of eligible citizens who

[7] Crotty, *Political Reform,* pp. 49–52.

[8] Report of the Committee for the Study of the American Electorate, December 18, 1978.

[9] Frank Lynn, "Voter Apathy Found Throughout 3 States of Metropolitan Area," *The New York Times,* January 22, 1979, p. 1. © 1979 by The New York Times Company. Reprinted by permission.

registered and voted in these three states in 1978 ranged between 38 and 47 percent of those eligible.[10]

One other distressing fact needs to be reported. Although voter turnout has consistently decreased, the social and demographic factors associated with a higher turnout have actually become more prevalent in the population. Norman Nie has found that although participation rates did not improve between 1952 and 1968,

> during this same period, however, many of the variables which we know to be highly correlated with levels of political participation have been rising, and rising rapidly. Median years of education have risen in this sixteen-year period from 9.5 to 12.1, and the proportion of the population who have completed college has just about doubled. Income, which opens the way for a greater variety of leisure activities, has risen dramatically, and the proportion of the population in white-collar occupations has increased by almost 10 percent. Yet levels of participation which are so highly correlated with these factors (income, occupation, and education jointly explain as much as 20 percent of the variance in rates of participation in the United States) have not been substantially altered.[11]

These demographic characteristics continue to become more prevalent, while actual voter participation continues to drop.

OTHER POLITICAL ACTIVITY

If people do not vote, they are not at all likely to engage in any of the other forms of political activity.[12] Table 1.3 illustrates the tendency. The number of individuals engaging in each of the activities is overreported (e.g., more claim to have voted than actually do). Nonetheless, the proportionate differences between the types of political behavior engaged in should be approximately

---

[10] Ibid.

[11] Norman H. Nie, "Future Developments in Mass Communications and Citizen Participation," in Albert Somit (ed.), Political Science and the Study of the Future (Hinsdale, Ill.: Dryden, 1975), p. 141, as quoted in Harry Holloway and John George, Public Opinion: Coalitions, Elites and Masses (New York: St. Martin's Press, 1979), p. 59.

[12] For analysis of different "modes," or patterns of participation, see Verba and Nie, Participation in America.

TABLE 1.3
Political Activity of the American Electorate, 1980

I. Activities	Engaged in Activity	
	Yes	No
Voted[a]	54%	46%
Tried to influence others (how to vote)	36	64
Attended political meetings, dinners, rallies, etc.	7	93
Worked for a political party or candidate	4	96
Wore a campaign button or put a sticker on the car	7	93
Took a tax check-off for a contribution to the presidential campaign fund	33	67
Gave money to a presidential candidate	6	94

II.   *Summary Index of Political Activities*[b]
      (based on above activities)

	Voters	Nonvoters
No activities	36.6%	55.2%
One activity	36.0	29.9
Two activities	17.5	10.7
Three activities	5.4	2.7
Four activities or more	4.6	1.5

[a] Voters are validated voters in the sample.
[b] Figures do not add to 100% because of rounding.
Source: Data supplied by the Center for Political Studies.

correct. The vast majority of respondents claim to have voted. One-third of the voters tried to influence others as to how they should vote, and one-fifth to one-fourth wrote public officials or newspaper editors or contributed money to political campaigns.

Nonvoters, in contrast, were not even this moderately involved in political life. In fact they appeared to have little interest in any political input. Better than one-half took no part in campaigning in any form, including wearing a candidate's button or placing bumper stickers on their cars. Better than 80 percent do not contribute financially to anyone's campaign, and between 70 and 80 percent have not, at any point in their lives, written public officials or newspapers on matters of consequence. Two-thirds of the nonvoters do not become involved at even the lowest and easiest level of participation, by attempting to influence someone they come in contact with as to how they should vote. Most of the nonvoters engage in no activities whatsoever. The bulk of the rest participate in few activities. Two-thirds of the voters, on the other hand, become involved in one or more political acts, beyond voting.

When asked what response they had taken to either national or local problems, nonvoters by and large report taking none. One-third of the voters on the national level and one-half on the local level engage in some activity to make their wishes known to political authorities. On the local level, voters appear particularly involved in alternative forms of political expression. Nonvoters are basically inactive on all levels. If people do not vote, the chances are excellent they will not participate in any other form of political processes. In effect, they remain outside the political system, unrepresented and ignored.

THE NONVOTERS

Nonvoters are a fairly predictable lot (Table 1.4). Traditionally, the South, the border states, and rural areas have a lower voter turnout than do other localities. Youth is definitely correlated with low rates of political involvement. Individuals thirty-five and under vote considerably less than those thirty-six to sixty-five, and first- and second-time eligibles are the least involved of any. The Center for Political Studies reported a substantial difference (16 percent) between 18–20-year-olds and 21–24-year-olds in their participation rates in 1972.[13] Similar differences were evident in 1976 and 1980. Young voters, and particularly those eligible for the first time, do not participate in large numbers.

Generally speaking also, people of lower occupational achievement, people who are not union members, those who identify

[13] Arthur H. Miller and Warren E. Miller, "Issues, Candidates, and Partisan Divisions in the 1972 American Presidential Election," *British Journal of Political Science* 5 (1975): 429.

TABLE 1.4
Voting and Nonvoting in the 1980 Presidential Election[a]

I.   Demographic Characteristics

Region	Voters	Nonvoters
New England	67.1%	32.9%
Middle Atlantic	52.5	47.5
East North Central	51.9	48.1
West North Central	68.0	32.0
Solid South	46.5	53.5
Border States	54.8	45.2
Mountain States	68.8	31.3
Pacific States	59.7	40.3

Size of Place	Voters	Nonvoters
Twelve largest cities	54.3%	45.7%
Other large cities	49.0	51.0
Suburbs of twelve largest cities	55.3	44.7
Other suburbs	56.1	43.9
Adjacent areas	54.7	45.3
Outlying areas	58.6	41.4

Age	Voters	Nonvoters
18–24	33.3%	66.7%
25–35	47.4	52.6
36–50	62.8	37.2
51–65	63.2	36.8
66 and over	60.9	39.1

Education	Voters	Nonvoters
Eighth grade or less	46.2%	53.8%
Some high school	40.5	59.5
High school	44.7	55.3
High school plus noncollege schooling	60.0	40.0
Some college	57.5	42.5
College graduate	71.6	28.4
Advanced degree	78.0	22.0

Self-Report Ideology	Voters	Nonvoters
None	45.7%	54.3%
Extreme liberal	52.0	48.0

(Continued)

TABLE 1.4 (continued)

I.   Demographic Characteristics

Self-Report Ideology	Voters	Nonvoters
Liberal	64.1	35.9
Slightly liberal	60.2	39.8
Moderate	54.5	45.5
Slightly conservative	58.7	41.3
Conservative	64.8	35.2
Very conservative	57.6	42.4

Union Membership	Voters	Nonvoters
Member	56.5%	43.5%
Nonmember	53.9	46.1

Class Identification	Voters	Nonvoters
Average working class	45.3%	54.7%
Working class	40.0	60.0
Upper working class	54.2	45.8
Average middle	60.6	39.4
Middle class	53.3	46.7
Upper middle	70.7	29.3

Income Level	Voters	Nonvoters
Under $3000	49.2%	50.8%
$3000–5999	49.8	50.2
$6000–10,999	47.6	52.4
$11,000–16,999	58.0	42.0
$17,000–25,000	64.5	35.5
Over $25,000	72.1	27.9

Religion	Voters	Nonvoters
Protestant	55.0%	45.0%
Catholic	54.3	45.7
Jewish	66.0	34.0

Sex	Voters	Nonvoters
Male	56.2%	43.8%
Female	52.9	47.1

TABLE 1.4 (continued)

Race	Voters	Nonvoters
White	56.0%	44.0%
Black	43.5	56.5

II.   *Party and Political Measures*

Party Identification	Voters	Nonvoters
Strong Democrat	66.1%	33.9%
Weak Democrat	54.1	45.9
Independent Democrat	49.3	50.7
Independent	36.8	63.2
Independent Republican	60.5	39.5
Weak Republican	65.3	34.7
Strong Republican	73.3	26.7

III.   *Information on Politics*

Interest in Campaign	Voters	Nonvoters
Very interested	70.7%	29.3%
Somewhat interested	56.5	43.5
Not interested	31.4	68.6

Watch Evening National News Broadcasts on Television	Voters	Nonvoters
Every evening	57.3%	42.7%
3–4 times a week	53.6	46.4
1–2 times a week	50.9	49.1
Less often	53.0	47.0
Never	48.5	51.5

Read a Daily Newspaper	Voters	Nonvoters
Yes	62.9%	37.1%
No	44.2	55.8

[a] Voters are validated voters.

Note: The difference between voters and nonvoters according to size of place, union membership, and religion are not statistically significant as computed by the chi-square statistic.

Source: Data supplied by the Center for Political Studies.

themselves as working-class or below, and those of lower incomes vote less than others. Jews, whites, and males have comparatively higher turnout rates than others.

The impact of education on turnout and the role of education more generally in explaining the increasing issue orientation of the electorate has been a matter of some debate.[14] People with less education vote and participate less in politics. This much is accepted. In Table 1.4, for example, education is strongly associated with voting. People with a high school education or less are markedly less likely to vote than those with some college or advanced degree work. Arthur Miller, Warren Miller, and their associates at the Center for Political Studies have reported that turnout fell disproportionately between 1964 and 1972 for the lower-educated while holding relatively stable among the higher-educated. Voting was down ten percentage points for the grade-school-educated, eight points for the high-school-educated, and only two points for the college-educated.[15] They suggest that the drop in participation rates is due mostly to those with the least formal education, in effect accentuating the trend toward the underrepresentation of those of low socioeconomic status.

Miller, Miller, Raine, and Brown's explanation for the increasing importance of education as a predictor of turnout has significance for the discussion of the increasing importance of issues in elections:

> As the focus of analysis moves across educational levels from grade school to college, the bulk of the explanatory power shifts from candidate image to issues and ideology. Voters with college educations are better informed politically, generally more cognizant of policy differences between the candidates and, therefore, more likely to make a decision on the basis of policy preferences than are

[14] For different perspectives, see *ibid.*; Philip E. Converse, "Public Opinion and Voting Behavior," in Fred I. Greenstein and Nelson W. Polsby (eds.), *The Handbook of Political Science*, Vol. 4 (Reading, Mass.: Addison-Wesley, 1975), pp. 75–169; Norman H. Nie, with Kristi Andersen, "Mass Belief Systems Revisited: Political Change and Attitude Structure," *Journal of Politics* 36 (1974): 540–87; and Lester W. Milbrath and M. L. Goel, *Political Participation*, 2nd ed. (Chicago: Rand McNally, 1977), pp. 98–102.

[15] Arthur H. Miller, Warren E. Miller, Alden S. Raine, and Thad A. Brown, "A Majority Party in Disarray: Policy Polarization in the 1972 Election," *American Political Science Review* 70 (1976), as reprinted in Richard G. Niemi and Herbert F. Weisberg (eds.), *Controversies in American Voting Behavior* (San Francisco: Freeman, 1976), pp. 176–95.

less well educated individuals. It is apparently far easier for college-educated individuals to translate issue attitudes into a vote decision than for the relatively less well educated who use the candidate as an intervening focus for their ideology.[16]

An issue-oriented electorate has less room for the poorly educated. One of the functions of a strong party system includes mobilizing the vote, expanding the electorate to represent as many people as possible. The American party system did this imperfectly, but apparently a good deal better than other less vigorous party systems now in the offing.

Another function of the party for the individual was to structure the vote; to allow him a point of reference in making his choice that minimized the need for an extensive investment of time and effort to acquire information, organize it, and relate it to the political world. Perhaps an electorate in which the party system no longer fulfills the function of structuring information and providing powerful cues to influence the individual's vote is one that makes the costs and personal investment needed to participate too high for those with fewer resources (in this case, formal educational achievements) to meet. Electoral decision making may become increasingly uncomfortable for them, and they may drop out to join the expanding ranks of the nonvoters.

In terms of attitudinal measures, independents and weak Democrats are among those least likely to vote. Strong party identifiers, led by the especially impressive vote of strong Republicans, have the highest participation rates. People who are weakly socialized to politics — that is, whose parents had little political interest — vote decidedly less than those who report one or both parents with a good deal of interest. Correspondingly, among those individuals with least interest themselves in political events, less than one-half vote. Among the most interested, 70 percent vote. More generally, individuals with low levels of trust, those who can find little to be proud of in American government, those who have little concern about the election outcome, and those who either sporadically or rarely follow public affairs, have a depressed voter turnout.

The informational questions indicate that those who watch Roger Mudd, Dan Rather, or John Chancellor on the evening

[16] *Ibid.*, p. 193.

news frequently are likely to vote. An even stronger predictor of the vote may be the newspaper. People who habitually read a daily newspaper appear to be considerably different from those who do not. In terms of the vote, 63 percent of the newspaper readers as against only 56 percent of the nonreaders vote.

Overall then, those on the lower end of the social ladder — the less-educated and those of lower economic status, occupational achievement, and income potential — and the young are disproportionately represented among the nonvoters. These are the same people with less input into the political system — through such things as contributions to campaigns, personal access to party officials and public officeholders, outlets for their views through the media and representation through established professional and economic interest groups — than others. It is a fact of political life that those least likely to vote are also those least likely to participate in politics in any other form.

REASONS FOR NONVOTING: STRUCTURAL

It is presently unfashionable to blame registration requirements for the low voter turnout. The rules have been improved significantly since the passage of the Voting Rights Act in 1965, and its reenactment each five years (as required in the original law).[17] Congress has made an effort to lighten the requirements for qualifying to vote in federal elections, and it has also attempted to modernize some of the procedures (as, for example, in filing absentee ballots). However, it has been most reluctant to go much further. It has proved hostile in the late 1970s to the Carter administration's proposals to reduce registration barriers to the bare essentials and to require only election-day registration in federal contests. If Congress had adopted such a plan, many (perhaps most) states and localities would have been forced to go along for reasons of practicality and the added cost of administering two separate systems (state and national).

Congress refused to adopt the plan and, after the initial rebuff, the Carter administration abandoned it. The Reagan administration has no interest in pursuing such reforms. Both Congress and the state legislatures — and, in fact, most practicing poli-

---

[17] Crotty, *Political Reform*, pp. 72–100.

ticians — fear the impact of drastic registration changes that would redefine the electorate by substantially increasing its numbers. Politicians are content to maintain an electorate they understand and with which they have had success. Self-interest favors retention of the familiar and the safe.

There is another reason also for the antipathy to registration reform. Congress and most of the states still distrust schemes promoting too easy participation. Meeting the hurdles posed by registration practices is seen as a matter of faith. The privilege (as against right) of being eligible to participate in elections is perceived as something a citizen should gain on his or her own initiative. The concept is a throwback to a theme that has dominated the thinking concerning registration and one that has produced a strain between the nation's democratic impulse and the desire for a restricted franchise.[18]

The present jumble of registration practices was introduced between 1890 and 1920. These practices were adopted in response to the political muscle exercised by an odd coalition of reformers and practical politicians. The Progressives wanted strict standards for qualifying voters in order to institutionalize within the electorate the middle-class virtues they represented. Through these measures they hoped to correct many of the machine abuses of the day by, in part, denying the vote to the urban ethnic groups that constituted the machine's base. Machine politicians accepted registration requirements as a means for ensuring a restricted and controllable electorate, sensitive to their wishes. Machines feared large voter turnouts that could result in unpredictable election outcomes. Finally, there were the southern whites who wanted to regain control of their region's politics. Stiff registration standards allowed them constitutionally to disenfranchise blacks (and lower-class whites also, if need be) and to again assume the political reigns within their states. All three elements of the coalition gained what they wanted with the resultant jumble of procedures and requirements coming on down to our own time.[19]

[18] *Ibid.*, pp. 3–45.

[19] *Ibid.*, pp. 11–42; Philip E. Converse, "Change in the American Electorate," in Angus Campbell and Philip E. Converse (eds.), *The Human Meaning of Social Change* (New York: Russell Sage, 1972), pp. 263–337; Walter Dean Burnham, "Theory and Voting Research: Some Reflections on Converse's 'Change in the American Electorate,' " *American Political Science Review* 68 (1974): 1002–23; and Jerrold G. Rusk, "The American Electoral Universe: Speculation and Evidence," *American Political Science Review* 68 (1974): 1028–49.

Registration practices were not invented in the Progressive era. They were universally applied to elections during that time, however. The idea underlying the institution of such rules went back to colonial times and to the belief in the qualitative vote: an individual should prove himself worthy of participation in community affairs. Voting, in effect, was a reward for good citizenship. The practice goes back to pre-Revolutionary times, when the right to have a voice in community decisions was restricted in some colonies to the company shareholders who put up the money for the venture and in other colonies to the members of the recognized church ("the elect"). Admission to these ranks was not bestowed frivolously.

At various points in American history, qualifying provisions were adopted that related to property holding, wealth, moral behavior, education (or the ability to read and interpret parts of a state or federal constitution to the satisfaction of an election official), and so on. Such laws disenfranchised at various times the poor, ethnics, blacks, Orientals, members of various religious groups (Jews, for example), institutionalized populations, the highly mobile, unmarried couples, Indians, and people who committed certain types of criminal acts. Many of those laws and the screening procedures used to enforce them are still on the books. The registration barriers have given way reluctantly. It took the civil rights revolution in the South in the early 1960s to bring about fundamental change and to spearhead the attack against the worst vestiges of the old order.

Over the last decade, the courts have become increasingly unsympathetic to registration barriers. The present rule of thumb in the federal courts is that registration laws that do not serve "a compelling state interest" are voided under the "equal protection" clause of the Fourteenth Amendment. The Supreme Court took this position in *Dunn* v. *Blumstein* (1972), a case that struck down unreasonably long residency requirements (of six months' to two years' duration) in state and local elections. The ruling brought state practices in line with federal procedures as mandated in the Voting Rights Act of 1970.[20]

---

[20] Crotty, *Political Reform*, p. 35. See also W. Crotty, ed., *Paths to Political Reform* (Lexington, Mass.: D. C. Heath, 1980), for a discussion of alternative registration strategies.

Nevertheless, the old traditions die hard. Congress has rejected attempts either to minimize the barriers or to facilitate registration through governmental initiatives in reaching and enrolling voters (as is done in most other democratic nations). As a consequence, registration formulas persist that deny each citizen equal access to the polls.

A study by Steven Rosenstone and Raymond Wolfinger of turnout in the 1972 presidential election estimated that registration laws reduced voting by about 6 to 10 percent. The regulations had their greatest impact in the South and more generally on the poorly educated. Less restrictive procedures could increase the participation of southern blacks by approximately sixteen percentage points and southern whites by almost as much. Elsewhere, the authors estimate that an increase in turnout across the board of roughly nine percentage points would constitute a reasonable expectation.[21] Arthur Hadley, who executed the most comprehensive analysis of nonvoting in the 1976 election, feels that more facilitative registration procedures might increase turnout among some groups by up to eighteen percentage points.[22]

The biggest structural barrier to the vote continues to be registration requirements. Registration has priority over voting and is a more difficult challenge to meet. Registration provisions are poorly understood, and enrollment periods often occur at times when people's political interest is dormant. By the time many prospective voters become aware of the candidates, their platform, and the issues of the day, and develop some interest in the election, it is often too late for them to meet registration requirements. As a consequence, they are unable to vote. This is more true of past elections when registration practices were more onerous, but it is still a problem. Data on the 1980 presidential election compiled by the Census Bureau indicate that 89 percent of the people who registered did actually vote (Table 1.5). Seemingly, the first and most obvious step in increasing turnout would be to simplify the registration barriers or possibly to eliminate them altogether. Curiously, such barriers are the ones most amenable to immediate relief, if the politicians so willed it.

[21] Steven J. Rosenstone and Raymond E. Wolfinger, "The Effects of Registration Laws on Voter Turnout," *American Political Science Review* 72 (March 1978): 22–45.

[22] Hadley, *Empty Polling Booth*, p. 119.

TABLE 1.5

Reasons for Not Registering and for Not Voting in the 1980 Presidential Election (In percentages)

I.   *Registration and Voter Turnout*

A.	Registered	66.9%	Not registered	33.1%
B.	Voted	59.2	Did not vote	40.8
C.	Registered, voted	88.6	Registered, did not vote	11.4

II.   *Reasons for not Registering (100%)*

A. Unable to register:

Recently moved	9.2%
Permanent illness or disability	4.1
Hours or place inconvenient	5.1
Other reasons unable to register	7.7

B. Did not want to register:

Did not prefer any of the likely candidates	8.5
Not interested, don't care, etc.	38.6

C. Other:

All other reasons for not registering	17.8
Don't know and reason not reported	8.8

III. *Reasons for not Voting When Registered (100%)*

A. Unable to vote:

No way to get to polls	4.1%
Could not take time off from work	7.6
Out of town or away from home	12.6
Sick or family emergency	17.1

B. Did not want to vote:

Did not prefer any of the candidates	16.0
Not interested, don't care, etc.	11.2

C. Other:

All other reasons for not voting	17.2
Don't know and reason not reported	14.1

Source: U.S. Department of Commerce, Bureau of the Census, "Voting and Registration in the Election of November 1980," *Current Population Reports, Population Characteristics* (Series P-20, No. 370, April 1982).

Registration alone, of course, is not the total cause of the problem. Its effects cannot be dismissed, but the malaise that has infected all aspects of American political life has certainly influenced the willingness of people to both register and to vote.

REASONS FOR NONVOTING: ATTITUDINAL

A principal cause of nonvoting clearly is the psychological malaise that dominates contemporary politics. Simply put, American voters appear "turned off" to virtually everything associated with politics. This theme pervades the current studies of the subject. Political parties, candidates, and elections are seen as irrelevant to the personal concerns of citizens and to the problems that plague the nation. People distrust governmental institutions, and they feel that they exercise no influence over what their government does and whom it serves. Voting, for such people, becomes a meaningless act. Robert Teeter, a pollster prominent in Republican-party circles, reported to a meeting of the nation's governors in the late 1970s that the most prevalent attitude found among prospective voters in his polls was the feeling that the individual could no longer influence the course of government action.[23] The result was that many people simply dropped out of the electorate. His Democratic counterpart told the same group, "The voter sees no link between his taxes and government spending." Although young people have failed to participate in large numbers, the most bitter group were those "between the ages of 50 and 64 who had planned for their retirements and now find their futures plucked from their hands."[24] The latter group should represent the core of a stable, reasonably satisfied electorate. It appears that little has changed.

Follow-up analyses of voter attitudes concerning elections pretty much support the pollsters' assertions. Some examples of voter attitude follow. A former peace activist in the 1960s: "Politi-

[23] F. Richard Ciccone, "Voters in Sour Mood, Pollsters Tell Governors," *Chicago Tribune*, August 29, 1978, Section 1, p. 5.
[24] *Ibid.*

cians are not doing their job. I don't give two cents for the whole lot of them. I've just lost interest in politics. Apathetic, I guess that's the word. I won't sit around arguing for the next ten years the way I did for the last ten."[25] A clerk in a department store in New Jersey: "You don't get anything for your taxes; it's just a bunch of garbage. I'm off today. I have no excuse, but I just don't feel like voting."[26] A nurse in Maryland: "It doesn't matter who gets elected. They can't do what they want. They're controlled by the people around them. So it doesn't matter whether I vote."[27] A patron of a beauty salon in New Jersey: "I really don't think there's much you can do about anything. It's getting to be frustrating. I'm just a little person who doesn't have much pull. But that's the way of the world, I guess."[28]

The message seems clear enough. The confusion, disinterest, and frustration of the individual are apparent. The government and its leaders appear remote and unconcerned with the problems of the person in the street. The thought of controlling politicians, making them responsive to the citizen, and directing the course of government through the vote seems incomprehensible.

Curtis Gans of the Committee for the Study of the American Electorate believes that nonvoting is associated with fundamental weaknesses within the political system. These include

> the decay of political and social institutions, most notably the political party; the growing impotence felt by the citizen in the face of large public and private institutions and increasingly complex problems; [and] the role that mass media, especially television, has in creating confusion in the minds of some.[29]

In short, they include almost everything related to modern American politics. Walter Dean Burnham, a political scientist who specializes in election analyses, predicts that if turnout "gets much

[25] Steven V. Roberts, "Electorate's Majority Prefers Sidelines," *The New York Times,* November 8, 1978, p. 18. © 1978 by The New York Times Company. Reprinted by permission.

[26] *Ibid.*

[27] Steven V. Roberts, "100 Million Didn't Vote — Some Express Disillusions," *The New York Times,* November 12, 1978, p. 26. © 1978 by The New York Times Company. Reprinted by permission.

[28] *Ibid.*

[29] Quoted in Adam Clymer, "Nov. 7 Voter Turnout Was 37.9%, Lowest Since 42," *The New York Times,* December 19, 1979, p. A13. © 1979 by The New York Times Company. Reprinted by permission.

lower, we will hit rock bottom."[30] Another academician and a political activist, historian Richard Wade, can see no reason why the slide will not continue. What can be done about it? "The first thing to do is to let people know how bad it is."[31] It does not seem like much, but perhaps it is a start.

[30] Robert Reinhold, "Portrait of American Electorate: It Is Large, Young, and Reluctant," *The New York Times*, November 8, 1978, p. 1. © 1978 by The New York Times Company. Reprinted by permission.

[31] Quoted in Lynn, "Voter Apathy Found."

2

Party Loyalty

PARTY IDENTIFICATION

Party identification is a psychological measure of voter identification with a political party. It is grounded in the individual's personal development and his exposure to such things as the influence of his parents, schooling and its impact, the views of business associates and the demands of making a living, and the network of friends and acquaintances that comprise the social setting in which a person lives and matures. Among all of the influences acting on partisan identification, the family is the strongest. The political ties picked up from one's parents and then influenced by later learning and life experiences form the basis for a number of political attitudes. Among the strongest of these is party identification. Because the socialization to political parties begins so early and because the attachments once formed are both strongly resistant to change and highly predictive of political behavior, partisan affiliation can be compared to religious choice or ethnic ties. Party identification is an important measure of the stability and vitality of the party system.

The indicator of party identification is used in voting analyses to gauge the direction (Democrat, Republican, or independent) and intensity (strong, weak) of support for the political parties. It is a powerful measure not subject to random fluctuation and, since its introduction in the early 1950s, it has proven to be the most significant of the three indices (issue orientation and candidate appeal being the other two) devised to explain voting behavior.[1]

The evidence is that party loyalty, as measured by party identification, is changing. The trend is obvious and has been continuous since the measure was introduced. Personal identification with a party is becoming less common and less important. Fewer people are identifying with either of the political parties, and even among those who do, the intensity of their identification is falling off markedly. The newest members of the electorate have the weakest ties to the party system. And for most people who have identified with either of the parties in the past, the strength of their identification has atrophied over the years. As a consequence, party identification has become less meaningful for predicting the vote. Loyalty to a party and its candidates has declined seriously. The electorate has begun to lose the factor of greatest significance in producing an order and predictability to election behavior. As party identification has declined in importance, the number and significance of independent voters has increased substantially. In return, the unpredictability and volatility of the vote returns attest to the weakening of party ties and the decline of party loyalty.

Survey data collected by the Center for Political Studies of the Institute for Social Research of the University of Michigan document the erosion of support for the parties. As Table 2.1 and Table 2.2 show, the attachment to the parties has decreased both in the proportion of those identifying and in the intensity of the affiliation over time. Three out of four adults identified with the major political parties in the 1950s. The attachments eroded slightly during the 1960s, but the significant decline became evident in the 1970s. The fall off was pronounced among strong party identifiers, down from 35 percent to 26 percent over two decades. The data from the 1980 election are virtually identical to those from the 1970s.

---

[1] Angus Campbell, Philip Converse, Warren Miller, and Donald Stokes, *The American Voter* (New York: Wiley, 1960).

TABLE 2.1
Partisan Identification by Decade

	1950s	1960s	1970s	1980 election
Partisans	74.2%	72.2%	63.5%	64.3%
Strong	35.5	33.0	26.0	26.6
Weak	38.7	39.2	37.5	37.7
Independents	21.8	25.8	34.8	35.7

Source: Data supplied by the Center for Political Studies.

The trend has affected the parties differently. The Republican party's coalition is small to begin with and can be expected to have strong and persistent ties since they have remained stable in the face of social pressures that have worked since the New Deal to the advantage of the Democrats. Apparently, this is the case. The overall decline in Republican identifiers is modest at best. Where the party has lost support is among the "strong" identifiers, whose proportions have decreased from 13 to 15 percent during the earlier years to 8 or 9 percent in more recent elections. The number of "independent Republicans" (people who claim to be independent but favor the Republican party) has increased slightly to where it now about equals the strong identifiers. The modal group among Republicans is the "weak" identifiers.

The Democratic party's coalition is considerably larger (claiming 16 to 20 percent more of the party identifiers over time) and far more malleable than the Republican party's. Although the same pattern holds true for the Democrats as for the Republicans, the losses for the former are more severe. The proportion of party identifiers found among "strong" party identifiers has declined. The number of "independent Democrats" is about the same, and the party's modal group is "weak" identifiers. The trend, then, is for fewer people to identify and for those who do identify (or are already psychologically committed to support the party) to have their ties loosen as time passes.

Independents have increased markedly in number to the point where they now rank in some polls as equals to or slightly behind the Democrats and well ahead of the Republicans. The day is not far

TABLE 2.2
Strength of Party Identification, 1952–1980

	Year														
	1952	1954	1956	1958	1960	1962	1964	1966	1968	1970	1972	1974	1976	1978	1980
Strong Democrat	22%	22%	21%	23%	21%	23%	26%	18%	20%	20%	15%	17%	15%	15%	18%
Weak Democrat	25	25	23	24	25	23	25	27	25	23	25	21	25	24	23
Independent Democrat	10	9	7	7	8	8	9	9	10	10	11	13	12	14	11
Independent	5	7	9	8	8	8	8	12	11	13	13	15	14	14	13
Independent Republican	7	6	8	4	7	6	6	7	9	8	11	9	10	9	10
Weak Republican	14	14	14	16	13	16	13	15	14	15	13	14	14	13	14
Strong Republican	13	13	15	13	14	12	11	10	10	10	10	8	9	8	9
Apoliticals: Don't Know	4	4	3	5	4	4	2	2	1	1	2	3	1	3	2
	100%	100%	100%	100%	100%	100%	100%	100%	100%	100%	100%	100%	100%	100%	100%

Source: Data supplied by the Center for Political Studies.

off when independent will clearly be the identification preferred by most Americans. In fact, there is nothing to indicate a substantial reversal or leveling off of the trend shown. Thus, independents will most likely continue to increase in significance and number with each passing election year. From an electorate in which 75 percent of its members loyally associated themselves with the major parties to one (in future elections) in which the majority may well claim to be independents is a major transition that, in itself, has changed, and will continue to change, the practice of American politics.

The decreasing frequency and intensity of identification with the parties is alarming (for party sympathizers) on a number of counts. The figures presented in Table 2.1 and Table 2.2 probably underestimate the extent of the defections. Party attachment is, as noted, an attitudinal force of considerable strength and durability. It is nurtured in the family and transmitted through the parents (primarily) to the emerging adult. The dynamics of the process are not unlike those through which other traditional and social values that earmark the individual's personal world are passed on in a society. The socialization process is strong enough that values once passed on are not easy to modify. Attitudinal identification with a party would be the one indicator of party loyalty most resistant to change. Yet an individual has to make some concession to a changing political environment and, potentially at least, to the perceived failure of the parties to offer him meaningful choices in elections and a continuing sense of direction for his political activity. The individual's life experiences and the political climate of the times in which he matures politically would influence the direction and nature of his political affiliations.

The process would be gradual. The likelihood is that pressures created by the perceived political environment in conflict with the family socialization processes would lead first to a change in behavior (in this case, the vote) and only later, as the behavior and the attitude conflict, to a gradual decrease in importance of the attitude. This, in turn, would lead to a modification of the attitude (a decrease in intensity of the identification or a drift from a "strong" or "weak" identification toward independence). The process of reconciling attitudes and behavior may take years, and, because of the intensity of the socializing forces, probably several generations.[2] Attachments would weaken over time, and new members entering the electorate would exhibit far weaker partisan ties, products of changing socialization cues and a restructured political environment. Thus, although the decline in party identification shown here is troublesome enough, it may in actuality mask both the actual extent of the erosion and its seriousness.

There is evidence to support these contentions. The data presented in Table 2.3 suggest an increasing disparity between identification and the vote. There is an increasing willingness on the part of many party members to break with their party and its candidates and to vote for the opposition. An examination of the trend in these regards makes the development unmistakable. The strength of party identification has traditionally proven to be an excellent prediction of the individual's vote. The number of defections by even weak party identifiers (Table 2.3) was small during the 1950s and up through most of the 1960s. A vote for the opposition by a strong party identifier was virtually unthinkable. Approximately 80 percent of the weak identifiers and well over 90 percent of the strong identifiers consistently voted for their party's presidential candidate during these years.

The pattern is changing (Table 2.3). Both the 1976 and 1980 presidential elections appeared to represent a return to a stronger party-based vote than either of their two predecessors. Better than one-third to one-half of the weak Democratic identifiers voted for the Republican nominee in 1968 and 1972, and they were joined in the latter election year by one out of four strong Democratic identifiers. In the same election years, almost half of the "independent Democrats" supported the Republican presidential candidate.

The larger Democratic coalition is more likely to defect than is the smaller group of Republican identifiers. The strong Republican identifiers remain a solid, if embattled, group of party believers with a consistently impressive 96 percent of its dwindling members religiously supporting its party's standard-bearer. Weak Republican defections are variable, peaking in the Goldwater race of 1964 with 43 percent. Only one-tenth (9 percent) broke ranks in

[2] Paul Abramson, *Generational Change in American Politics* (Lexington: D. C. Heath, 1975); Kristi Andersen, *The Creation of a Democratic Majority, 1928–1936* (Chicago: University of Chicago Press, 1979); and Abramson, *Political Attitudes in America* (San Francisco: W. H. Freeman, 1983).

TABLE 2.3
Defection Rates Within Categories of Party Identification, 1952–1980 (*In percent*)[a]

I.   By Year

Democrat	1952	1956	1960	1964	1968	1972	1976	1980	Average 1952–80
Strong	17	15	9	5	11	26	9	9	13
Weak	39	37	28	18	38	52	25	31	32

Independent	1952	1956	1960	1964	1968	1972	1976	1980	Average 1952–80
Democrat	40	33	15	11	49	44	24	25	30
Independent	—	—	—	—	—	—	—	—	—
Republican	7	6	13	25	19	14	14	11	14

Republican	1952	1956	1960	1964	1968	1972	1976	1980	Average 1952–80
Strong	1	1	2	10	3	4	3	1	3
Weak	6	7	13	43	12	9	22	9	13

II.   By Decade

Democrats	1950s	1960s	1970s	1980 election
Strong	4.3	8.0	17.5	9
Weak	18.2	22.4	38.5	31

Republicans	1950s	1960s	1970s	1980 election
Strong	3.7	1.2	3.5	1
Weak	16.2	19.6	15.5	9

[a] Entry is the proportion of the voters whose vote for president was other than for the candidates of the party with which they identified.

Source: Data supplied by the Center for Political Studies.

1980 to vote for Jimmy Carter. "Independent Republicans" defect at about the same rate as weak Republicans. Ronald Reagan generally appeared to be a strong candidate among Republican identifiers.

The progressive decay in party allegiance is most apparent from a comparison of the rates of defection for party sympathizers by decade (Table 2.3). Allowing for variations introduced by the response to individual candidacies, the Republican figures are fairly consistent over time. The Democratic rates are not. The proportion of strong party identifiers who defected doubled from the 1950s to the 1960s, and doubled again from the 1960s to the 1970s, whereas the proportion of weak Democratic identifiers voting Republican increased by over twenty percentage points to where an average of one out of three supported the opposition party in the 1970s. The rates of defection for the late 1970s and early 1980s appear to have stabilized.

John Petrocik has extended this analytic avenue by comparing the strength of partisan identification with the individual's vote over time in presidential, House, Senate, and gubernatorial races.[3] Defections range on the average between 5 percent and 35 percent for the various types of contests, and the trend is toward less consistency between the psychological attachments of an individual and his party vote. Exceptions do appear in the 1976 and 1980 presidential vote, both of which seem to show at least a short-run drop in defections. In Petrocik's analysis, the pattern evidenced in the presidential elections may be close to that found in the 1950s. The elections may be aberrations. This is not true for the House, Senate, or gubernatorial contests in 1976 (the last election year Petrocik analyzed) when the defections equaled or exceeded those for the 1960s. Petrocik goes on to plot the correlation between party identification and the vote. The decline is consistent and dramatic for all races (president, House, Senate, governorships) over time (1952–76). The author concludes:

> Party identification is no longer the robust predictor of the vote that it was in the 1950s. The evidence for this is so overwhelming and

[3] John R. Petrocik, "The Changeable American Voter: Some Revisions of the Revision." Paper presented at the Annual Meeting of the American Political Science Association, New York, August 31–September 3, 1978.

widely recognized that the point is easily belabored. . . . Through 1960, party preference accounted for about fifty percent of the variance of the vote for these offices, by the late 1960s it was down to about thirty-six percent of the variance, and in the 1976 election party identification accounts for barely a third of the variance in the vote for the different offices.[4]

The trend line developed by Petrocik appears relevant to the dynamics of voter attitudinal change in the 1980s.

UNPREDICTABILITY IN THE VOTE

If this thumbnail sketch of the decline in party identification is relevant for elections, it is reasonable to expect party to be less meaningful as a referent in structuring the vote. This is exactly what happens. Voters, as noted earlier, are not inclined to turn out, but when they do vote, they are considerably less likely to vote the party label for all offices on the ballot. The changes are striking. Unequivocal party support appeared to be the norm in the 1950s and early 1960s. For example, it seems extraordinary within the context of today's politics, but among Democrats and Republicans better than 70 percent supported their party's presidential candidates in the 1950s. In the 1960 and 1964 presidential elections, the figure for partisan identifiers still hovered at an impressive two out of three. By the 1970s it had dropped to roughly one-half. In other words, the odds are not much over fifty-fifty today that a party identifier will vote for his party's presidential nominee. Republicans are little different from Democrats in this regard.

SPLIT-TICKET VOTING

Party members are also considerably more likely to split their tickets (i.e., to vote for candidates of different parties) at successive levels of contests. The frequency of split-ticket voting, another measure of the instability of partisan attitudes and con-

[4] *Ibid.*, p. 18.

temporary politics, has increased significantly since the beginning of systematic academic surveying in the 1950s.

About a third of the Republicans and half of the independents and Democrats (in the Eisenhower victory of 1952, the percentage rose for Democrats) split their tickets between the parties. Goldwater's candidacy created difficulties for some Republicans, but it was not until the election of 1968 that split-ticket voting clearly began to claim a majority of participants. In the 1970s and 1980s, between two-thirds and three-quarters of the independents and the Democrats and one-half of the Republicans divided their ballots between the parties at one point or another. Split-ticket voting has replaced the straight party vote as the norm for the American electorate — one further sign of the volatility present within the electorate and of the decay of party influence.

Charles Hadley and Susan Howell have pressed the examination of split-ticket voting further than most.[5] Political scientists have argued that split-ticket voting is not only a sign of political instability, but that it may also be the forerunner of major upheavals within the electorate and possibly of a political realignment. Increases in the amount of split-ticket votes, for example, appeared in the 1890s and the 1920s, periods that preceded a major, and even crucial, shift in electoral alignments.[6]

With this in mind, Hadley and Howell have probed below the surface of national politics to investigate whether there are differing patterns of voting loyalty associated with regions of the United States. They found that most Americans tend to vote for the same party in presidential and congressional races. From 1952 through 1968, on the average only 15 percent of the people divided their vote between the parties for these offices. To emphasize how rare splitting the ticket was, they point out that the region with up to

[5] Charles Hadley and Susan Howell, "Split Ticket Voting in the Northeast, 1952–1976: Partisan Realignment, Dealignment, or Status Quo." Paper delivered at the Annual Meeting of the Midwest Political Science Association, Chicago, April 20–22, 1978.

[6] Walter Dean Burnham, *Critical Elections and the Mainsprings of American Politics* (New York: Norton, 1970); Burnham, "The Changing Shape of the American Political Universe," *American Political Science Review* 59 (March 1965): 7–28; and Burnham, "The Appearance and Disappearance of the American Voter." Paper prepared for the Conference on the Future of the American Political System, Center for the Study of Democratic Politics, University of Pennsylvania, April 12–13, 1979.

five times as great an incidence as the others in presidential and congressional races was the South. The area was just beginning to evidence results of the powerful transformation toward a more competitive two-party politics closer to the national model.[7] In 1952, over 90 percent of non-Southerners consistently voted for the same party at the presidential and congressional level.

By the 1970s split-ticket voting in these contests had increased to one-quarter or better for the nation as a whole (27 percent on the average). The pattern was pronounced in all regions, although the South and the Northeast had the highest rates of defection.

In state and local races, the trend was similar. Less straight party voting could be expected in these contests, and less occurred. Nonetheless, the figures testifying to party loyalty for the early period (1952–60) are impressive. Only about one in four (27 percent) split their votes at these levels in these races. The trend is quite different after that. In the elections from 1960 to 1972 (the question was not asked), first 40 percent, then 48 percent after that, and, by 1972, 58 percent, had divided their support between the parties in lower level contests.[8] The evidence of party instability is not confined to the national races only. It has permeated all levels of politics.

INDEPENDENTS

The most noted aspect of the changing allegiance to political parties has been the rise in numbers and influence of the independent voter. The trend has been remarkable and has helped change the American political landscape from one dominated by party loyalties to one increasingly subjected to the whim of unattached and uncommitted (in partisan terms) electors.

The growing ranks of independents introduce an increasing unpredictability into election outcomes. The party label anchored the vote for identifiers. It was (as shown in Table 2.2) a reliable guide to the individual's political intentions. In what Philip Converse has

[7] William C. Havard (ed.), *The Changing Politics of the South* (Baton Rouge: Louisiana State University Press, 1972); Jack Bass and Walter DeVries, *The Transformation of Southern Politics* (New York: Meridian, 1977).

[8] Hadley and Howell, "Split Ticket Voting," pp. 7–12.

called the "steady-state" period of party hegemony (1952–64),[9] it was both difficult and unusual for a member to break with his party to support an opposition candidate. Independents operate under no such constraints. By definition, their vote (and, for that matter, whether they choose to vote at all) is not anchored by party ties. It responds to short-term influences associated with the candidates and the issues in the campaign or the political climate peculiar to the given election year. It is an unstable vote (and turnout) that is basically unpredictable over time, and introduces into elections an increased volatility that today's fluid politics do not need.

The increasing number of independents cannot be disputed. As Table 2.1 demonstrates, independents have increased from about one-fifth of the electorate in the 1950s to better than one-third in the 1980s. The independents stand in numbers just behind the Democrats and well ahead of the Republicans. The trend is clear, and the future favors the independents. It is likely that each successive election will witness a swelling of their ranks.

The independent vote is up for grabs. It has no allegiances. Its volatility and malleability does little to ease the concern of those who value stability and order in American politics. As Table 2.4 illustrates, the turnout of "pure" independents is normally well below that of partisans. This has been particularly true of the elections from 1964 onward. The effects of the expansion of the electorate through the introduction of the eighteen-year-old vote can be seen in 1972, 1976, and 1980. Not only did the number of independents grow, but their participation fell to modest levels (52 percent on the average), comparable in many respects to the poor turnouts following the advent of female suffrage in the 1920s.[10]

The independent vote is fluid. The intensity of its support tends to drift from one candidate and party to the other, depending on what happens to excite the fancy of the voter. Apparently, the independents were strongly attracted to Dwight Eisenhower in 1952 and 1956, awarding the Republicans better than 80 percent of their vote (Table 2.5). The independents reacted negatively to Barry Goldwater in 1964 and George McGovern in 1972. In both cases, their opponents received 70 percent or more of the inde-

[9] Philip Converse, *The Dynamics of Party Support* (Beverly Hills: Sage, 1976).
[10] William Crotty, *Political Reform and the American Experiment* (New York: Crowell, 1977), pp. 20–22.

TABLE 2.4
Voter Turnout in Presidential Elections and Partisan or Independent Affiliation, 1952–1980[a]

	1952	1956	1960	1964	1968	1972	1976	1980
Partisans	79%	77%	85%	83%	81%	79%	77%	78%
Independents[b]	74	77	77	62	65	53	57	52

[a] Figures are based on self-reported voters.

[b] "Independent Democrats" and "Independent Republicans" (or "leaners") have been omitted.

Source: Data supplied by the Center for Political Studies.

pendent vote. Richard Nixon (in both 1968 and 1972) benefited from the independent vote, and Ronald Reagan in 1980 proved to be highly attractive to the independents. The surges and the equally pronounced drop-offs in the proportion of votes cast for the parties and their candidates from one election to the next indicate the changeability and unreliability of this increasingly significant bloc of electors.

To add to the confusion, not only is the number of independents increasing, but their composition is changing. The new independents coming into the electorate are not the same as the old independents. Originally, it was felt that independents were the classic

TABLE 2.5
Swings in the Independent Vote, 1952–80, as Measured by Support for the Democratic Presidential Nominee

1952	1956	1960	1964	1968	1972	1976	1980
20%	16%	46%	77%	31%[a]	30%	43%	30%[b]

[a] 20 percent of the independent vote supported Wallace in 1968.

[b] 12 percent of the independent vote supported Anderson in 1980.

Source: For 1952, 1956, 1960, 1964, and 1972 from Herbert B. Asher, *Presidential Elections and American Politics: Voters, Candidates, and Campaigns Since 1952.* © The Dorsey Press, 1976. Reprinted by permission. For 1968, 1976, and 1980 from Center for Political Studies 1968–1980 presidential election survey.

embodiment of the democratic spirit. It was believed that in the best civics textbook fashion they voted the man, not the party, and that they did so on the basis of issues and the common good. The assumptions were that they were not blinded by party, that they weighed the issues and candidates in a campaign, and that they then made their choice based on their own values and the information received from the media and other sources during the campaign.

The early voting studies demolished the myth. The independent voter was found to be the individual with the weakest ties to the political system (hence his failure to identify with one of the major parties), the least interest in and knowledge of politics, and the greatest likelihood not even to vote. The picture was not a pleasant one.

Political conditions have changed, and many people have begun to question the bleak assessment of the independent found in the traditional voting studies. The reexamination of the independent is not intended to disown the commonly accepted characterization. Rather, it is intended to suggest that the picture drawn of the independent may not be accurate for substantial numbers of independents. The group is too large and too complex for that.

Beginning with an analysis of the 1964 election, Walter Dean Burnham has suggested the emergence of a "new" independent, quite different in social characteristics and political concerns from the "old" (or traditionally described) independent. The "new" independents, says Burnham, "may have declined to identify with either major party not because they are relatively politically unconscious, but because the structure of electoral politics at the present time turns upon parties, issues, and symbolism which do not have much meaning in terms of their political values or cognitions."[11]

Burnham finds that independents, although as a group ranking low in income, occupational achievement, and education (as would be expected from the classical model), have a bloc of highly educated adherents. It is also true that independents rank low on participation, but (and this could not be predicted from the earlier voting studies) they exhibit both a high and a low distribution on indices of political efficacy, a measure of perceived ability to affect

[11] Burnham, *Critical Elections,* p. 127.

the political environment. The measure is important for understanding political behavior and correlates highly with involvement, political competence, and knowledge. The bloc that scores high in efficacy ranks second only to "strong" Republican identifiers, a surprising outcome. He also found that the policy views of independents are not as inchoate as had been assumed. Rather, they normally fell somewhere between the two parties' positions, a location that gives some credence to Burnham's views.

Finally, Burnham looked at those defecting from Democratic ranks to independent status. He found them to be among those who rank the highest on social and demographic measures of socioeconomic status. Additionally, the young seemed particularly attracted to the independent category.[12]

An examination of data from the recent presidential elections appears to support the depiction of a new, evolving, and younger independent coalition. For example, in examining the proportion of independents by age group (Table 2.6), one finds a strong association between age and partisanship. The older the person, the more likely he is to have identified (and to continue to identify) with a political party. Conversely, the younger the person, the greater the likelihood that he will be independent.

Recent elections show a much greater incidence of first-time electors claiming independent status.[13] The change is sharp and is not explained by the eighteen-year-old vote, whose impact was first felt in 1972. On the contrary, the jump in independents became pronounced between 1964 and 1968 and has held steady since then. This suggests that changes in the political environment fundamentally affected the way people viewed politics and their willingness (or lack thereof) to associate with either of the major parties. Once the move toward independence gathered momentum, it continued to be strong. With approximately 8 percent of the electorate new each presidential election year and with the refusal to identify with parties strongest among the young, continued growth in the proportion and importance of the independent vote is highly likely.

[12] *Ibid.*, pp. 123–26.

[13] See Norman Nie, Sidney Verba, and John R. Petrocik, *The Changing American Voter* (Cambridge, Mass.: Harvard University Press, 1976), Table 4.3, p. 60, and text discussion, pp. 59–73.

TABLE 2.6
Age and Party Status, 1980

Party Identification	18–20	21–25	26–30	31–35
Democrats	34%	30%	35%	42%
Strong Democrat	(9)	(7)	(9)	(14)
Weak Democrat	(25)	(23)	(26)	(29)
Independents	46%	49%	43%	37%
Independent Democrat	(22)	(17)	(13)	(12)
Pure Independent	(10)	(20)	(16)	(16)
Republicans	17%	20%	22%	19%
Strong Republican	(2)	(4)	(8)	(11)
Weak Republican	(15)	(16)	(14)	(8)
N	67	154	174	98

Party Identification	36–40	41–50	51–60	61 and older
Democrats	37%	44%	41%	48%
Strong Democrats	(11)	(14)	(23)	(28)
Weak Democrats	(26)	(30)	(18)	(20)
Independents	41%	33%	36%	22%
Independent Democrat	(9)	(9)	(11)	(6)
Pure Independent	(16)	(12)	(9)	(7)
Independent Republican	(16)	(12)	(16)	(9)
Republicans	22%	25%	23%	31%
Strong Republican	(9)	(10)	(9)	(15)
Weak Republican	(13)	(15)	(14)	(16)
N	127	182	208	308

Note: Totals may not add up to 100 percent as a result of rounding error.
Source: Data supplied by the Center for Political Studies.

YOUTH AND THE PARTIES

It has been argued that as people mature and assume the economic and familial responsibilities of life, their political views become more conventional and they begin to assume their political responsibilities The argument could be extended to contend that the young adults will then associate with one of the political parties and the trend toward independence will be blunted; in effect, that trend is an artifact of an extended and an increasingly younger electorate Clearly, the strength of party identification is significantly different among age groups as Table 2.6 shows.[14] Comparing the oldest and youngest age cohorts in the presidential electorate in Table 2.6, one uncovers some remarkable differences in affiliation. Half of those under thirty claimed some type of independent status, and the other half affiliated with a political party. Among the oldest voters (those first eligible to vote in 1920 or before), 79 percent identified with a political party, and of these 43 percent were classified as "strong" identifiers. Only 11 percent of the most recent voters could be called "strong" identifiers. A relatively small 22 percent of the oldest category claimed independent status.

Any change toward increased partisanship by the new voters of the last decade is unlikely. The point cannot be proven, obviously, but it is likely that strong partisanship for older voters is a product of the time and political conditions in which they entered the electorate. Different generations of voters are socialized in different states of political party significance. As they mature, their political ties become stronger. New voters have weaker ties. The political situation at present encourages independence; the political parties do not attract the new voters. Unless there is some unforeseen upheaval, these conditions are not likely to change. Partisanship is dying. The strongest party identifiers are consistently being phased out of the electorate. Time is on the side of the independents.

ELECTORAL SWINGS

Let us look at one further piece of evidence on the decreasing impact of political parties in elections. Party loyalty tended to

[14] For comparative data and related findings, see Arthur H. Miller and Warren E. Miller, "Partisanship and Performance: 'Rational' Choice in the 1976 Presidential Election." Paper presented at the 1977 Annual Meeting of the American Political Science Association, Washington, D.C., September 1–4, 1977, p. 25.

anchor an electorate. Drastic changes in the vote from one election to the next were unlikely. If party support is less important to the voter, then sharp (even wild) swings in the proportion of the vote cast for each of the parties would appear a likely consequence. This, again, is happening (Figure 2.1). Historically, elections go through different phases. A period of highly competitive and close elections will be followed by one in which one party has a distinct advantage. The distinguishing characteristic, however, has been the consistency of a given pattern for an electoral era.

FIGURE 2.1
Changes in the Two-Party Vote, 1916–1980

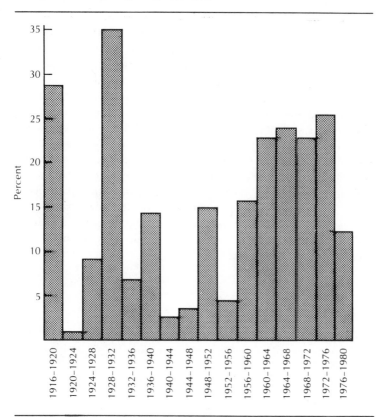

This is not true for the contemporary period. Beginning in 1960, there has been a dizzying succession of close elections followed by landslides, then by toss-up races, and so on. To confuse matters further, the shifts can benefit one party or the other, almost on whim. In 1960 the Democrats won an extraordinarily close contest. Four years later they won in a landslide. Could the party have been on its way to recouping its losses and establishing itself as the dominant party in a one-party era? Not so. In 1968 Richard Nixon and the Republicans came back to win the presidency in a very close contest. Four years later Nixon won in a landslide comparable to Johnson's in 1964. Perhaps the Republicans were on their way to reemerging as the dominant coalition, as many of their adherents claimed. However, the party's immediate fate was much the same as that of the Democrats in the mid-1960s. Four years later the Republicans lost a close contest to Jimmy Carter and the Democrats. Four years later (1980) Ronald Reagan won a decisive victory (51% to 41%) over Jimmy Carter in the two-party division of the vote, an outcome that was not predicted (the election was supposed to be close) and one lopsided enough as to be heralded as the beginning of a new conservative era in American politics.

The wild variations in the vote are further indications of the rootlessness of contemporary American politics. Party loyalty has declined precipitously. Nothing has replaced it that could give elections the structure and certainty evident only a few decades ago. For better or worse, the contemporary scene is one of fluidity and uncertainty with no change in the dominating patterns in sight. The politics of the present, whatever its shortcomings, will be the politics of the immediate future. If anything, the changes traced here and their ramifications should become more pronounced.

3
The Rising Significance of Issues in Elections

ISSUE VOTING

As party has become less important in structuring the individual's vote, policy questions have been assuming a new significance. Researchers have found that voters have a new coherence in evaluating issues, and that they attach more significance to issues in making their decisions.[1]

Most of the contemporary debate over issues and their importance in elections revolves around methodology such as the conceptualization of such studies, the proper wordings of questions and interpretation of replies, the appropriate criteria for accepting and judging an issue-related vote, and the assumptions the researcher brings to the analysis. The debates are technical and have

[1] The literature on this point is extensive. See, as examples: Norman H. Nie, Sidney Verba, and John R. Petrocik, *The Changing American Voter* (Cambridge, Mass.: Harvard University Press, 1976); Gerald Pomper, *Voters' Choice* (New York: Dodd, Mead, 1975); and Benjamin I. Page, *Choices and Echoes in Presidential Elections* (Chicago: University of Chicago Press, 1978).

a good deal to do with the way in which the research findings are evaluated and the weight that should be given the results.[2] The general trend is clear, and virtually everyone involved in investigations of voting behavior would agree: voter reliance on the issues in campaigns and the stands taken by the candidates has significantly increased since the mid-1960s. As party identification has declined, voters have relied more on issues to fulfill the functions once served by the parties. That trend began in the election of 1964 when voters were offered clear choices on a policy basis between candidates (Barry Goldwater and Lyndon Johnson) and political parties. The break with the past elections studied in depth by academicians since the advent of modern survey technology (1952–60) was sharp. In this sense 1964 may have represented something akin to a "critical" election: one that provokes (or institutionalizes) a break with the past that endures beyond the immediate election.[3] In effect, a critical election redirects the course of American electoral behavior.

The trend toward an increased reliance on issues has endured. The elections of 1968, 1972, 1976 and 1980 saw a greater consistency and predictability among individual beliefs and a greater impact of these on the election. The exact causes (and their relative impacts) that explain these changes are debated, and the comparative importance of issues as against party identification in con-

[2] As examples, see: James A. Stimson, "Belief Systems: Constraint, Complexity, and the 1972 Election," *American Journal of Political Science* 19 (1975): 393–417; David RePass, "Issue Salience and Party Choice," *American Political Science Review* 65 (1971): 389–400; Gerald Pomper, "From Confusion to Clarity: Issues and American Voters, 1956–1968," *American Political Science Review* 62 (1972): 415–28; Benjamin I. Page and Richard A. Brody, "Policy Voting and the Electoral Process," *American Political Science Review* 66 (1972): 979–95; Richard W. Boyd, "Popular Control of Public Policy: A Normal Vote Analysis of the 1968 Election," *American Political Science Review* 66 (1972): 429–49; John H. Kessel, "The Issues in Issue Importance," *American Political Science Review* 66 (1972): 459–65; and David M. Kovenock, James W. Prothro, et al., *Explaining the Vote*, 2 vols. (Chapel Hill, N.C.: Institute for Research in Social Science, 1973).

[3] Pomper, "From Confusion to Clarity"; Mark A. Schulman and Gerald Pomper, "Variability in Electoral Behavior: Longitudinal Perspectives From Causal Modeling," *American Journal of Political Science* 19 (1975): 1–18; John C. Pierce, "Party Identification and the Changing Role of Ideology in American Politics," *Midwest Journal of Political Science* 14 (1970): 25–42; John Field and Ronald Anderson, "Ideology and the Public's Conceptualization of the 1964 Election," *Public Opinion Quarterly* 33 (1969): 380–98; and Walter Dean Burnham, "American Voting Behavior and the 1964 Election," *Midwest Journal of Political Science* 12 (1968): 1–40.

tributing to the election outcome is argued by "revisionists" (those who emphasize the change toward an issue-oriented electorate) and "traditionalists" (those whose past concern has been with the dominant role of party identification in influencing vote outcomes).[4] The controversy may be one of degrees rather than trends. The greater reliance on issues in affecting the vote decision and thus the election outcome is clear enough and, as a trend, not a basic point of dispute.

Essentially, recent investigations have found that the public's awareness of issues and their relevance to the vote has increased markedly since the 1950s; that the public has a better conception of the differences between the two parties on the issues; and that issues are assuming a greater importance in explaining the voter's decision. Although party identification is still a potent contributor to the voter's decision, the increasing impact of issues has coincided with a decline in significance of party identification in explaining election outcomes. And, surprisingly, the changes observed have come about in a relatively short period of time (since the election of 1964, as noted) and contrast sharply with the interpretations of voting behavior of an earlier period (1952–1960).

Gerald Pomper has been a leader in the line of inquiry. He has shown in his work the sharp divergence between two sets of presidential elections, 1956–1960 and 1964–1968, in the perception of party differences on policy matters of traditional concern to the Democratic and Republican party coalitions (i.e., aid to education, medical care, job guarantees, fair employment, school integration, and foreign aid). These are issues that have provided a basis for continuing cleavage between the national parties. Beginning with the 1964 election, far greater numbers of voters began to perceive the contrasting party stands on these issues, and the individual voter's party identification and policy support positions began to be more consistent than in the past.[5] In a related investigation, Pomper and Mark Schulman were able to show for the presidential elections of 1956, 1964, and 1972, that though the correlation of

---

[4] The debate is reviewed in Philip E. Converse, "Public Opinion and Voting Behavior," in Fred I. Greenstein and Nelson W. Polsby (eds.), *Handbook of Political Science*, Vol. 4 (Reading, Mass.: Addison-Wesley, 1975), pp. 75–169; and Herbert Asher, *Presidential Elections and American Politics* (Homewood, Ill.: Dorsey, 1976).

[5] Pomper, "From Confusion to Clarity."

party identification with the vote declined 30 percent, the association between issues and voting increased almost fourfold.[6] Figures of this nature can be misleading, especially because of the complexity of the analysis being done and the uncertain extent to which parties and candidates themselves are perceived in an issue context. In the Pomper and Schulman analysis, party identification and candidate appeal maintained formidable associations with voting, even exceeding that for issues. The direction of the changes, nonetheless, is the important clue to the way in which the electorate is moving.

Norman Nie, Sidney Verba, and John Petrocik have written the most comprehensive reexamination of voting behavior since the classic *The American Voter*, published in 1960.[7] In their book (suitably entitled *The Changing American Voter*), they have put the matter simply and well:

> Party voting has declined for two reasons: the number of Independents (who cannot cast a party vote) has risen, and the number of party identifiers who defect when they vote has gone up as well. At the same time, issue voting has increased for two similar reasons: more citizens have consistent issue positions on the basis of which they can vote; and more citizens are guided by these issue positions in casting their vote.[8]

Norman Nie and Kristi Andersen have examined voting behavior for 1956–72 in an attempt to determine the associations among issues, voting, and attitudinal constraint (a measure of ideological conceptual ability).[9] Their analysis is broader than the efforts to associate individual sets of issues with voting. By introducing attitudinal constraints in reexamining the assumptions concerning the electorate's conceptual abilities found in the pioneering work of Philip Converse,[10] the authors are attempting to chart the movement in consistency and predictability among, for exam-

[6] Schulman and Pomper, "Variability in Electoral Behavior."

[7] Nie, Verba, and Petrocik, *The Changing American Voter* (Cambridge, Mass.: Harvard University Press, 1976); and Angus Campbell, Philip Converse, Warren Miller, and Donald Stokes, *The American Voter* (New York: Wiley, 1960).

[8] *Ibid.*, p. 291.

[9] Norman H. Nie with Kristi Andersen, "Mass Belief Systems Revisited: Political Change and Attitude Structure," *Journal of Politics* 36 (1974): 540–87.

[10] Philip Converse, "The Nature of Relief Systems in Mass Publics," in David Apter (ed.), *Ideology and Discontent* (New York: Free Press, 1964), pp. 206–61.

ple, domestic, foreign, and civil rights clusters of issues and their association with both party identifications and the vote.

Nie and Andersen found, as have others, that the correlation between party identification and the vote fell consistently between 1956 and 1972. For the elections of 1956–60, the association between the vote and party identification averaged a very high 0.89 and for the elections of 1964–72, 0.69. Meanwhile, the association between political attitudes and the vote rose from lows of 0.16 and 0.21 in 1956 and 1960, respectively, to an average of 0.52 for the elections of 1964–72. [11]

The changes observed do not appear to be transitory. They mark a pronounced shift in correlates of voter decision making that, since 1964, have seen the increase in importance of issue stands in voter choice. Correspondingly, although this need not be the case (an individual's party affiliation and his position on issues could reinforce each other, and both could correlate strongly with the vote), party identification has declined significantly as an influence on voting.

The changes in voter response have resulted from a different political climate. The relative complacency of the 1950s was shattered by a series of major social and economic upheavals during the 1960s that have continued to this day. The following have left their mark:

the civil rights revolution
the Vietnam War
demonstrations and civil violence
concern over crime in the streets
the burning of cities
the bitter disappointment over the Great Society programs
government misconduct
the excesses of the FBI, other governmental invasions of the rights
    of individuals (e.g., wiretapping)
CIA involvement in the overthrow of the Chilean regime
the assassinations of John and Robert Kennedy
three attacks on incumbent presidents (Ford two, Reagan one)
the assassination of the preeminent civil rights leader (Martin
    Luther King)

---

[11] Nie and Andersen, "Mass Belief Systems Revisited."

the shame of Watergate and the resignation in disgrace of a president
the decay of the cities
the rise in taxes
the women's rights revolution
the pollution of the environment
the energy crisis
recession, unemployment, and inflation
the greatest budget deficits in American history
a stagnant economy

and so on. Americans became issue-conscious, and issues became more closely associated with their vote choices.

As the political environment changed, so did the nature of the candidates. Presidential contenders began to take stands on issues of broad concern and to offer voters a choice. When they did, and as voters began to perceive differences of consequence on policy concerns between parties and candidates, their views on questions of policy began to exercise an increasing influence on their votes.[12]

Table 3.1 provides some background for these developments. The table presents the major issues, as seen by the public and identified in the Gallup polls, for the years 1948–1980. From drugs to crime to war, the range of issues put before the electorate has been considerable. Interestingly, the relative dispersion of concerns evident in most other election years was less apparent in recent elections. In both 1976 and 1980, three out of four believed that the economy (the high cost of living and unemployment) represented the major problem, a dissatisfaction that may have more to do with the outcome of these elections than any other factor.

There is some confirmation for this position in Figure 3.1 which examines the public's perception of the political party best able to handle the problem identified as the nation's most significant. Generally, the presidential candidate of the political party seen as most competent in the area won the election. This was true of the economic issue in 1976. In 1980, there appeared to be some doubt, although the Republicans held a slight edge. More significantly, the Democrats' traditionally superior appeal on this type of domestic issue (in part, a carryover from New Deal-Fair Deal days)

[12] Pomper, "From Confusion to Clarity"; Page, *Choices and Echoes*; Nie and Andersen, "Mass Belief Systems Revisited."

TABLE 3.1
The Public's Perception of the Nation's Most Important Problem During Election Campaigns, 1948–1980

Date of Opinion Poll	Problem	Percent indicating that it is the most important problem
June 1948	Foreign policy	44%
	High cost of living	23
	Domestic policies (includes presidential election, education, racial problems)	9
	Strikes, labor problems	5
	Housing	4
June 1952	Russia	32%
	Economic problems	21
	Korean war	19
	Foreign policy, war, threat of war, defense	9
	Communism/socialism in government	7
October 1956	War, threat of war, Suez, foreign policy	48%
	High cost of living	13
	Civil rights, desegregation	12
	Farm problems	7
	Unemployment	3
June 1960	Threat of war	22%
	Relations with Russia/threat of war	15
	Foreign relations	15
	Threat of communism	11
	Racial problems	6
September 1964	International problems, cold war, war problems	46%
	Racial problems	35
	High cost of living	6
	Unemployment	4
	Too much goverment control	4
August 1968	Vietnam	51%
	Crime (includes looting, riots)	21
	Civil rights	20
	High cost of living	7
	Poverty	3

(Continued)

TABLE 3.1 (continued)

Date of Opinion Poll	Problem	Percent indicating that it is the most important problem
September 1972	Vietnam	27%
	Inflation, high cost of living	27
	Drug use, abuse	9
	International problems	10
	Crime, lawlessness	8
	Pollution, environment	4
October 1976	High cost of living	47%
	Unemployment	31
	Dissatisfaction with government	6
	Crime	6
	Foreign affairs	6
September 1980	Inflation, high cost of living	61%
	Unemployment	16
	International problems	15
	Dissatisfaction with government	6
	Energy	4

Note: Totals may be less than 100% because of additional miscellaneous categories not included in the table; totals may exceed 100% because of the allowance for multiple responses.

Source: The Gallup Poll, as reported in *The Gallup Opinion Index,* September 1980, p. 11. Used by permission.

eroded between 1976 and 1980, one indicator of the dissatisfaction with the Carter Administration's performance.

Although party identification supplied the primary explanation for the outcomes of presidential elections during the 1950s and early 1960s, the tide had begun to turn in 1964. By 1972, the Center for Political Studies of the University of Michigan, the group whose work was employed as the cornerstone of the debate and the most consistent defender of the traditionalist position, was willing to concede that major changes had taken place. The Center used multivariate analytic techniques that included "proximity measures" (an assessment of where an individual stood on an issue compared to where the candidate or political party was perceived to stand) to measure voters' conceptual abilities and policy con-

FIGURE 3.1
Political Party Which Is Best Able to Handle the Nation's Most Important
Problem According to Public Perceptions, 1948–1980

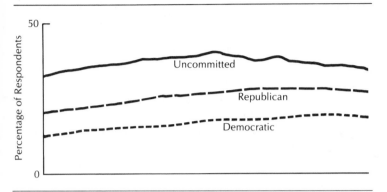

Source: Data from The Gallup Poll, as reported in *The Gallup Opinion Index*,
September 1980, p. 13. Used by permission.

cerns and to correlate these with the vote decision. The authors of
the Center's report on the 1972 election wrote, "The proximity
measures, when taken together as reflecting ideology [conceptual
abilities] and policy voting, were substantially more important as
direct explanations of the vote than was party identification."[13] The
researchers went on to test their conclusion through a path analytic
approach and concluded that "we found the total effect of party
identification to be .51, whereas the issue effect was .55. *As an
explanation of the vote in 1972, issues were at least equally as
important as party identification*" (emphasis in the original).[14]

The 1976 presidential election seemed to feature a return to a
stronger party-based vote. Any assumptions of a decrease in issue
voting may be misleading, however. The Center for Political
Studies's report on the 1976 election, prepared by Arthur Miller

[13] Arthur H. Miller, Warren E. Miller, Alden S. Raine, and Thad A. Brown, "A
Majority Party in Disarray: Policy Polarization in 1972 Election," *American Political Science Review* 70 (September 1976): 753–78, as reprinted in Richard G. Niemi
and Herbert F. Weisberg (eds.), *Controversies in American Voting Behavior* (San
Francisco: Freeman, 1976), p. 190.

[14] *Ibid.*, pp. 191–92.

and Warren Miller, makes a number of points.[15] First, between 1972 and 1976 the level of attitudinal consistency and ideological thinking among the American voters remained essentially unchanged. Party association, nonetheless, appeared stronger in its correlation with the vote. The authors explain the apparent paradox as follows:

The presidential candidates in 1976 (as opposed to 1972) chose to deemphasize issues. Jimmy Carter, in particular, may have obscured his position on many policy concerns. An assessment of candidate strategy in this regard is somewhat conjectural.[16] Voters did not perceive the clear differences between candidates that they had four years earlier. In such uncertainty, voters tend to return to their party moorings for direction. Since there are more Democrats than Republicans, such strategy clearly helped Carter's candidacy.

The issues that were stressed in the campaign tended to relate to economic concerns, the basic dividing point between the Democratic and Republican coalitions. This emphasis would again reinforce a party-oriented vote. It served another function for the Carter campaign, in that it provided the one solid rallying point for the large and heterogeneous Democratic coalition and, at the same time, avoided inflammatory concerns such as those introduced into the McGovern campaign, which severely divided Democrats.

Issue perceptions and party affiliations may be more closely associated than many believe. The authors conclude that their research has provided

solid evidence for the theoretical expectation that when voters are uncertain about the issues positions espoused by the candidates, they employ a partisan issue ideology in their electoral decision-making. The important point here is not simply that this partisan ideology is used to reduce uncertainty and resolve the electoral choice, but that it is apparently based upon policy considerations, and not an empty and habitual response to party labels.[17]

[15] Arthur H. Miller and Warren E. Miller, "Partisanship and Performance: 'Rational' Choice in the 1976 Presidential Election" (Washington, D.C.: Annual Meeting of the American Political Science Association, September 1–4, 1977).

[16] James Wooten, *Dasher* (New York: Summit Books, 1978); Jules Witcover, *Marathon* (New York: Viking, 1977); and Martin Schram, *Running for President 1976* (New York: Stein and Day, 1977).

[17] Miller and Miller, "Partisanship and Performance," p. 62.

By 1980, the emphasis had turned 180 degrees in the other direction with most political observers proclaiming an ideological election, based on a dissatisfaction with and reaction to liberal policies. The 1980 presidential vote combined with the sizable gains by Republicans in the Congress was interpreted as signaling the emergence of a conservative "New Right" dominance in American politics. The Reagan Administration claimed, and the Congress and political pundits were quick to concede, a "mandate" to institute fundamental changes in the direction of American policy and American government. The changes to be introduced would be the most comprehensive since the New Deal of Franklin Roosevelt and would include attempts to roll back the social legislation of the New Deal-Great Society (Lyndon Johnson's domestic program) days; reduce government regulation of business and the environment; decentralize programs and responsibilities from Washington to the states (the "New Federalism"); balance the budget; cut back on education programs and abolish the new Department of Education; reduce taxes; substantially expand the armed forces and military expenditures; and take a hard-nosed stance toward communist expansion in Central America or any place else that appeared to warrant it.

Could all of these changes in policy direction result from one election? The key, of course, to the Reagan Administration's approach and to its repeated policy successes with the Congress during its first year was the interpretation placed on the 1980 voting results. Was the election policy-oriented? And did it constitute a mandate for "New Right" conservatism? The 1980 presidential election did offer a clear choice on policy questions between a moderately conservative President, pushed to the left by his party's coalition, and a more extreme "New Right" candidate from the conservative wing of the policy spectrum. The choice appeared as clear-cut as that in either 1964 or 1972. Issues were important in the 1980 election, although the direction of public preferences did not always divide along liberal-conservative lines or break in favor of the pronounced conservative solutions offered by candidate Ronald Reagan. At best, the picture was mixed.

If there was a mandate, it was muted. The 1980 election results may best be explained by a combination of factors which includes an emphasis on "retrospective" or "performance-based" voting (i.e., a judgment as to how well the incumbent has done in office). By this gauge, there was a mandate: to replace the Carter Administration with another, potentially more capable of meeting the country's serious economic needs. The verdict went against the party in power, and the only realistic alternative in the general election, despite John Anderson's third party candidacy, was Ronald Reagan.

Ronald Reagan's closing appeal, in the last of the televised debates, that the voter judge whether he or she was better off than he or she had been a year earlier and then to vote accordingly, may have had as much to do with the outcome as anything. According to some polls, as the tail end of the 1980 campaign approached, up to one-third of the electorate remained undecided, the highest proportion in contemporary (post-1950) polling history. This appeal may well have proven persuasive within this group. Those believing that the nation's business condition was at that time worse than it was a year before, rose to 71 percent in 1980; the approval rating of Carter's performance in office, low at the end of his term, sank further during the election campaign by thirty-six percentage points (ending as a dimension favoring Reagan); and the voters' perception of the Administration's ability to handle both the economy and unemployment, likewise already weak, declined substantially during the campaign (ending also as factors influencing a vote for Reagan).[18] A preference for policy change and the negative evaluation of the Carter Administration's performance are the two biggest factors contributing to the Reagan vote.[19]

This is not to say that party identification was not a factor. As in 1976, it was a factor, although it contributed more to Carter than to Reagan. Ideological predisposition was also influential in the vote,

[18] Warren E. Miller and J. Merrill Shanks, "Policy Directions and Presidential Leadership: Alternative Interpretations of the 1980 Presidential Election," *British Journal of Political Science* 12 (July 1982), pp. 299–356. On the 1980 election, see also: Arthur H. Miller and Martin P. Wattenberg, "Policy and Performance Voting in the 1980 Election." (New York: A Paper Prepared for Delivery at the Annual Meeting of the American Political Science Association, September 3–6, 1981); Donald R. Kinder, "Enough Already About Ideology: The Many Bases of American Public Opinion" (Denver: A Paper Prepared for Delivery at the Annual Meeting of the American Political Science Association, September 1–4, 1982); and John R. Petrocik and Sidney Verba, with Christine Schultz, "Choosing the Choice and Not the Echo: A Funny Thing Happened to *The Changing American Voter* on the Way to the 1980 Election" (New York: Prepared for Delivery at the Annual Meeting of the American Political Science Association, September 3–6, 1981).

[19] *Ibid.*, p. 351.

helping Reagan more than Carter. All other factors — including the personal perceptions of the candidates and related measures of "like/dislike" favored Carter (and not, as the media presumed, Reagan).[20] Overall then, it is safe to say that issues, as well as other factors such as party preference, were important in influencing the 1980 election outcome (although not quite in the manner reported in the media). The broad outlines of the 1980 election are consistent with those elections that immediately preceded it.

Issue voting lives. If the association between issue positions and party choice is as relevant as it appears, then it would behoove the parties to take clear and attractive stands on the major policy concerns of the day. In the past, political parties have not served well as vehicles of policy representation and articulation. They will have to change. In an age of increased issue concern, the very existence of the parties may well depend on it.

While the trend toward the increasing importance of issues in presidential elections is clear, a few caveats are in order. Initially, candidate orientation was posited as one of the three most important influences on the presidential vote (along with party identification and issue orientation). Candidate image is a short-run factor influencing individual elections. Its effect from one presidential race to the next could be expected to vary greatly. It is a difficult concept to measure and may in fact be associated in national elections with the voter's issue perceptions. As an example, a voter who strongly favored a law-and-order position in 1972 would have supported Richard Nixon, whom he would also have been likely to perceive personally in favorable terms; a voter strongly opposed to the Vietnam War in 1972 would have backed George McGovern, and this support could color, to a degree, his perception of the candidate and his qualities. Because of the ambiguities inherent in the concept (both Reagan and Carter had negative assessments in 1980, although Carter's were less intense than Reagan's) and the increasing emphasis on issues in presidential elections, candidate orientation as a factor in explaining presidential election outcomes has been stressed less, and at present the concept is undergoing experimental attempts to redefine it as a measurement tool. The end result could be a clearer indication of its impact on national-level voter decision-making.

[20] *Ibid.*, pp. 351–52.

It should be noted also that in congressional (and perhaps other levels of elections) both the voter's perceptions of the candidates and a habitual party vote may assume greater importance. This tendency is discussed later in this book in relation to congressional elections where policy positions are often of far less importance in explaining election outcomes. On the presidential level, however, there has been a decided move in voter decision making toward an increased reliance on issues in determining for whom to vote.

4

Liberalism/Conservatism

An increasing turn toward conservatism, many observers believed, marked elections from the late 1960s and to the early 1980s. Early on, the conservatism was focused on the revolt against lawlessness; the decline in adherence to traditional moral and social values; crime in the streets; the campus disruptions; cities in flame; the hippie life style and the "me generation" syndrome; the disrespect for authority and the vilification, in particular, of the police; and the mass demonstrations and continuing acts of civil disobedience sparked by the Vietnam War. The nation's social fabric seemed to be unraveling. The revolt coincided with, and helped feed, an increasing cynicism concerning the value and objectives of the massive government spending programs and the social welfare priorities of the Johnson-Kennedy years. The beneficiary of this revolt in its first stages was Richard Nixon, the Republican nominee for president in 1968. Nixon won narrowly, but he did beat the dominant Democratic party, and he ended its eight-year control of the presidency.

As president, Nixon interpreted his "mandate" broadly and attempted to build a conservative coalition of sunbelt states, Republicans, and about anyone dissatisfied with the Democratic programs and the seeming moral decay and political anarchy rampant in the society. The chief focus of the new conservative resurgence was to be the "silent majority" — those quiet Americans, basically conservative in social and fiscal policy, that Nixon's people believed represented the mainstream of political thinking.

Nixon and his policies went too far, resulting in a repressive government posture that eventually forced the president's resignation under threat of impeachment. Gerald Ford, the vice-president, assumed the top office. Ford, a conservative, was a twenty-six-year veteran of the House of Representatives who had faithfully mirrored the values of his midwestern constituency.

Ford, in turn, went down to a narrow defeat in 1976 at the hands of Jimmy Carter, the Democratic candidate. Carter appeared to be a moderate. In office, his policies of fiscal restraint, reduced social programs, tight money, decontrol of the oil industry, and moderately increased defense spending placed him closer to the Ford-Nixon policy emphasis than to that of the more traditional Democratic programs of Johnson and Kennedy.

By the late 1970s the rise of interest rates, a decade of increasing inflation, and the corresponding decline in the standard of living had voters in a sour mood. Although the off-year election of 1978 was hailed as a victory for conservatism, the Republicans did not significantly increase their seats in either the House or Senate. The election year did, however, give birth to the Proposition 13 mentality. There was an effort to limit taxation through legislative initiative, or state or national constitutional amendment if necessary. The Kemp-Roth bill was introduced in the Congress to cut taxes across the board by one-third. It quickly became a popular political debating point. Who could be for taxes? California Governor Jerry Brown, one of Carter's rivals for the 1980 Democratic presidential nomination, endorsed the idea (favored mostly by rightists and some Republicans) of a new constitutional convention to rewrite into the Constitution limits on taxation and possibly federal spending. The hero of the new public mood was Howard Jarvis, a previously unknown conservative activist, who in his later years (he was over seventy) had risen to prominence as cosponsor and principal lobbyist for Proposition 13. With the ratification by California voters of the proposition, Jarvis became the highly publicized political guru of the new revolt. The media proclaimed the rise of conservatism among voters and the new mood that had taken control of political life. Were Americans becoming more conservative? Had a conservative philosophy of government come to dominate the views of Americans?

The characteristics of the period appeared to be the following:

the move to cut taxes
the belief that social welfare and spending programs did not work
the reactions to big government
a "get-tough" attitude toward crime and criminals
renewed support for the death penalty and its reconstitution in
    many states
the prolonged opposition to busing and new civil rights legislation
support for defense spending
the antiabortion crusade
the faltering drive for ERA (Equal Rights Amendment)
a hardening line toward the Soviets and any SALT (Strategic Arms
    Limitation Treaties) pacts

The climax of this movement came with the election of Ronald Reagan to the presidency in 1980. Reagan was the most visible spokesman for the "New Right"-conservative orthodoxy. His election was seen as a turning point in American history: the emergence of the conservative right as the dominant force in American politics. However, this impressionistic vision of political events was forced to give way to a more complex reality. A review of the factors influencing voter decision making in the 1980 election reveals that the American voter was more pragmatic than perceived either by the media, with their immediate reaction to issues, or by the political pundits, with their instant analyses of political results.

First, in regard to the conservatism of the American population in general, conservatives do appear to outnumber liberals (Figure 4.1). According to Gallup, the margin of liberals to conservatives is 31 percent to 19; the National Opinion Research Center (NORC) places it at 34 to 26 percent; and, in figures not shown, the Center for Political Studies' 1980 election survey reports a 27 to 16 percent edge for conservatives.[1] A 1980 *Time* magazine poll gives the most decisive edge to conservatives, 44 to 13 percent. In both the Gallup and NORC surveys the modal group are the moderates or

[1] Center for Political Studies, 1980 Presidential Election Study.

FIGURE 4.1
Counting Conservatives: The Polls Disagree

I. Gallup

Question: People who are conservative in their political views are referred to as being right of center and people who are liberal in their political views are referred to as being left of center. Which one of the categories (respondents handed a card: Far left, substantially left, moderately left, just slightly left of center, just slightly right of center, moderately right of center, substantially right of center, far right) best describes your political position? (1980)

	Liberal	Middle-of-the-Road	Conservative
April 1972	27%	34%	39%
March 1976	20	47	33
September 1980	19	49	31

Note: For earlier question wording, see *Public Opinion,* December/January 1981.

II. National Opinion Research Center (NORC)

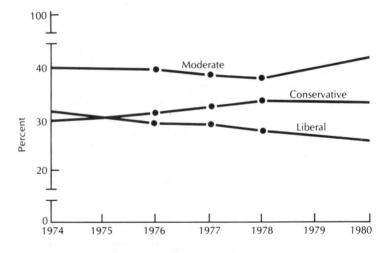

III. *Time*/Yankelovich, Skelley, and White

Question: Do you think of yourself as: Conservative, Moderate, Liberal, Radical?

Source: Public Opinion, February/March 1981, p. 20. Part I: Surveys by the Gallup Organization, latest that of September 9–12, 1980. Part II: Survey by National Opinion Research Center, General Social Surveys, latest that of 1980. Part III: Survey by *Time*/Yankelovich, Skelly and White, August 26–28, 1980. Used by permission.

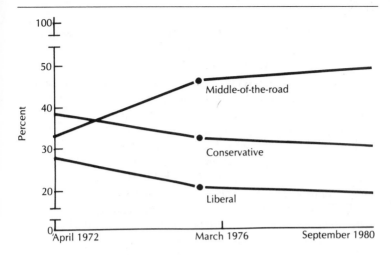

Question: We hear a lot of talk these days about liberals and conservatives. I'm going to show you a seven-point scale on which the *political* views that people might hold are arranged from extremely liberal – point 1 – to extremely conservative – point 7. Where would you place yourself on this scale?

	Liberal	Moderate	Conservative
1974	31%	40%	30%
1975	30	40	30
1976	29	40	31
1977	29	39	32
1978	28	38	34
1980	26	41	34

Note: Liberal = Extremely liberal, liberal, and slightly liberal; Moderate = moderate, middle-of-the-road; Conservative = slightly conservative, conservative, and extremely conservative.

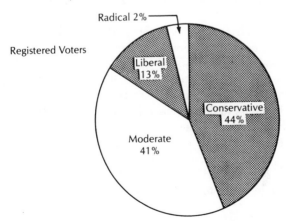

Registered Voters

"middle-of-the-roaders" at 49 and 41 percent in the respective polls. The modal group in the Center for Political Studies' 1980 survey are those unwilling or unable to place themselves on an ideological scale (38 percent). Nineteen percent said they thought of themselves as centrists. Again, the *Time* magazine poll is at odds with the others. In this, 41 percent consider themselves moderate, slightly less than those calling themselves conservative. In the Gallup, NORC and *Time* polls, either the respondents were not given the option of placing themselves on the scale, or the results were not reported. Overall, it is probable that many Americans have trouble seeing themselves in an ideological light and intelligently defining what was meant by liberal, conservative, or centrist. Most, in fact, may well be unable to commit themselves seriously to such a position and, to the extent that they did, might well position themselves between the polar extremes.

As to the argument that there has been an increase in the number of conservatives, Gallup actually reports a decline in the proportion of adults willing to characterize themselves as either conservative or liberal (both down 8 percent) between 1972 and 1980. The NORC figures show a modest increase in the proportion of conservatives (up 4 percent since 1974) along with a related drop in those labeling themselves liberal. The Center for Political Studies' data demonstrate a slight drop in the proportion of liberals (from 19 to 16 percent) but no change in the proportion considering themselves conservative (steady at 27 percent) in both 1972 and 1980. If there has been a move in a conservative direction, it has been subtle and probably not significant enough to account for the election outcomes and policy changes often attributed to a changing public ideology.

As to the personal characteristics of those who consider themselves left, right, or center, moderates predominate among those with the least formal education and the lowest income levels (Figure 4.2). Men are slightly more conservative than women. A conservative political orientation is more associated with higher incomes, and a willingness to declare oneself either conservative or liberal is strongly related to higher levels of formal education. In fact, among those attending post-college graduate and professional schools, only 23 percent chose to identify themselves as moderates. Information levels should increase with formal education, which in turn should relate to a clearer perception of one's own

FIGURE 4.2
Characteristics of Liberals, Moderates, and Conservatives

Question: Regardless of the party you may favor, do you lean more toward the liberal side or the conservative side politically?

Voters as they left the polls*

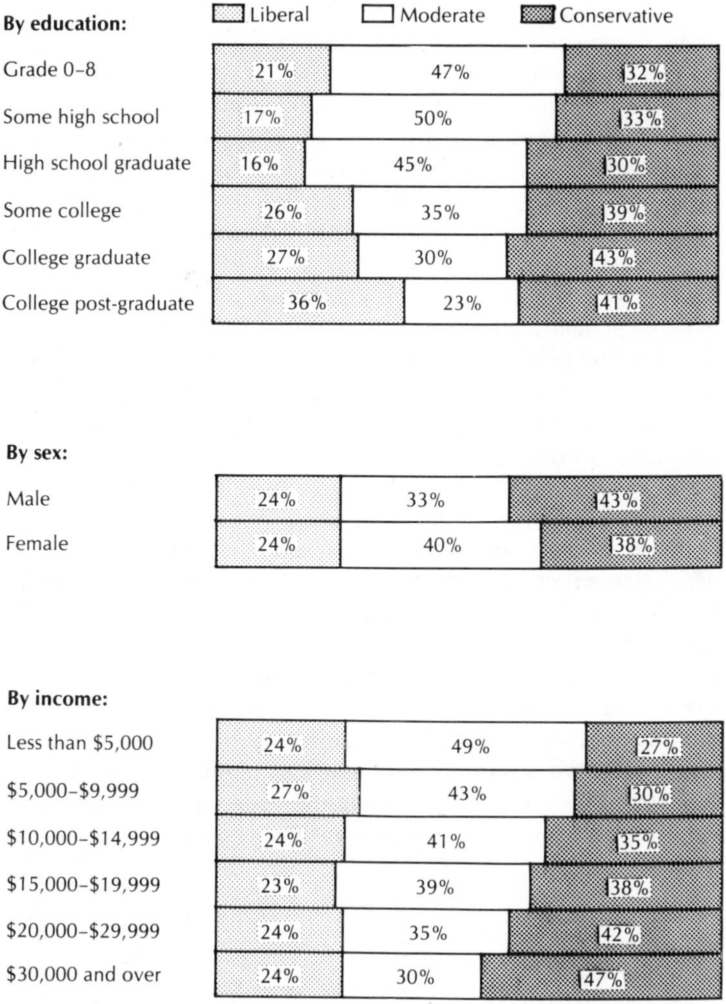

By education: ☐ Liberal   ☐ Moderate   ▨ Conservative

	Liberal	Moderate	Conservative
Grade 0–8	21%	47%	32%
Some high school	17%	50%	33%
High school graduate	16%	45%	30%
Some college	26%	35%	39%
College graduate	27%	30%	43%
College post-graduate	36%	23%	41%

By sex:

	Liberal	Moderate	Conservative
Male	24%	33%	43%
Female	24%	40%	38%

By income:

	Liberal	Moderate	Conservative
Less than $5,000	24%	49%	27%
$5,000–$9,999	27%	43%	30%
$10,000–$14,999	24%	41%	35%
$15,000–$19,999	23%	39%	38%
$20,000–$29,999	24%	35%	42%
$30,000 and over	24%	30%	47%

Source: Public Opinion (February/March 1981), p. 21. Used by permission.

views and where those views stand in relation to those of others and in response to the political alternatives offered in elections. A clearer perception of the policy alternatives being offered by the political parties and the candidates for elective office and a better appreciation of one's own issue priorities, both of which are associated with higher levels of formal education, could — and, some would argue, do — lead to a higher incidence of issue voting and a clearer definition of ideological position.

The picture is complex. Americans do appear frustrated and angered in recent election years with big institutions of every kind over which they exercise little control. Their faith in government, in particular, has declined to all-time lows (for the post-1950 modern era of polling). The proportion of adults finding government "very responsive" to their needs declined from roughly one out of three to one out of twelve between 1964 and 1980 (see Figure 4.3). Correspondingly, the proportion of those feeling that congressmen pay a good deal of attention to the views of those who reelect them was down by twenty-five percentage points or that political parties help keep those in power accountable declined similarly. The American electorate has been disillusioned with the performance of its governing institutions. If there is encouraging news in all of this, it is that by 1982 the faith in government had begun to creep back up (to 33 percent from 25 percent, for example, in those who believed that the government in Washington could be trusted to do what was right all or most of the time). The government's ability to cut inflation and interest rates probably accounts for the change.[2]

That is the good news. The bad news is, as political scientist Arthur Miller observed, that the increase in public confidence should not be overstated: "The American public remains predominately negative toward government and public officials, but the shift toward a more positive attitude is historically and politically important."[3] How important and where it goes from here, remain unclear.

[2] Adam Clymer, "Poll Finds Trust in Government Edging Back Up," *The New York Times,* July 15, 1983, p. 1. © 1983 by The New York Times Company. Reprinted by permission. See also: Stephen Earl Bennett, "Changes in the Public's Perceptions of Governmental Responsiveness: 1964–1980," A Paper Prepared for Delivery at the Annual Meeting of the Midwest Political Science Association, Milwaukee, April 29–May 1, 1982.

[3] Quoted in Clymer, *op. cit.*

FIGURE 4.3
Changing Attitudes Toward Government

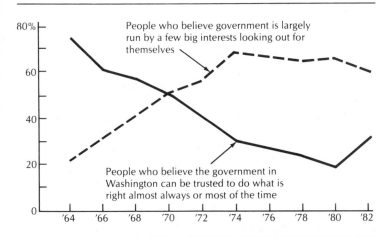

Source: Center for Political Studies, as appearing in *The New York Times,* July 15, 1983, p. B6. © 1983 by The New York Times Company. Reprinted by permission.

In specific issue areas the public tends to strongly support government-sponsored social welfare programs. Three out of four Americans believe that the government should help everyone who wanted a job to find work and that it should assume responsibility for assisting people to acquire low-cost health care. Although sentiment favoring the death penalty increased, so has support for liberalized positions on such social concerns as legalization of marijuana, the propriety of premarital relations, careers for married women, and a woman for president. Those favoring the ERA resolution remain a majority. The number of those willing to make divorce easier, another indicator of the attitude toward permissiveness and moral questions in the society, has fluctuated, but continues to stay well ahead of the comparative levels of response of two decades ago.

Attitudes toward racial questions (outside of busing) appeared to have liberalized remarkably. Better than 70 percent of the population disapprove of state laws against interracial marriage (up from 49 percent in 1965); 84 percent would support a black for president (up from 51 percent in 1963); and 93 percent believe that blacks have a right to live any place they chose (up from 71 percent in 1960). These statistics represent pronounced changes in attitudes toward blacks. They are paralleled by the rise in support for civil liberties. In 1954, at the height of the McCarthy era, a social scientist, Samuel Stouffer, surveyed Americans as to the strength of their support for libertarian qualities in a variety of projected situations (permitting antireligion or socialist speakers to address gatherings in the community; keeping antireligion or socialist books in the local library; allowing a socialist to be a teacher). The mean level of support favoring the civil liberty positions was 43 percent in 1954. Two decades later, a survey asking the same questions found that the support level had risen to a mean of 65 percent.

To confound matters, a majority of conservatives supported many liberal positions. These included government guarantees of jobs and housing for blacks, restrictions on the sale of handguns, approval of sex education courses, and allowing pornographic materials to be sold to adults. Conversely, on such issues as quotas for minorities, support of government regulation of business, increases in domestic spending, and a belief that the Great Society programs made life better, a majority of liberals took positions normally associated with conservatives. On the other issues (government-supported abortions; restrictions on the sale of marijuana) conservatives were conservative, and liberals were predictably liberal.[4]

If anything, in most of the issues surveys Americans appear to be moderately liberal. Yet there is some truth to talk of a conservative revival. Surely, the rhetoric of the 1970s and easily the 1980s involved typically conservative issues (inflation, economic recession, decreases in the standard-of-living, government spending), and the solutions proposed by Democrats and Republicans alike tended to be conservative (cut taxes, restrict government expenditures, balance the budget, tighten the money supply, trim social welfare programs). Liberals and traditionally liberal programs were very much on the defensive.

Perhaps the answer lies more in the changing nature of politics in the last decade than in any pronounced shift in voter attitudes.

[4] The specific figures can be found in William J. Crotty and Gary C. Jacobson, *American Parties in Decline* (Boston: Little, Brown, 1980), Table 4.2, pp. 56–58.

It is true that conservative issues dominated political debate. It is also clear that conservative groups and causes became better organized and aggressively militant. Such groups benefited from the political exhaustion of the times and the seeming disarray of liberal groups. They also made quick use of the new campaign laws that encouraged business and ideological group financing and used extensive media campaigns to retake the political initiative during a confused and party-weakened period. Although the number of conservatives may not have increased over the last twenty years, the proportion of conservatives becoming attached to the more ideologically militant wing of the group did appear to increase. Warren Miller and Teresa Levitin report, for example, that the proportion of "strong conservatives" in their study of political activists (those in the electorate who tried to persuade others to support their candidate or views) rose by 50 percent between the 1972 and 1976 presidential elections to where this group accounted for almost half of all conservatives (47 percent) and approximately a fifth of all political activists.[5]

Whereas liberal assumptions and programs appeared under sustained attack, the conservative movement was buoyed by the emergence of the American Enterprise Institute (AEI), a conservative Republican-oriented think tank in Washington, D.C. Within a few years, and with sustained financial support from conservative groups and Republican administrations (such as the Nixon administration), AEI became aggressively outspoken on political issues confronting the nation. Its staff increased to over one hundred of the best-known academics and political figures on full-time status and a large number of others under contract for specific projects. Its $8 million budget exceeded that of its older, somewhat staid and moderately liberal rival, the Brookings Institution.[6]

One writer has described the conservative (or, as he calls it, neoconservative) intellectual and policy-oriented movement as

> a child of the Sixties — the Other Child, the one that didn't turn on, tune in, and drop out; that didn't join the commune in California, march on Washington, or boo Hubert Humphrey in Chicago. Neoconservatism sets itself against the Sixties, against social turbu-

[5] Warren E. Miller and Teresa E. Levitin, *Leadership and Change: Presidential Elections from 1952 to 1976* (Cambridge, Mass.: Winthrop, 1976).

[6] Peter Steinfels, "The Reasonable Right," *Esquire*, February 13, 1979, p. 29.

lence, political conflict, and cultural experiment. From its beginnings, neoconservatism has been fiercely attached to political and cultural moderation, committed to stability, pessimistic about the possibilities for long-range — or even short-range — change in America, and imbued with a foreboding sense of our civilization's decline. Because neoconservatism didn't fit the conventional image of the times, its gathering strength was ignored. Yet in the end, neoconservatism may be the most enduring political legacy of the "radical Sixties," of the very Eden so many liberals claim as their own. [7]

In a period of intense voter disillusionment and continuing public apathy, conservatives at least were on the move. It may be that a low level of political involvement coupled with a political situation (the ineffectiveness of parties, the rise of new sources of business and ideological funding) provides a receptive climate for conservative politics. Or, it may be that the issues of the day favored conservatives; that the liberal coalition was in turmoil, a continuing legacy of the divisive 1960s; and that in the vacuum that evolved, a well-financed and intellectually aggressive conservative voice drew new attention.

[7] *Ibid.*, p. 29.

II
THE DECLINE OF THE
PARTY IN CAMPAIGNS

Introduction

The role of the political party in campaigns has given way to the technology of television-centered campaigns built on polls and run by media and public relations experts. The evolving politics is a candidate-centered, technocratic exercise in impersonal manipulation. It is also a politics of extraordinary expense.

The new technology costs a great deal of money and, as a result of the recent campaign financing laws, a new source of funds has emerged: the Political Action Committees (PACs). These business, labor, and ideological groups constitute a new and continually more significant source of funding for political races. Most often they invest in candidates to secure specified economic or other policy ends. Since 1974 they have completely overshadowed the party organizations in supplying campaign funds. The PACs and the modern campaign technology have encouraged the emergence of new single-interest groups (on abortion, the gun lobby) and ideological interest groups that have an increasing impact on the parties, the conduct of campaigns, and the nature and policy commitments of elected public officials. These developments are all very recent (since 1974), but their impact is already clear. Although a growing source of political influence, these groups —

their motives and methods — are just beginning to receive serious attention.

The partyless campaign is a slick and expensive exercise that can often result in forceful, well-built, and highly professional candidate organizations. As soon as the election is over, win or lose, the candidate organizations are disbanded, and the professional consultants move on to their next job. A similar expense of money and effort in creating permanent party organizations would result in lasting benefits. Unfortunately, that cannot happen. By definition, the professionalized candidate organizations are bought by one person's money and committed to only one person's success. They are basically antiparty and contribute one more factor to the eroding base of the party in campaigns.

In this section we will look at television and the politics of the media; polling and other professional consulting services; the escalating cost of politics and the role of the business and labor PACs and ideological issue groups in funding political contests; and, briefly, the efforts to equalize resources and return political races to the public domain. The latter is the concern behind the present efforts to legislate federal (and to a lesser extent, state) funding of congressional and other elective races. The section concludes with an analysis of the parties' response to the realities of a changing political environment.

5
Television and the Politics of the Media

Television is the new political god. It has supplanted the political party as the main conduit between candidate and voter. It is the principal influence acting on the voter in a campaign and his chief source of information. It is the medium of information he is most dependent on and the one he trusts most implicitly. However, it is both an expensive and unpredictable master.

Television allows those candidates who can command the necessary financial resources to mount impressive challenges to incumbents at all levels. Such candidates are not dependent on the political party to sponsor their careers. A political organization and the mastery of a ladder-like succession of political offices are no longer prerequisites for nomination and election to higher political offices. A prospective candidate with sufficient personal wealth or PAC resources can run for office whenever he decides. He need have no previous political experience, no ties to the party whose nomination he seeks, and no particular roots in the community or bonds to the people he seeks to represent. All he needs is the ability to use television, to follow the advice of his consultants, and to pay for the services rendered. The last is the most important.

THE PERVASIVENESS OF TELEVISION

Television is the great American pastime. Americans have become television junkies to an alarming extent. The Federal Communications Commission reveals that 97 percent (73.3 million) of American homes (of a total 75.3 million) contain at least one television set. The average home has its set(s) turned on about six hours a day. With such a communications vehicle available, it is not surprising that politicians have been quick to take advantage of it.

The rise in television's influence can easily be documented. The presidential election of 1952 saw the first, tentative use of television on a broad scale in national campaigns. Republican Dwight Eisenhower's campaigners experimented in this election year (and later in 1956) with employing television to humanize the general and to personalize his virtues. Through television use the Republicans attempted to communicate a sense of Eisenhower's integrity, honesty, and forthrightness. The efforts largely succeeded. Adlai Stevenson chose to focus on televising polished oratorical addresses on issues of national concern and delivered before large audiences in auditoriums or prescheduled rallies. The approach was conventional and it was stilted. It is fair to say that the Stevenson people, unlike Eisenhower's, never fully utilized the new medium and, in fact, failed to grasp its potential.

Building on the Eisenhower success, other candidates evolved strategies that came to depend more and more on television as the centerpiece of their campaign efforts. At the same time, television began to emerge as the dominant source of campaign information for the voter. Between 1952 and 1956 alone, the number of voters identifying television as the most important source of their political information jumped from 36 to 56 percent. By the 1960s two-thirds of the electorate relied mostly on television. Newspapers came in a poor second, commanding approximately one-fourth of the voters' allegiance; and radio declined from about one-third to where it, along with magazines, became relatively insignificant as a source of campaign news.

Yet it can be argued that those who depend on newspapers for their news receive a quite different level of information: more thorough and sophisticated, with the issues and the contending positions and their implications sharply defined. Those relying on newspapers tend to have a stronger informational base and are more resistant to transitory opinion changes than are those who depend on television for guidance.[1] They tend also to be of higher socioeconomic status, which may account for their choice. Concurrently the use of television has paralleled a decrease in reliance on multiple sources for political news. It would appear that as television has become more prominent in political campaigns, it has also fostered a dependence on it that works to the increasing exclusion of other sources of information. It is a safe, easy, and sanitized way to acquire political information.

The hegemony of television in transmitting political news is singularly unfortunate. There are a number of things about television that help place in perspective its role in communicating political information. First, television and television news are big business. The corporations that control the major networks are multibillion-dollar conglomerates whose interests, in addition to owning networks and individual television and radio stations nationwide, extend to publishing houses, entertainment parks, real estate, movie corporations, sports franchises, and about anything else that will return a profit and is not illegal.

Individually owned television stations return a handsome profit also. A representative of a consumer federation told Congress in mid-1979, "The average station earns about 100 percent on investment every year, and network-owned stations earn three times that. . . . [Advertising] rates for time go up every year; 1980 is substantially sold out at all-time high prices."[2]

Entertainment programming, of course, is a highly profitable venture. But the profits extend also to news. Such programming is both prestigious and quite lucrative. It is a moneymaking enterprise that networks and independent stations have no intention of jeopardizing. Unfortunately, the entertainment psychology extends to much of news programming. Entertain, Amuse, and Do Not Shock (or worse, Bore) appear to be the rules of the day. Controversial issues are watered down in presentation, and the

---

[1] See Thomas E. Patterson and Robert D. McClure, *The Unseeing Eye* (New York: G. P. Putnam's Sons, 1976); and Patterson and McClure, "Television and Voters' Issue Awareness," in William Crotty (ed.), *The Party Symbol* (San Francisco: W. H. Freeman, 1980).

[2] Joan Hanauer, "New Look at Old Law," *Boston Globe*, June 12, 1979, p. 29.

less conventional side usually receives limited attention. The "happy talk" news shows on local stations epitomize the tendency, but the network news programs — the most prestigious of television programs — show the same tendencies.

The examples are many. Despite the euphoria and self-congratulations spawned by the (eventually) successful investigations and revelations of the *Washington Post* reporting team of Carl Bernstein and Bob Woodward on Watergate, their type of reporting (and impact) is far more the exception than the rule.[3] The results were duly (and rightly) lionized. It is not by accident that Woodward and Bernstein's reports appeared in a newspaper. Television (and for that matter most newspapers) confined itself to reporting the official White House rebuttals to the Bernstein-Woodward accusations and only tangentially addressed themselves to the serious charges of criminal and governmental misconduct that they revealed. Television, in time, was a major influence in educating the country to the extraordinary constitutional abuses of the Nixon Administration: a sign of its tremendous potential for developing an informed and responsive electorate. It did this, however, only after the revelations concerning Watergate refused to disappear. And television did this by covering live the Ervin Committee hearings documenting the allegations and the Rodino Committee deliberations on impeachment. In effect, it could not avoid covering in depth what then was the biggest news story of the decade and one of the most disturbing in the nation's political history.

Television likes to justify its dominant public role and think of itself as providing a public service of extraordinary consequence. Luckily, both the Ervin and Rodino hearings were good theater as well as good news, and both were good public relations. It is more fruitful to ask what role CBS, NBC, and ABC news played in revealing the basic abuses of governmental and constitutional safeguards by Richard Nixon and his associates before the major governmental agencies acted. What did television contribute to the education of the public on these issues before national concern forced major congressional investigations?

[3] Carl Bernstein and Bob Woodward, *All the President's Men* (New York: Simon and Schuster, 1974); and Woodward and Bernstein, *The Final Days* (New York: Simon and Schuster, 1976). On Watergate more generally, see: J. Anthony Lukas, *Nightmare: The Underside of the Nixon Years* (New York: Viking, 1976).

In these areas the contribution of television is far less impressive. Individual television reporters (Dan Rather and Daniel Schorr of CBS come to mind) did take the lead in forcing revelations and placing the Nixon Administration on the defensive for its actions. They were atypical. More prevalent would be the approach of the news anchors and the television news editors on the major networks. Walter Cronkite, the long-time anchor of the "CBS Evening News," can be used as an example. For years, the best-known and most trusted newsman in the country, Cronkite was a celebrity in his own right; his personal life and avocations were covered by the media for their own news value. Cronkite is a centrist with a sense of obligation to the role and mission of television as he sees it. His approach and sensitivities on what constitutes acceptable news programming were not significantly different from those of corporate heads such as William Paley, who directed the CBS network. Network executives are more concerned with bottom-line profits, the noncontroversial presentation of issues, and good relations with political leaders. They are aware that such leaders can do much through the Federal Communications Commission and congressional legislation to punish unfriendly television outlets.

Watergate is as good an example of the role of television in news reporting and its extraordinary sensitivity to political pressures as any. CBS news decided to do a more in-depth analysis of the Watergate scandals immediately prior to Election Day 1972 in an effort to tie together the various reports of political abuse and to place them in a context meaningful to the voter. The report was to be delivered in several relatively lengthy installments on the "CBS Evening News" (the average story runs thirty to ninety seconds). The principal reporters were to be Daniel Schorr and Dan Rather.

The report did not uncover more information, and it did not add much to the pool of knowledge available. This was not its purpose. It was an attempt to apply perspective to the problems addressed and, as originally filmed, it was explicit. "They [spokespersons for the Nixon Administration] keep issuing general denials; they are depending on that, and silence, to make the allegations go away," reported Rather.[4]

The first segment was broadcast. The remaining reports had

[4] Daniel Schorr, *Clearing the Air* (Boston: Houghton Mifflin, 1977).

been scheduled to follow immediately but were postponed. Eventually they did appear in highly abbreviated form with much of the substance and commentary deleted.

Why this occurred is a matter of controversy. The White House did contact Paley at CBS and various other news officials who had power over news programming. This much seems clear. What exactly the role of the White House was and how much weight the CBS officials placed on its threats is in debate. Nonetheless, the Nixon Administration got most of what it wanted, and the presentation was seriously cut. The episode illustrates the sensitive role of television news reporting and its vulnerability on matters of importance to official pressures.

The Nixon Administration used threats against individual reporters (for example, through FBI investigations into the background of media critics such as Daniel Schorr) and networks. It threatened CBS with a variety of reprisals, from loss of access to government decision makers to support for policies that would strike directly at the financial base of the networks (encouragement of challenges to the licensing renewals of network-owned stations; divestiture of company-owned stations; proposals for the federal licensing of networks; government promotion of alternative communication channels such as cable TV).[5] The administration's successful efforts to weaken public broadcast television and to move its emphasis from public affairs (potentially a source of embarrassment to the administration) to nonpolitical cultural and local programming illustrates the extent to which it was willing to go.[6] Television is particularly vulnerable to these types of official retribution.

Nixon, in his campaigns and while in office, received generally good press, despite his beliefs to the contrary and his sensitivity to any criticism, however mild. His attacks on the commercial networks paid dividends. The emasculation of the Rather and Schorr

[5] Other accounts of relevance to this discussion include: *ibid.;* David Halberstam, *The Powers That Be* (New York: Knopf, 1979); William S. Paley, *As It Happened: A Memoir* (New York: Doubleday, 1979); Dan Rather and Mickey Herkowitz, *The Camera Never Blinks* (New York: Morrow, 1977); Gary Paul Gates, *Air Time* (New York: Berkley, 1979); William Crotty, *Political Reform and the American Experiment* (New York: Crowell, 1977), pp. 139–67; *The Senate Watergate Report,* 2 vols. (New York: Dell, 1974); and *The Impeachment Report* (New York: New American Library, 1974).

[6] "A Bid to Establish a Nixon Network," *The New York Times,* February 2, 1979, p. 4E.

report is but one example. The other two networks did far less than CBS. As a consequence, the news source most listened to and most trusted by the American people did little in the 1972 campaign to foster an understanding of an issue that would eventually topple a president.

Nixon also managed to command national air time for news conferences, speeches, and announcements, as do all presidents. The opposition (whether it be Republican or Democrat) is rarely given a meaningful chance to employ television to rebut a president or his stand. Such was certainly the case with Nixon. His opponents were afforded little or no opportunity to speak before national television audiences to counter the president's messages.

The Nixon White House managed to stifle a good deal of dissent — specifically as voiced on national television. The administration even orchestrated a campaign against the network reviews and assessments ("instant analysis," as the White House pejoratively referred to it) that followed major Nixon addresses, successful enough to force them to drop those efforts to inform the public and to place the events that had transpired in some context.

The Nixon assault on television raises questions about the role of the nation's most powerful communications medium in transmitting ideas and subjecting these to informed criticism and debate. Television did not fulfill this function well during the Nixon years.

Nixon's job in controlling the media, or at least in forcing a more receptive hearing for his position, may not have been as difficult as it seemed. The media have an image of themselves as independent, fearless, and professionally neutral conveyors of information: vital links in the chain of democratic governance. In reality, as already noted, journalism is corporate business at the highest level. It is also a business heavily dependent on the good will and access provided by official decision makers. How much publishers and electronic and print reports rely on official entrée is just beginning to be understood. Herbert J. Gans, a sociologist, has recently completed an assessment of what becomes "news" and how the choice process operates.[7] He found, among other things, that in two of the nation's most prestigious newspapers, the *New York*

---

[7] Herbert J. Gans, *Deciding What's News* (New York: Random House, 1979).

Times and the *Washington Post,* 78 percent of the 2850 domestic and foreign stories he examined came directly from public officials.

Gans divided the stories examined into "knowns" and "unknowns" in terms of the source and/or subject categories. The political, business, social, and cultural celebrities account for 70 to 85 percent of the final news content. "Unknowns" manage to break into print usually for criminal offenses. Gans comments that those who are powerless on important issues must often resort to civil disturbances to obtain access to news outlets. [8]

This may not be too surprising. It may be more impressive, and worrisome, that the president alone accounts for 20 percent of all domestic news and that the president's cabinet accounts for another 20 percent. A monopolization of news channels to this extent raises serious questions, again, about the role and contribution of television, and the news media more generally, to an informed contemporary electorate.

Beyond the problems of access and establishment monopolization of communications channels, there is another: the superficiality of television news reporting. This problem is also serious. In part, it is a function of the medium, and in part it relates to the cultural role television has carved for itself in society. Either way, it directly affects the quality of political decision making and the intensity and relevance of information shared by voters.

Americans turn to television for relief from the tension of their daily lives. They seek diversion and amusement, and television has proven very successful in providing a low-level escapism. More than entertaining its viewers in any provocative manner, television fills up their time: it anesthetizes them, blocks out other sensations, and provides for the passage of time. Television entertainment — the "$1.98 Beauty Show," "The Love Boat," the "Gong Show," and so on — strives for (and obtains) the lowest common denominator. A listing of the top shows for the 1980–1981 television season makes the point (Table 5.1). The most popular television fare included "Dallas," "The Dukes of Hazzard," and "That's Incredible." Only one news program, CBS' popular "60 Minutes," cracked the top thirty. It would be surprising if the psychology of show business values, and quick profit turnover from

[8] See the review by Richard Rovere in "Political Books" in *The Washington Monthly,* March 1979, pp. 60–61.

TABLE 5.1
Most Popular Television Programs, September 1980 through September 1981

Rank	Program	Network
1	"Dallas"	CBS
2	"60 Minutes"	CBS
3	"The Dukes of Hazzard"	CBS
4	"M*A*S*H"	CBS
5	"Private Benjamin"	CBS
(tie) 6	"NBC Movie of the Week" and "NBC Tuesday Night Movie"	Both NBC
8	"The Jeffersons"	CBS
9	"Best of the West"	ABC
10	"The Love Boat"	ABC
(tie) 11	"NFL Monday Night Football" and "Three's Company" and "House Calls"	ABC, ABC, and CBS
14	"Brady Girls Get Married"	NBC
15	"Too Close for Comfort"	ABC
16	"The Two of Us"	CBS
17	"Alice"	CBS
18	"Diff'rent Strokes"	NBC
19	"That's Incredible"	ABC
20	"Trapper John, M.D."	CBS
21	"Real People"	NBC
22	"The Facts of Life"	NBC
(tie) 23	"Hart to Hart" and "The Little House on the Prairie"	ABC and NBC
25	"Fantasy Island" and "Happy Days" and "Laverne and Shirley"	All ABC
28	"One Day at a Time"	CBS
29	"Lou Grant"	CBS
(tie) 30	"The Greatest American Hero" and "Magnum, P.I."	ABC and CBS

Source: Nielsen Prime Time Audience Rating. Reprinted by permission of the A. C. Nielsen Company. Used by permission.

television's entertainment ventures, did not affect its approach to the news.

Technically, television is a visual medium. It needs pictures — and the more active and personalized the better — to tell its story. It does not deal well with issues, the varying positions on a dispute, the arguments and evidence available to the protagonists, and the implications of the proposed alternatives. This is a cerebral and fairly abstract type of information better conveyed on the printed page. Television demands movement, color, and associations made with the eye. This has led to a certain type of news orientation. Issues are crammed into a brief (minute or so) segment. An edited tape of a proponent making a quick statement and someone speaking on the other side is shown, and the show moves on. It would be extraordinarily difficult for a viewer to pick up any meaningful information that would help him to make an informed judgment from such an exposure. Yet this is what he must cope with.

An example will make the point. An individual turns on the television and finds that there is an oil crisis. Long lines of car owners seeking gasoline in eastern states are shown; violence at several stations is reported; a story is presented on many service stations restricting fuel purchases to three or five dollars; and a reporter says the situation is likely to get worse. A story is then introduced about independent truckers striking against higher diesel prices. Reports show truck stops and major highways blockaded by truckers; the state police in several states are shown trying to break the blockade; a trucker is reported killed in one state; and, in another, the governor calls out the national guard. The president is shown demonstrating a solar heating system on the roof of the White House to supply part of its energy load and lauding it as a future possibility. The secretary of energy comes on to say that the crisis will get worse as oil import prices increase, but there should be plenty of gasoline for the summer. The televised news moves on to other subjects.

What is a viewer to think? What has he learned? He knows there is a gasoline shortage. He realizes that people are angry and that violence has occurred. He can associate the shortage with OPEC, but that may be as far as his knowledge goes. He will learn little from this television program on matters concerning the role, profits, and alternatives of the oil companies; the potentially competing energy proposals and their feasibility; the long-run implications of the crisis; the differences in proposals being put forth in Washington by oil, government, and consumer groups; and so on. Yet, to reemphasize, television is the dominant source of news. It communicates headlines and feelings about problems but little beyond this. This is the level of information on which most people, not exposed to other sources of news, must rely.

Television has further reduced the role of the political party as a communicator of news and as a shaper of the public will. It has replaced the political party and the printed media as the dominant source of issue information. Yet television gives news a certain, often superficial, emphasis, and it is open to subtle, but powerful influences on its operations. Whether the reliance on television is an improvement over the old ways is debatable.

TELEVISION AND POLITICAL CAMPAIGNING

Television's coverage of political campaigns is much the same: superficial with emphasis on the visual. Television focuses on the obvious. It is not concerned with the extended exploration of policy issues, relative differences in positions, or even thorough investigations of an individual's background and previous policy stands. In the pre-nomination phase, the media focus on the primaries and, specifically, the first of these, New Hampshire.[9]

Overall, the media — and television would be the leader in this regard — emphasize the sporting aspect of races. They are concerned with transmitting the lowest level of information — who is ahead, who is catching up, what tactics are being used, what the latest developments are.

Thomas E. Patterson, who has made a comprehensive study of this area, reports that more than half of the media outlets he analyzed, and over 60 percent of the reports given on television's evening news, stressed the "horse-race" aspect of the campaigns at the expense of issue analyses, thorough reports on candidates or developments, background briefings, or much of anything else of substance (Table 5.2).[10]

Doris A. Graber has analyzed media coverage in the 1968, 1972,

[9] Michael J. Robinson, "Media Coverage in the Primary Campaign of 1976: Implications for Voters, Candidates and Parties," in Crotty, *The Party Symbol;* and Rhodes Cook, "Media Coverage of the 1976 Nominating Process," in Crotty, *The Party Symbol.*
[10] Thomas E. Patterson, "The Media Muffed the Message," *Washington Post,* December 5, 1976, p. B1, as quoted in Harry Holloway and John George, *Public Opinion: Coalitions, Elites, and Masses* (New York: St. Martin's, 1979), p. 250. See also Patterson and McClure, *The Unseeing Eye;* Ron Powers, *The Newscasters* (New York: St. Martin's, 1977); and Ben H. Bagdikian, *The Information Machines* (New York: Harper Torchbooks, 1971).

TABLE 5.2
Press Coverage of the 1976 Presidential Campaign[a]

	Network Evening News		Los Angeles Times		Erie (Pa.) Times		Time and Newsweek	
The Horse Race:								
Winning and losing		16%		17%		25%		19%
Strategy, logistics, and support	62%	22%	51%	19%	57%	18%	55%	28%
Appearances and crowds		24%		15%		14%		8%
The Substance:								
Candidates' issue positions		10%		13%		6%		9%
Candidates' characteristics and backgrounds	24%	6%	30%	7%	24%	7%	31%	13%
Issue-related (e.g., party platforms		8%		10%		11%		9%
The Rest:								
Campaign events calendar		2%		4%		6%		3%
Miscellaneous (e.g., election procedures)	14%	12%	19%	15%	19%	13%	14%	11%

[a] Figures based on random selection of at least 20 percent of the coverage by each news source. Figures include opinion and analysis as well as regular news reports.

Source: From Thomas E. Patterson, "The Media Muffed the Message," *The Washington Post,* December 5, 1976, p. B1. © 1976 The Washington Post. Reprinted by permission.

1976, and 1980 elections. In 1980, her examination of the reporting of the presidential election campaign in the *New York Times,* possibly the most prestigious and influential newspaper, showed that over one-half of the coverage was given to campaign events (Table 5.3). The next most significant coverage was given to domestic problems. Foreign policy, economic concerns, and social problems trailed significantly in the newspaper's attention. These results were roughly similar for each of the four election years examined. The major exception was 1968. At the height of the

TABLE 5.3

Newspaper Issue Coverage in the 1968, 1972, 1976, and 1980 Campaigns
(figures are in percentages for the last campaign month)[a]

	1968	1972	1976	1980
Campaign events	14	42	51	52
Domestic politics	21	24	19	29
Foreign affairs	30	18	14	5
Economic policy	13	10	11	7
Social problems	22	7	5	6

[a] Percentages are based on the following number of issues: 1968: 3,538; 1972: 11,187; 1976: 11,027; 1980: 147. The data come only from the *New York Times*. Data for the earlier elections come from twenty newspapers. Since news distribution patterns are quite similar among all papers, the data for a single paper are representative.

Source: Doris A. Graber, "Hoopla and Horse-Race in 1980 Campaign Coverage: A Closer Look," A Paper Prepared for Delivery at the Annual Meeting of the Midwest Association for Public Opinion Research, Chicago, November 19–20, 1982, Table 1, p. 4. Used by permission.

Vietnam War, the internal domestic debate over it, and the civil disruptions that characterized the late 1960s, more attention was given to foreign and domestic policy and to social problems.

Graber concludes that three major features dominate in media coverage:

> Most significantly the media devote the bulk of their stories to campaign hoopla and the horse-race aspects of the contest. Second, they slight political, social, or economic problems facing the country and say little about the merits of the solutions proposed, unless these issues can be made exciting and visually dramatic. Finally, information about issues is patchy because the candidates and their spokesmen address only issues that will help their campaign. Newspeople rarely investigate neglected issues on their own. The issue positions of vice-presidential candidates remain virtually unexplored, for example.[11]

[11] Quoted in Doris A. Graber, "Hoopla and Horse-Race in 1980 Campaign Coverage: A Closer Look," A Paper Prepared for Delivery at the Annual Meeting of the Midwest Association for Public Opinion Research, Chicago, November 19–20, 1982, Table 1, p. 4.

Graber wrote this on the basis of the media coverage of the elections for 1968 to 1976. For 1980, she added "little has changed."[12]

If the *New York Times* leaves room for improvement, Pulitzer-prize-winning author David Halberstram finds television significantly less satisfying in its coverage. Television's preoccupation with ratings and its concentration on the format in which stories are presented does a disservice to the nation, according to Halberstram. The end result is a condensation of the news to the point where "it is like printing the *New York Times* on a postage stamp."[13]

There is also a reasonable question as to the seriousness with which viewers approach television news in particular. David B. Hill has examined "how well" the audience watches political news on television.[14] He found that most viewers — 80 to 90 percent or more — did not watch the comprehensive, analytic news programs such as "Face the Nation" or the "MacNeil/Lehrer Report" (Table 5.4). About two out of three did watch the local and national evening news, and slightly less than one-half watched CBS's slick, magazine-style "Sixty Minutes" on Sundays, a news feature program that is among the most popular on television. It is difficult to ascertain why some people rather than others watch quality news programs or to determine the attentiveness and impact of these programs on their thinking and behavior.[15] What does seem clear is this: whatever its deficiencies, the general evening news program is the most heavily subscribed source of political information.

Candidates for office, of course, are well aware that television is a visual and entertainment-oriented medium. It wants action-oriented shots and simple messages, and they supply them. The best way to achieve television exposure is not to give a speech on a major policy concern or to issue position papers. The most direct course is to do something that is colorful and has human interest potential. Candidates are concerned with television's needs and become highly skilled in attracting as much TV exposure as possible.

[12] *Ibid.*, p. 5.

[13] Address of David Halberstram at Northwestern University, November 29, 1982, as reported in Jim Nousek, "Facts Suffer in TV News: Prize-Winning Journalist," *The Daily Northwestern*, November 30, 1982, p. 3.

[14] David B. Hill, "The Audience for Political Television: How Well Does It Watch?", A Paper Prepared for Delivery at the Annual Meeting of the Midwest Political Science Association, Milwaukee, April 29–May 1, 1982.

[15] *Ibid.*, pp. 12–14.

TABLE 5.4
Frequency of Exposure to Political Television Programs (in percent)

Programs	Number of Exposures During Month Preceding Interview					
	0	1	2	3	4	5+
Sunday interview						
Meet the Press	87%	2%	4%	2%	4%	1%
Face the Nation	88	2	3	3	3	1
Sixty Minutes	52	9	11	10	16	2
Newscasts						
Local News	32	3	3	5	14	43
National News	38	2	4	4	12	40
Public television						
Washington Week in Review	95	1	2	1	1	—[a]
MacNeil/Lehrer Report	97	—[a]	1	—[a]	—[a]	2
Black Perspective on the News	98	1	—[a]	1	—[a]	—[a]
Entertainment/Current events						
Good Morning America	89	2	2	1	3	3
Today Show	87	1	2	2	4	4
Washington Behind Closed Doors[b]	83	4	2	3	5	3

[a] less than 1 percent.

[b] This program did not fall into every respondent's reporting period; therefore, the figures presented here do not accurately represent total exposure to the program.

Source: David B. Hill, "The Audience for Political Television: How Well Does It Watch?" A Paper Prepared for Delivery at the Annual Meeting of the Midwest Political Science Association, Milwaukee, April 29–May 1, 1982, Table 1. Used by permission.

GETTING THE MEDIA'S ATTENTION

Free Television

It is possible for a candidate of some public standing or with substantial backing to receive free television exposure to make a statement of consequence on a national issue of major concern. However, this process happens rarely. Incumbents, and especially presidents, dominate the news. Others need to develop ways to dramatize what they say or what they stand for. Inventing such means has become something of an art. Attracting media attention is a vital part of any candidate's run for office.

Here are a few guidelines for the aspiring politician:[16]

1. Assignment editors, not reporters, determine what stories or candidates will be covered and what gets on television. Cultivate the assignment editor.

2. Schedule the event you want covered so that it is convenient for television to cover it. The best time is between 10:00 A.M. and 2:30 P.M. on weekdays. This allows for TV crews to record and edit the session for the 5:00 and 6:00 evening news. Most news seen on the late news (10:00 or 11:00 P.M.) is a rehash of the earlier programs. Weekends are normally poor times for news coverage. Most stations operate with skeleton crews.

The scheduling of events to maximize television coverage is sometimes carried to extremes. Reporters covering the civil war in Lebanon between Christians and Moslems reported that both sides in Beirut would wait for the television crews to arrive and the cameras to be in place before shelling the enemy. They would also position their guns to get the type of pictures and background effect they wanted recorded. In this case, and many others, the images sent via television to the world were more important than any immediate military advantage from the bombardment.

Daniel Schorr told how the late Hubert Humphrey called him and asked him if he could set up a spare television camera in his committee room. It turned out that Humphrey was holding a hearing, and no other senators had turned up. He reasoned that if a television camera were present, the absent senators would troop in and the business of the Senate could go on.

In another case, a congressional aide called Schorr to warn him of an upcoming committee meeting on a health and welfare issue that would have witnesses from women's groups, blacks,

[16] Based on a study by Rick Neustadt and Richard Paisner, "How to Get on TV," as reported by Bob Greene, "How Politicians Get That Free TV Time," *Chicago Tribune*, April 10, 1979, Sec. 2, p. 1; and Neustadt and Paisner, "How to Run on TV," *New York Times Magazine*, December 15, 1974, pp. 20ff.

Hispanic-Americans, and Native Americans in full Indian dress. When Schorr's crew could not make the meeting, the aide offered to reschedule it for television's convenience.[17]

3. Come up with good visuals. The job here is to make the visuals attractive to television and its audience and, secondly, to make sure they get across the message the candidate wants. The wrong visual can draw attention away from the candidate and what he is saying, or even contradict his message.

4. If a television crew is scheduled to cover the event, wait until it arrives. Usually these crews run late. Rather than pressing them to speed up or going ahead with the event as scheduled, wait. The print media and the audience may be inconvenienced, but television is the target. Most people depend on it for news; the other groups are secondary concerns.

5. Keep your statement short (usually about ninety seconds). In this way you can dictate what television will run on the evening news. Do not introduce confusing facts and figures. Pause every twenty seconds to allow for easy editing and cutting. Pass out a press release that repeats what you said. More often than not whatever is read to accompany the story will come directly from what you release.

6. If you are asked tough or embarrassing questions by reporters while the cameras are on, be vague, unstructured, and longwinded in your replies. This will make the television film or tape unusable.

7. End the event or press conference quickly. Say what you have to say and terminate the proceedings. This guards against mistakes.

8. If you did make a mistake and let something slip that was not intended, do not worry. Often it is buried in the long answers to the unscheduled questions, and television reporters, in particular, are unlikely to realize its significance or news value. Television reporters usually do not know anything about the stories they cover. Their job is to record and report on a variety of occurrences for the evening news. These range from traffic tieups and local crime news to political races. Unlike newspaper

[17] Reported in David B. Wilson, "Medium Not the Message; It's the Power," *Boston Globe*, December 3, 1978, p. A7.

reporters, they are not well prepared, and they are not familiar with the implications of any one story.

Television favors men and women who look attractive on camera. Journalistic ability is not the major concern in their hiring. This affects their preparation for every news story and the amount of critical editing they are likely to do.[18]

Finally, approximately ninety seconds of air time is allotted to a story. The television reporter is concerned with introducing the event and briefly touching on its significance. The margin for candidate error in such a situation is limited.

Gimmicks

To attract free television time and to distinguish themselves from the welter of other contenders and their demands, candidates are willing to try almost anything. The flashier and more novel the event, the likelier the media attention. With more candidates than ever running (for example, from the 1960s to the 1980s candidacies for congressional seats increased by 40 percent *in toto* and for open seats by 75 percent), the competition for the valuable television exposure has become stiffer. Incumbents normally have little difficulty in attracting attention for official statements and for the coverage of official duties. For the challenger, however, TV time is a problem.

In the 1970s, the major gimmick appeared to be walking from one end of a state to the other. The candidate would dress in work clothes and then trek from town to town and media market to media market. The idea was to show a populist concern with the people and their wishes and to contrast the folksy challenger with the seemingly remote officeholder. The strategy worked. Lawton Chiles, an unknown, won a Florida Senate seat at the beginning of the decade in this manner. Others were quick to copy his success. In a major upset, Dick Clark defeated a Republican Senate incumbent in Iowa in 1972 with the same approach. Dan Walker, a maverick Democrat, won his party's gubernatorial nomination and the Illinois governor's office in another upset by exploiting the tactic.

[18] Powers, *The Newscasters*.

As the novelty of walking candidates faded, others searched for new gimmicks to replace it. Cliff Finch, a Democratic candidate for governor of Mississippi, needed to build an identification with the working class in his state, a constituency he hoped would propel him into the governorship. He succeeded by scheduling "blue-collar workdays" in which he would work at different blue-collar jobs on selected days. These efforts received wide television coverage.

Bob Graham, a successful candidate for the Democratic nomination for governor in Florida, refined the approach. Graham was an underdog in a crowded six-candidate field. To attract attention and build a constituency, he vowed to work in 100 jobs before the primary. In the course of his efforts he worked on the sponge docks in Tarpon Springs, as a Tallahassee policeman, a nursing home orderly, a shrimp fisherman, a stable boy, and an airline attendant. As part of one stunt he appeared as a corpse in a college theater production, an effort that attracted national TV attention. In another he substituted as a bellboy and ended up carrying the luggage of the wife of one of his principal opponents.

The efforts may appear frivolous. Graham did not think so. He combined the free television with a well-designed television advertising campaign that was built around the film clips of the work sessions. He also used the outings to attack the state administration and make his own policy positions known (greater support for the police, renewed efforts to promote the state's fishing industry, and so on).[19]

The approach worked. Graham finished second in the primary field and qualified for the run-off. He beat the favorite and went on to win the governorship in the general election. He had overcome a lack of name recognition, the absence of a broadly based constituency, and an association with large wealth (he had a personal fortune of $4 million made in real estate and the dairy business).

Other candidates try other tacks. James "Big Jim" Thompson, the incumbent governor of Illinois and a media favorite, took his newborn daughter to the state fair. The event captured widespread coverage in his reelection bid. Unfortunately, the child caught pneumonia. She recovered in time to spend the evening in

---

[19] Charles W. Hucker, "Political Stunts: Working Replaces Walking," *Congressional Quarterly,* October 21, 1978, pp. 3060–61.

front of the television lights at her father's campaign headquarters, bottle in mouth, with the band playing "Rock-a-Bye Baby," the night he won the election.[20]

Lee Dreyfus, an unconventional contender for the Wisconsin governorship in 1978, proved a formidable candidate. Dreyfus was a college administrator with no political experience or basis of support. With little funding ($36,000 — "not even gas money" according to his campaign manager[21]) and despite the pleas of his friends and political associates, Dreyfus ran. A year before the election 97 percent of the state's population did not even recognize his name.

Dreyfus proved to be a personable candidate with a good sense of comic timing. What he needed was media exposure. He gained this by wearing a red vest and campaigning across the state from the back of an old school bus redesigned to look like a steam engine. The modified bus had a platform for speech-making and room for bands and entertainers. The bus attracted the media attention Dreyfus needed to get his message across to the voters. He went on to win his party's nomination and become the state's first Republican governor since 1966.

Strom Thurmond, whose political versatility is legendary, added another chapter to his personal saga. Thurmond, in his seventies, sought reelection to his Senate seat from South Carolina. He was facing a young and articulate Democrat with a proven vote-getting ability in the state (he had been denied a chance for victory in the governor's race a few years earlier on a residency technicality). Thurmond's age became an issue in the campaign.

The senator bought a "Strom-trek" van and took his family barnstorming across the state. He outfitted his wife, a thirty-one-year-old former beauty queen, and his four young children in campaign T-shirts. The children's shirts read "Vote for my Daddy." During the campaign he held a birthday party for one of his children and to the delight of the TV cameramen repeatedly slid down the firepole to show how fit he was.

---

[20] Sean Foolan, "Samantha Jayne Aids in Dad's Victory Scene," *Chicago Tribune*, November 8, 1978, p. 15.
[21] Joseph Sjostram, "Gov.-Elect in Wisconsin is a Man of Blunt Words," *Chicago Tribune*, November 12, 1978, Sec. 3, p. 24.

His efforts were sufficient to turn back the age issue and to convince the voters of South Carolina of his physical durability. Thurmond, a Republican, went on to win another term with 56 percent of the two-party vote.

More conventional is the effort to attract media attention through endorsements from sportspeople and other celebrities. Joe Garagiola, a network baseball announcer and former ballplayer, campaigned with President Gerald Ford in 1976 and served as master of ceremonies for many of his paid television programs. Former St. Louis Cardinal and University of Oklahoma football coach Bud Wilkenson had performed the same function for Richard Nixon in his presidential campaigns. Among other celebrities, football's Fran Tarkenton, the Boston Red Sox's Carl Yastrzemski, the Angel's Reggie Jackson, former Los Angeles Dodgers Steve Garvey and Don Sutton, and boxing's Muhammad Ali have all campaigned for candidates for political office. A number of Bill Bradley's old New York Knicks teammates backed his successful bid for the Senate in New Jersey. Other athletes, including Pete Rose, Johnny Bench, Arnold Palmer, Sonny Jurgenson, Billy Kilmer, Chris Evert, Dorothy Hamill, Peggy Fleming, and Richard Petty, have campaigned for various candidates during elections.

There is a certain predictability to this. Sports figures command media attention. Simply receiving their endorsement is news. Many athletes appear regularly in campaign after campaign, and several (Jack Kemp for one) have cashed in their fame to the extent of running for office (congressman). Most athletes tend to favor the conservative alternative in any race. There are exceptions, but the general rule holds true. Perhaps this should not be surprising. As one commentator wrote, except for Jackson and those who supported Bradley, and with the "partial exception" of Ali,

> Every sports superstar I know of who brought his influence to bear upon a congressional or gubernatorial race favored the more conservative choice, whether Democrat or Republican. Famous athletes tend to have a lot of money and to feel they deserve it, they tend to be involved with good-sized business concerns, and they tend to have spent the afternoons of their formative years with Tom Lasorda or Woody Hayes.[22]

[22] Roy Blount, Jr., "Late Returns," *The New York Times*, November 13, 1978, p. C6. © 1978 by The New York Times Company. Reprinted by permission.

A Massachusetts GOP state chairman attempting to draw early support for his candidate for president in 1980, the little-known conservative, Congressman Phil Crane, had his wife do a belly dance for four hundred Republican leaders in Michigan. The stunt did attract attention.[23] Richard Cheney, a Republican candidate for Congress in Wyoming, came up with an unusual, and unwanted, means of attracting public attention. He had a heart attack. He was only thirty-seven, but it looked like his yet-to-be-born political career was finished. Surprisingly, polls taken after the attack showed that as a result of the publicity his name had become a household word in the state. It helped rather than hurt him in the campaign, and he went on to win the office.

Gimmicks sometimes can backfire. One gubernatorial candidate hired a baseball stadium and held a barbecue for sixteen thousand people. They ate his food, but they voted for his opponent. Another candidate for the Senate in New York was hospitalized with an infection that severely limited his campaign time. He had become ill diving into the Hudson River for the television cameras to dramatize his concern with water pollution.

"Big Jim" Thompson, in the wake of public support for Proposition 13-type amendments to restrict taxation, came up with Proposition "0." It was to be put before the state's voters in the election. In it they were to indicate whether they voted yes or no to have their taxes cut. Unfortunately, the proposition was only advisory and had no power over any governmental body. Thompson received a good deal of publicity over the amendment before its full nature became known. As interest slackened, pressure was put on party workers to come up with the necessary signatures to qualify the proposition for a ballot position. In their haste, party workers forged a large number of signatures. As this became known, it presented one of the few obstacles to Thompson's reelection.

Television exposure is crucial. The more free TV time for a campaign the better, and candidates will go to great lengths to attract it. When all else fails, a person running for office could do what Evelle Younger, a Republican candidate for governor of California, did and declare himself "normal, usual, unstrange."[24]

---

[23]"GOP Chairman's Wife Does the Belly Dance," *Boston Globe*, July 23, 1978, p. 21.
[24] *Chicago Sun-Times*, November 8, 1978, p. 6.

This did attract media notice. Younger was then running against Governor Jerry Brown, a maverick politician, a former seminarian, and a practitioner of Zen. Among other idiosyncrasies, Brown dated rock star Linda Ronstadt and forsook the governor's mansion to sleep on a mattress in an inexpensive apartment. Brown was good copy. Against that caliber of competition for media attention, Younger was reduced to declaring himself "normal."

Buying Media Exposure

A second way to get on television is to buy time for commercial advertising. This can be an expensive undertaking.

The first and fundamental rule is that adequate media exposure costs a great deal of money. In the Chicago area television costs alone have increased 600 percent over the last decade. These figures are probably not out of line with those nationwide. A thirty-second commercial in prime time (7:00 to 10:00 P.M. in the midwestern market) on Chicago television costs $5250. This is for air time alone, of course, and does not include production costs, media consultants, script writers, cameramen, equipment, and so on. A "minimum buy" of $30,000 for a two-week period is considered necessary to have any effect.

Robert Agranoff estimates that a one-time showing of a spot commercial on network television costs upward of $20,000 and one half-hour of network air time upward of $75,000 to $80,000.[25] Production expenses run about 20 percent of the air-time costs of the TV program, although they can run as high as the time costs. The advertising agencies that arrange for the placement of TV commercials charge roughly 15 percent of the air costs, in addition to such expenses as travel and creative costs.

To complicate matters, many television stations do not want political advertising. They do not need the money — the air time is much desired by less controversial clients — and they find commercial advertisers more dependable and predictable (although all television advertising must be prepaid). NBC in Chi-

---

[25] Robert Agranoff, "The New Style of Campaigning: The Decline of Party and the Rise of Candidate Centered Technology," in Robert Agranoff (ed.), *The New Style in Election Campaigns* (Boston: Holbrook, 1972), pp. 31–33. See also Agranoff, *The Management of Election Campaigns* (Boston: Holbrook, 1976).

cago permits only one spot per week in prime time, and the other stations have similar, if less stringent, restrictions on prime-time political advertising. The stations also can limit the total number of political commercials they will accept, and many do. In Chicago, the CBS outlet permits only nine per week, NBC five, and ABC eight.

For comparison purposes, the cost of a one-page advertisement in a magazine such as *Time, Newsweek, U.S. News and World Report*, or *Sports Illustrated* would range from $18,000 to $37,000. A one-page, black and white advertisement in the Chicago edition of one of these magazines would cost about $3500. The Chicago ad would reach an estimated 106,000 readers. Television has the capability of reaching almost everyone in the 3.5 million-person metropolitan area.

On a different level, it would cost about $6000 a week in a densely populated congressional district for major advertisements in all weekly newspapers. Each paper would reach about sixty thousand people per issue. A newsletter statewide runs about $125,000. At the very lowest level, car-top advertisements cost only $12 per automobile and, of course, would be seen by the fewest number of people.

There is a certain economic logic for the larger races in focusing on television. However, a major problem with television, beyond cost, is that it indiscriminately reaches many viewers not in the intended market area. For example, many major media markets encompass several states. New York City television reaches people in Connecticut and New Jersey. Chicago television has viewers in Indiana, lower Wisconsin, and western Michigan. Boston TV reaches parts of all of the New England states. A candidate for statewide office, in effect, "wastes" a good deal of the exposure he is paying for if the voters cannot participate in that state's election. Similarly, in congressional campaigns, television advertising can reach voters in dense market areas that cover many congressional districts. Nonetheless, despite this relative inefficiency and its cost, the recent trend is toward a greater reliance on television in congressional campaigns. Its lure and its potency cannot be ignored.

Gordon Humphrey, a little-known airline pilot and the conservative Republican candidate for the Senate in New Hampshire, bought large chunks of Boston TV to beam his message back to his state. This was a first for New Hampshire politics. It was costly, and most of the voters reached by Humphrey's advertising did not live in his state. His opponent, incumbent Democrat Thomas McIntyre, disdained the new departures, but Humphrey's tactics worked. In an upset Humphrey beat McIntyre by five thousand votes. Lessons like this are not lost on politicians. Whatever its cost, television is worth it. A serious candidate cannot afford to ignore it.

It is not unusual today for campaigns of any consequence (United States Senate, governor, and other statewide offices, president) to rely almost totally on the media. The emphasis has shifted from developing a party organization and conducting a door-to-door campaign to employing television to reach as wide a possible audience in the shortest possible time with the least organizational effort.

The new campaigns bypass the party and contribute to its further erosion. They do allow for an abundance of new candidates in any given election; there is no need to work through party channels or to satisfy party leaders in order to be slated for public office. The new technology also allows for a flexibility in campaign strategy not possible before. The strengths and weaknesses of a totally media-oriented campaign can be illustrated by reference to one contest.

A TELEVISION EXTRAVAGANZA: A CASE STUDY OF THE PERCY-SEITH CAMPAIGN

Charles Percy was a popular Senator from Illinois believed to be unbeatable in the 1980 election. He had entered the United States Senate in 1966 by defeating incumbent Paul Douglas, a much-respected liberal and a former professor of Percy's. He had won reelection in 1972 by overwhelming the Democratic candidate, a veteran congressman, Roman Pucinski, with 62 percent of the vote. No political figure of any stature in the Democratic party wished to damage his career by challenging Percy in 1978. As a consequence, he was conceded reelection by the media and by his opponents in both parties. His own thinking paralleled that of others, and he began by running a perfunctory campaign.

The prevailing conditions allowed Alex Seith, a young and wealthy lawyer, to win the Democratic nomination with little difficulty. Seith, a newcomer to elective politics, ran a media campaign to develop his name recognition. He also began a walking tour of the state's 102 counties a year before the election. The idea was to listen to the people and acquaint them with his two major proposals: a "take-home pay protector," which would tie taxes to inflation, and a "revenue-keeping" plank that would require more federal tax funds to stay within the state. Seith was attempting to capitalize on the voters' tax revolt mood and the increasing inflation. His proposals were obscure. His only previous political office had been as head of the Cook County Zoning Board of Appeals. It was a nonelective and little-publicized position. His earlier policy stands appear to have come from his experience and his concern with "tax indexing." They were little understood and did not play a role in the campaign.

Once he won the nomination, Seith had the funds to hire nationally known consultants and to launch a massive, and effective, media blitz. The television emphasis was crucial to Seith's campaign. Almost all of Seith's budget was projected for television. As Seith's campaign manager explained, "It's extremely important because Percy never had a challenger who could give to the voter information about Percy's record. [Television] gets Seith recognition and it provides information."[26]

Seith caught Percy unawares and eventually forced him on the defensive. As a new, and as it turned out, articulate candidate, Seith began to receive media attention. He used the opportunity to attack Percy for being out of touch with the state and its constituency. This argument would have a telling effect. The fact that Percy was seldom in the state to campaign, preferring instead to remain in Washington to attend to his legislative duties, did not help the senator's position. As the campaign went on, it was learned that Percy did not own a home in Illinois (he used his mother's residence for voting purposes). He did own a home in Washington, and he was actively engaged in a public lobbying effort in the District of Columbia to reduce his property taxes.

[26] F. Richard Ciccone and William Griffin, "TV Blitzes Give Contests Added Flavor," *Chicago Tribune*, October 22, 1978, Sec. 1, p. 48.

Seith had tapped a large reservoir of discontent with the senator and his performance. To capitalize on it, Seith decided to move to the right. His belief was that Democrats and liberals would likely vote for him because they had little place else to turn. He felt that by taking a conservative and essentially Republican position on taxes and the budget, as well as on social issues, he could isolate Percy and undercut his support. The strategy was not necessarily successful — there was little difference between Seith and Percy on most issues — but it did serve to demonstrate the topsy-turvy nature of politics in the late 1970s. In a more structured political situation the Democrat could be expected to present the more liberal alternatives and the Republican the more conservative. In Illinois the battle — to the extent issues were involved — was fought out on the moderate right. The left was unrepresented. Eventually, dissatisfied more with Seith's tactics than his murky positions, many Democratic liberals came out for Percy, a moderate. An examination of the voting results suggests this is how many Democrats voted, and their vote may have been decisive in the campaign.

Seith's most potent issue was that voters were disillusioned with politics in general and Percy in particular. Seith was a new face with no political ties. In 1978 this was an advantage. If he could have kept the pressure on Percy, been vague on policy questions, and not alienated significant blocs of Democratic voters (a strategy used successfully by Jimmy Carter in 1976), he might have pulled off the year's biggest upset. Unfortunately for him, he began to push too hard, and a reaction set in.

To capture the black vote, Seith recorded two radio messages to play on predominantly black radio stations. The first message linked Percy to Earl L. Butz, a Republican and former secretary of agriculture. Butz had been removed from office by President Gerald Ford after making an intemperate remark about blacks. Percy, in a speech during the 1978 campaign, well after Butz's removal from office, indicated he thought highly of Butz. Seith's commercial therefore linked Percy to Butz and through him, by inference, to racism. It said,

Do you think Senator Charles Percy is a friend of black people? Well, remember Earl Butz? He was secretary of agriculture who made a racist and obscene joke about blacks. We can't repeat his words on the air, of course, but they were so offensive that he had to

resign. . . . Senator Percy said of Earl Butz . . . "I wish he was
secretary of agriculture still today." . . . Senator Percy wants the
black vote. With friends like this, you don't need enemies.[27]

Seith then followed up with a second radio commerical. The
spot began,

Do you remember the commercial we ran a few weeks ago, the one
that told how Senator Charles Percy wanted Earl Butz back again?
Butz — the former secretary of agriculture who made such an out-
rageous racist joke that he had to resign? Well, since then, people
have asked what the secretary of agriculture has to do with people in
the inner city, anyway.

The spot went on to say that such programs as food stamps and
school lunches are administered by the Department of Agriculture. It then concluded,

But Earl Butz didn't care about these programs. He used them as
dumping grounds for excess agricultural products. And when the
present secretary of agriculture came to Chicago, he had to
straighten out the food-stamp and free-lunch programs, which suffered under Earl Butz's neglect. And Senator Charles Percy says he
would like to see Earl Butz back in office. All right. That's why this
is documented, paid for and authorized by the Seith for Senate
Committee. What does this say about Senator Percy?[28]

The ads caused an uproar. Many black leaders, including
Muhammad Ali and the Rev. Jesse Jackson, began to work on
behalf of Percy.

At about the same time the radio spots were causing controversy (the middle to end of October, 1978), a respected newspaper
poll, the *Chicago Sun-Times*'s Straw Poll, was published showing
Percy losing to Seith by seventeen percentage points. The commercials and the poll results suddenly focused attention on an
election most people had conceded to Percy. It became a hot item,
commanding headlines. Journalists followed both candidates and
reported on them in depth. Talk show hosts attempted to have
both appear. The events galvanized financial and voter support for

[27] G. Robert Hillman, "Seith Swaps Lie Charges With Percy," *Chicago Sun-
Times*, October 25, 1978, p. 3.
[28] G. Robert Hillman, "2d Seith Ad Pitch to Blacks Links Percy, Butz," *Chicago
Sun-Times*, October 27, 1978, p. 16.

Percy, both of which had been languid until this point, and allowed him to redirect his efforts in the last two weeks of the campaign. He was able to raise immediately $450,000 (mostly loans from his own funds) and to command between $1 and $1.5 million in the closing days of the campaign. It all went into a new media blitz.

Seven days before the election, Percy was able to put a totally new media campaign on the air. It had three themes. First, it showed a "humble" Percy saying he had "gotten the message." He admitted having been out of touch and not reflecting the wishes of the voters. He apologized and asked to be returned to the Senate to use his experience and knowledge to fight for what the voters wanted. This was the central thrust of the new media effort, and it appeared to work. Percy surged ahead and eventually beat Seith. The day after the election, Percy followed through on this theme by flying around the state to thank the people for their support and to tell them that he had received a "clear message."

A second thrust of the media campaign was Percy's prominence and experience. It was carried out in a series of commercials essentially similar to the earlier media efforts, except that they emphasized endorsements by television and radio stations and newspapers statewide. The new ads selected references in the endorsements that mentioned Percy as "one of the taxpayers' better watchdogs in the U.S. Senate" and "his outspoken criticism of inefficiency in government"; his fights for "reduction in the bureaucracy"; his "courageous" fight on behalf of the state and against "big-money pressure groups"; and his identification with the citizens of Illinois.

Third, and more controversially, Percy attacked Seith. Mike Royko is Chicago's favorite columnist. He had written several columns on Paul Marcy, who had been convicted of failure to pay taxes on a $55,000 bribe he took from a builder who wanted a zoning case fixed. This type of thing is not unusual in Chicago, and perhaps in most American cities. Marcy, however, was the brother of a known syndicate hoodlum. He was also secretary of the Cook County Zoning Board of Appeals, which Seith chaired, and according to Royko, Seith's "top aide" on the board. Seith had appeared as a character witness for Marcy.

In his own defense, Seith claimed no knowledge of the bribe. Seith said his position was appointive and nonsalaried and he had no power to fire Marcy, although he hoped Marcy would resign.

The Royko columns appeared on October 29 and November 1. The Percy campaign reprinted the columns during the final week of the election in full-page advertisements in the leading Chicago newspapers under the heading "Pulitzer Prize Winner Mike Royko Tells More About The Mobs, The Chicago Machine and Alex Seith."[29] The story and the controversy that followed were the major campaign news heading into election day.

Seith was enraged. He accused Percy of the same type of innuendo and lack of ethics that Percy had charged him with in the controversy over the ads to black voters. Percy replied that he saw nothing wrong with the ads, although he did subsequently delete the lead-in referring to the mobs and Seith.

Immediately preceding the election Seith and Percy appeared on radio and television interview programs on which they accused each other of cheap shots, gross distortions, and unethical conduct. One particularly bitter confrontation on a television program was recorded from the time the candidates entered the studio building until they departed, still hurling accusations at each other. To add to the drama, after leaving the studio (but while still being covered by TV cameras), Percy fainted. The session was treated as the major news of the day by the television stations, and the entire interview program was scheduled twice during the final weekend of the campaign.[30]

Percy recovered and won the election with 54 percent of the vote. The entire campaign, on both sides, was a creature of the media. It had all the elements — personalities, drama, horserace aspects — that make for exciting television. It had very little to do with issue positions, performance while in office, the representation of party coalitions, personal contact with the voter, or the major issues of the day. In these regards it is not dissimilar to the media-oriented campaigns being conducted in all parts of the United States.

After the election, Seith was asked why he, an unknown and a newcomer to politics, should have done so well against an established vote-getter like Percy. He made the point that he was the

[29] See, as examples, the full-page advertisements in the *Chicago Sun-Times* of November 3, 1978, p. 41, and November 5, 1978, p. 12.

[30] For one account of the episode, see Gary Deeb, "The Turning of the Tide for Percy, Via Video Stage Manager Jacobson," *Chicago Tribune*, November 13, 1978, Sec. 3, p. 9.

first candidate Percy had faced with the financial resources needed to hire first-rate consultants and launch the comprehensive media campaign needed to be effective. The cost was high for both sides. The Seith campaign cost approximately $1 million, and the Percy effort $2.4 million.

Seith's point is well taken. The first prerequisite of effective political campaigns in the media age would seem to be funding; the second, the luck to hire competent professional consultants; and the third, the ability to follow their advice.

After the campaign, Percy went to pains to assure Illinois voters that "he had gotten the message." He promised he would pay more attention to their needs and keep more in contact with his constituency. The extent to which he succeeded in these regards would be tested in the 1984 election. This time Percy would face opposition in the Republican primary from a New Right, Reagan-type conservative congressman. Democrats, also learning the lesson of the previous election, were eager to contest the senator. No longer would the party's nomination go by default to a relative unknown. Among the hopefuls for the Democratic party's nomination was Seith, promising this time to run a more issue-oriented campaign. Given the quality of the Democratic field and the entry of several better-known candidates, it was unlikely that Seith would get a second opportunity to challenge Percy.

IS THE MEDIA LIBERAL?

For years, it has been argued that the media is "liberal," biased toward a liberal perspective in reporting the news and divorced from the interests, assumptions, and values of most of the American population, which is assumed to be centrist or even conservative. Richard Nixon and Spiro Agnew used the theme repeatedly to good advantage, discrediting news stories that reflected unfavorably on them personally or on administration policy and constantly keeping the media on the defensive. Ronald Reagan has also used this argument in attempts both to discredit any media comments unfriendly to his administration and also to make the media more receptive to the government's position. On one occasion, Reagan even called Dan Rather of the "CBS Evening News" while Rather was on the air in order to present via telephone the administration's point of view on the issue being discussed.

Is the media *really* biased toward the "liberals" (however that term might be defined)? It could be argued, as it often has, that reporters are liberal and that the corporate owners of the media outlets are conservative. The implication of this argument is that news reports reflect a liberal bias, and that the editorial page and candidate endorsements reflect a management position. This purported division of counter-balancing biases is not a satisfactory resolution of the question. What appears on the editorial page is management's prerogative. But does the news itself contain a liberal bias?

Michael J. Robinson has studied the problem. Robinson quotes the conclusions of another study comparing media and economic elites:

> . . . the media elite — the Eastern press establishment — *think* more liberally than the nation's economic elite. . . . the national media are, in their personal opinions, decidedly more liberal than their national audience. Over half of the media elite were willing to label themselves liberal, twice the proportion of the public at large. Eighty-five percent of the sample of press people think that homosexuals should be allowed to teach in public school. The national figure is 57 percent. And over 80 percent of the press elite admitted to having voted for George McGovern in 1972, a statistic that, by historic contrast, makes even the voters of Massachusetts look reactionary.[31]

But as Robinson notes " . . . press behavior — not opinion — is the key."[32] How did the media *report* the news? To find out, Robinson looked at the "CBS Evening News" and the UPI wire, plus NBC, ABC, the AP, the *Boston Globe*, the Columbus *Dispatch*, and the Seattle *Times*. He concludes, "we failed to find that UPI or CBS (or any of the other six sources) behaved very ideologically in covering 1980 politics. They were cynical, yes; but liberal, no."[33] The press, according to Robinson, "was *especially* objective in covering issues";[34] it "failed to capture the subtleties of

---

[31] Michael J. Robinson, "Just How Liberal Is the News? 1980 Revisited," *Public Opinion*, February/March 1983, p. 55. Used by permission.

[32] *Ibid.*, p. 56.

[33] *Ibid.*

[34] *Ibid.*

the various [candidate] positions" in the prenomination races, but an analysis of its reporting failed also "to reveal policy preferences of the reporter involved";[35] the media gave equal time and attention to Republican and Democrat, Reagan and Carter in the general election; and it did *not* give extra coverage or unusually favorable reporting to the liberal, "new politics" candidacy of John Anderson, a finding that Robinson feels " . . . makes it even more clear that the press favored nobody and nothing."[36] In fact, the one bias of consequence in the analysis of the media reporting was against third party candidates. It simply refuses to report much of what the John Andersons, Barry Commoners (Citizen Party), or Ed Clarks (Libertarian Party) do.

Robinson's findings help to debunk the myth of a liberal prejudice in media reporting. The problem with media reporting is not bias, but superficiality. "Fair, if frivolous, coverage" seems to be the order of the day.[37] Robinson's conclusions are in line with those of other students of the media.

PROFESSIONAL CONSULTANTS

The number of consultants available to a candidate is enormous. Robert Agranoff, who has studied the new politics in depth, has listed the twenty-seven categories of consultants a candidate might wish to hire.[38] These range from advertising agents and advance men to graphic designers and computer programmers. The variety of types and the services they can perform are impressive. A campaign consulting firm, or an individual consultant with the necessary authority and funds, can create for a candidate an organization comparable to the most efficient and streamlined of modern political parties. President Nixon's Committee to Re-Elect the President in 1972 developed an organization on paper and in practice that far excelled anything available to the Republican or Democratic parties. The uses it was put to are, of course, a different matter. It does serve as the most elaborate of its type and a

---

[35] *Ibid.*, p. 57
[36] *Ibid.*, p. 59.
[37] *Ibid.*, p. 60.
[38] Agranoff, "The New Style of Campaigning," p. 17.

model (less the ethical connotations) that other candidates attempt to duplicate.

Senatorial candidates regularly develop, in effect, their own political parties. They are candidate-centered organizations established in the short run to serve the immediate end of an individual's election. Although impressive, they are expensive and wasteful. Immediately after the election the organization is dismantled, and the consultants move on to their next job. The same time and effort invested in political party organizations would have long-run beneficial consequences. This, however, is not the trend. If anything, the candidate-centered, technocratic, short-lived, and election-oriented organizations are on the rise. It is not unusual to see them now in congressional races.

In one year prior to the 1980 national nominating conventions, the Republican National Committee held its semiannual meeting. Normally, this would be a fertile ground for prospective presidential contenders to solicit votes among the movers and shakers of the party. However, the gathering was boycotted by a number of the principal contenders for the party's presidential nomination, including Ronald Reagan, Howard Baker, Jr., and John Connally. Why? The answer reflects the tenor of the times. One observer wrote, "Although those who stayed away gave various reasons for doing so, some party leaders said the contenders were so busy setting up organizations outside the party that they saw little point in making personal appeals to the regular party leaders."[39]

The Pollster and the Polls

The most publicly visible of the consultants are the pollsters. This is a tribute both to the importance polls have assumed in campaigns and to the ability of the pollsters to promote their own interests. Pollsters, unlike other campaign consultants, can become nationally known. Louis Harris, George Gallup, Daniel Yankelovich, Peter Hart, Robert Teeter, and, most recently, Patrick Caddell have acquired national reputations. They become celebrities in their own right, and all attract lucrative contracts for their polling services from corporations, trade groups, newspapers and

[39] John Herbers, "G.O.P. Ends Its National Meeting With An Optimistic View of 1980," *The New York Times*, June 27, 1979, p. A14. © 1979 by The New York Times Company. Reprinted by permission.

television stations, and even foreign governments. This is in addition to whatever party and candidate polling they might do.[40]

Polls are expensive. The least costly for a congressional district or state begin at $10,000 to $15,000, and the costs run up from there. Packages of polls delivered at specified times during a campaign can come to a quarter of a million dollars. Richard Nixon, who depended heavily on polling information in both 1968 and 1972, awarded individual polling agencies campaign contracts of over $400,000 and $200,000 respectively.

Whatever the price, polls are considered essential to a serious candidacy. They serve a number of functions. A candidate can use a poll to establish such things as his name identification and his prospects of victory in a race. How many people know him? What types of knowledge (personal? political?) do they have of him? Is it positive? Will it work to his advantage in a campaign? How well known are his opponents? What are their strengths and weaknesses? Where are they vulnerable? If the results are discouraging — a candidate is not widely known, and the incumbent looks unbeatable — he may decide not to make a race. In the long run, the time and money saved may well make the poll a bargain.

If a candidate is intent on running, a poll can identify his support in the electorate and the groups within which he is weak. It can tell him the issues that are of concern to the voters and the types of solutions they favor. A sophisticated poll analysis can project the support among groups a candidate is likely to pick up or lose with different types of policy stands.

A poll can point out the weaknesses in a candidate's image (or his opponent's) and suggest ways to improve it. It can tell a candidate if a stand of his is going over as anticipated or if it may need modification. It can reveal the voters' reaction to crucial events in a campaign (unanticipated charges of misconduct or corruption, for example) and indicate how best to handle these. A poll can demonstrate if a candidate is failing to educate a constituency to his positions or if a vague policy stand might actually work to his advantage. In these regards, a poll can dictate campaign strategy.

As an example, Hubert Humphrey entered the 1972 contest for the Democratic presidential nomination belatedly. He decided to

[40] A critical assessment of polling is contained in Michael Wheeler, *Lies, Damn Lies, and Statistics* (New York: Dell, 1976). See also Harold Mendelsohn and Irving Crespi, *Polls, Television, and the New Politics* (Scranton, Pa.: Chandler, 1970).

challenge the front-runner, George McGovern, in the last major primary of the nomination season, California. At this point, the battle looked hopeless. McGovern was far ahead in the delegate count, and it appeared that he had his party's nomination all but ensured. Humphrey, however, if he wanted any chance at the nomination, had to challenge in California. At this point several polls played a major influence in the race.

First, a respected statewide poll showed that McGovern would win a highly decisive victory. After the publication of the poll, anything less than an overwhelming McGovern vote would be taken by the media as a moral defeat. The poll also had the tendency to relax the McGovern activists. The outcome seemed foreordained.

Humphrey had his own pollster, the late Oliver Quayle, who conducted some private samplings on his behalf. What Quayle and Humphrey found was that much of McGovern's support was soft and many of his prospective voters did not know their candidate's stand on the issues. This decided Humphrey's strategy. He went after McGovern relentlessly on a series of issues and managed to provoke heated controversy in several head-to-head debates, televised in California and nationwide. In the course of his attacks, he showed that McGovern had not thought through the implications of several of his policies, a revelation that weakened his candidacy. McGovern won an unexpectedly close vote, but the initiative taken by Humphery helped undermine McGovern's credibility. McGovern captured the nomination, but the problems begun in California continued, and his candidacy never became a serious threat to incumbent Richard Nixon.

Michael Dukakis, governor of Massachusetts, encountered a situation in 1978 somewhat analogous to McGovern's in California. His early polls, as well as those published in the newspapers, showed him far ahead of any potential opponents. However, he lost the primary nomination to an opponent, Edward King, who had no experience in elective office and seemingly little support among Democrats. Dukakis believed the polls: "The early polls had me ahead so far in the primary that it was impossible to get the voters to take the race seriously."[41] The early poll returns also

[41] "Notes on People," The New York Times, January 19, 1979, p. 49. © 1979 by The New York Times Company. Reprinted by permission.

encouraged other major Democratic candidates who aspired to the governorship to bypass the race, believing Dukakis invincible.

Dukakis ran again in 1982, and again the polls showed him well ahead of the now incumbent, and unpopular, governor, Edward King. Dukakis called on his earlier experience to remind his supporters of what happened when they believed the polls under similar circumstances. This time Dukakis won the nomination easily and moved on to the governor's office in the November election.

Polls can also be used to measure a candidate's progress as the campaign wears on and, near the end, to predict which one is the likely winner. A private poll (on occasion, doctored poll results) can be released by a candidate if it shows him doing unusually well (or at least better than the published poll results). The intention is to build a wave of support, a "bandwagon effect," behind a given candidacy. Encouraging private poll results can also be used to stimulate activists and to bring in campaign funds. A campaign manual, typical of the breed, advises: "Reproduce a favorable poll, give a quantity of copies of it to your fundraising chairman and let him use it as a tool to generate money. Everyone likes to back the winner; if your poll shows you to be the frontrunner, those campaign dollars will come easier."[42] They surely will. Contributors like to invest in successful enterprises.

Polls and pollsters are vital to campaigns. They affect every aspect of it and in the process have restructured not only the campaign process, but (along with television) the entire communication process between voter and candidate.

The Future of Consultants

Political consultants are controversial. Many believe that their services lend themselves to abuse. Nonetheless, they can be highly effective. They can help, as consultant Michael Kaye of Los Angeles did, to turn a professional basketball player like Bill Bradley into a United States senator. Bradley employed television

---

[42] Hank Parkinson, *Winning Your Campaign: A Nuts and Bolts Guide to Political Victory* (Englewood Cliffs, N.J.: Prentice-Hall, 1970), p. 158.

commercials to emphasize repeatedly the special bond needed between officeholder and voter. The appeal was effective.

Consultants can also be employed, as in Nelson Rockefeller's campaigns, to turn a negative image into a strong endorsement for reelection. Rockefeller was an unpopular governor at the beginning of each of his reelection campaigns. In large part, he believed this resulted from people not understanding his accomplishments as governor. He had the money to do something about it, and the advertising campaigns that resulted are considered among the best and most effective in recent political annals.

The fears of those who mistrust political consultants and their influence in elective politics can be illustrated by the 1978 gubernatorial campaign of a candidate in Hawaii. His major campaign presentation was a thirty-minute film shown repeatedly on the state's television. In it, the candidate, George Ariyosha, was shown with his parents, falling in love, visiting various places on the island, and, in the film's major emphasis, courageously overcoming a serious speech impediment. Not mentioned was the policies Ariyosha supported or what he intended to do as governor. Yet Ariyosha at the time of the campaign had already served as governor for six years.

The tactic worked. The governor went from a 15 percent approval rating at the beginning of the campaign to victory in the general election. The consultant who engineered the project, Michael Rowen of San Francisco, happily reported that Ariyosha was the "perfect candidate because he never asked us what we were doing, never asked to see the file and read whatever lines we gave him to read."[43] The fears of many critics of the new campaign technology are implicit in that statement.

The future of consultants looks very promising. If anything, their influence appears to be spreading. As president, Jimmy Carter contracted with Robert Squire, previously associated with the presidential bids of Senator Edmund Muskie, to coordinate picture coverage of one of his administration's biggest accomplishments, the Camp David summit meeting between Israel and Egypt. As his administration continued to flounder, Carter turned to Gerald Rafshoon, an Atlanta advertising man who had handled

[43] Richard Reeves, "White House Gunslingers," *Chicago Sun-Times*, April 9, 1979, p. 32.

the president's media advertising during his 1976 election bid. Rafshoon's most striking contribution during the campaign had been an artistically and politically successful series of commercials and paid television programs personally introducing Carter the man. These showed Carter at his warehouse in Plains and walking through peanut fields, and introduced his military career, educational background, family and so on. The idea was both to introduce Carter to the American public and to develop a warm, positive, and personal feeling for him. The media work was considered ingenious.

Rafshoon was placed on the White House payroll and given the job of improving Carter's presidential image and coordinating the White House public relations in anticipation of the 1980 campaign. One of his earliest contributions was a theme to place administrative policies in some context. After rejecting such slogans as "Beloved Community," "Moral Force," "Bold Mission," and "New Progressivism," Rafshoon settled on "Building New Foundations." The new theme was introduced in the State of the Union message. [44]

Ronald Reagan as candidate and president has used to good effect the media and the symbolic gesturing of the public relations expert. His carefully rehearsed effort to transmit an image, rather than substantive points, in the last of the televised debates in the 1980 campaign may have won him the presidency. His use of well-publicized symbolic gestures in office to mobilize public support for his policies, at times in the face of unenthusiastic support from the Congress, the media, and constituency groups has served him well as president. His ability to symbolize concern, decisiveness, or leadership abilities as the situation demands, by dramatizing stands on television, making special appointments of individuals or commissions or through highly publicized offers of offficial help in personal emergencies has proved to be one of the White House's strongest resources in dealing with critics and in getting the Congress to support administration policy. Reagan has repeatedly used carefully scheduled media appearances (visits to schools or areas where unemployment was high), press conferences, and televised speeches to bypass the Congress to appeal directly to the voters for

[44] Harry Kelly, "Rafshoon Waves a Wand of Power," *Chicago Tribune*, April 15, 1979, Sec. 2, p. 14.

support. Generally, the tact has proven successful, most notably in the passage of the Reagan Administration's budget which included possibly the most significant reordering of budget priorities since the "Great Society" of Lyndon Johnson or the "New Deal" of Franklin Roosevelt, depending on what commentator you choose to believe or which standard you wish to apply.

Reagan relied heavily on consultants and his own superb sense of the uses of the media in his 1980 presidential campaign. The combination of consultants and personal instincts was nowhere better illustrated than in Reagan's approach to and performance in the last and most influential of the televised debates, already mentioned. As it turned out, Reagan's advisors had in their possession Carter's planning book, detailing his answers to questions and the policy positions he hoped to stress. The revelation caused a stir when it came to light three years after the election — some were to call the episode "Debategate" — and the Carter materials undoubtedly helped Reagan and his consultants to anticipate Carter's themes and to plan how best to rebut. Reagan's handling of himself — his professionalized stage manners and ability to project competence and trust — also had much to do with the favorable response to the televised image he developed. His success in these latter regards will not be lost on future candidates.

One has to wonder if a reaction of sorts against the excesses of the media-oriented, consultant-based campaign has begun to set in. "Debategate" may illustrate the point. No one denied that Carter campaign papers had been obtained by the Reagan camp and used to brief Reagan for his television encounters. Related materials had been offered to third-party candidate John Anderson. Anderson's advisors refused them and reported the matter to Carter's people, who apparently believed the offer to be an isolated incident and therefore dismissed it. The Reagan advisors, however, chose to take advantage of the Carter materials. In their own defense, they later said that the materials had not proved terribly useful or productive. There were charges that some of the Carter materials had come from the White House and from the National Security Council, indicating potential thefts or leaks of potential consequence to national security. The Carter advisors made such claims, along with charging that the papers outlining their strategy were crucial to their campaign.

At a minimum, it could be assumed, given Watergate and its impact on American politics and the nation's psyche, that the government would quickly follow up on such allegations. Such was not to be the case. The Reagan Administration was not about to indict itself. More surprising, however, was the response of the Democratic-controlled House. When a little-known congressman, Donald J. Albosta, from a rural Michigan district, announced that a subcommittee he headed would investigate the charges, his own party not only discouraged him but also opposed the investigation. The national party saw no reason to emphasize the allegations. The Democratic party's leader in the House, Speaker Thomas P. "Tip" O'Neill, did not believe that the incident was serious or that it was relevant to Carter's defeat. He actively and publicly opposed the House investigation, although it continued.

At the same time, the public attitude was quite different. According to a Washington *Post*/ABC poll, a majority (57%) believed both that the Reagan camp should have refused the papers and that those involved in the incident should be punished in some manner (Table 5.5). Party supporters differed, although a plurality in both parties disapproved of the Reagan's camp's response. A majority of those polled also felt such incidents to be common in politics, possibly the view held by politicians who wished to de-emphasize the incident. [45] It may be that the public is beginning to show less tolerance for such incidents, and to consider them potentially more serious, than does its political leadership.

The pervasiveness of consultants and the media in campaigns and governance are a continuing feature of present-day politics. All indications are that their influence and usage will increase rather than decrease. They have proven too valuable and too effective to be ignored. If anything, new and creative ways will be found to exploit their potential.

---

[45] For different accounts of the incident, see: Leslie H. Gelb, "Data-Gathering Efforts Described as Part of Campaign for Reagan," *The New York Times,* July 7, 1983, p. 1; David S. Broder, "Ethics are Flexible When Office Is the Prize," Washington *Post,* July 10, 1983, p. 1; Martin Schram, "Carter Aide Says Debate-Book Report Dismissed," Washington *Post,* July 10, 1983, p. 1; Philip Taubman, "Ethics of Using Carter Notes Were Little Weighed in 1980," *The New York Times,* July 16, 1983, p. 1; and Barry Sussman, "Carter Papers Should Have Gone Back, Survey Finds," Washington *Post,* August 6, 1983, p. A3.

TABLE 5.5
Public Attitudes Toward "Debategate"

Q. Before the 1980 presidential election debate between Ronald Reagan and Jimmy Carter, Reagan campaign workers obtained documents which revealed Carter's debate plans. Suppose you were a campaign worker who had been given materials on your opposing candidate's debate plans. Would you have returned those papers, or would you have used them to help prepare your candidate?

	Total	Democrats	Republicans
Returned papers	57%	62%	49%
Used them to help prepare candidate	34	30	40
No opinion	9	8	11

Q. Do you think Reagan administration officials who were involved in getting and using Carter debate materials should be punished or not?
(If "Yes"): Should they be fired or not?

	Total	Democrats	Republicans
Should be fired	40%	47%	27%
Should be punished, but not fired	17	18	14
Should not be punished	35	27	48
No opinion	8	8	11

Q. Some people say that incidents such as the Reagan people getting Carter's briefing papers occur often in presidential elections. Carter himself said he thinks such incidents have hardly ever occurred in the past. Which of those views is closer to your own?

	Total	Democrats	Republicans
Common	58%	49%	64%
Hardly ever happens	30	38	23
Somewhere in between	1	1	2
No opinion	11	12	11

Figures are from a Washington *Post*-ABC News telephone poll of 1,505 people nationwide from July 28 to Aug. 1, 1983.

Source: Washington *Post*/ABC News Poll, as reported in the Washington *Post*, August 6, 1983, p. A3. Used by permission.

6

The Spiraling Cost of Politics

The new political technology is very expensive. In fact, it is based on money. Without money, the new politics is not possible. The rise in campaign expenditures indicates the increasing reliance on new political technology.

Campaign costs rose dramatically from 1952 to 1972 in presidential races and continue to rise in other contests.[1] The Citizens' Research Foundation reported that campaign expenses came to $140 million in 1952. This figure had climbed to $425 million by 1972. Presidential races cost between $2 million and $5 million up through 1948. The Democratic and Republican presidential contenders combined in 1948, for example, spent a total of $5 million. This figure rose to $12 million in 1952, the first year that television played a major role in campaigns. With this race the escalation of costs had begun in earnest. In 1972 it topped out. The two presidential contenders in 1972 spent a total of roughly $100 million (Nixon $61.4 million; McGovern $42 million).

[1] For overviews, see: William Crotty, *Political Reform and the American Experiment* (New York: Crowell, 1977), pp. 103–90; Herbert E. Alexander, *Financing Politics: Money, Elections and Political Reform* (Washington: Congressional Quarterly Press, 1976); and Herbert E. Alexander (ed.), *Political Finance* (Beverly Hills, Calif.: Sage, 1979).

117

The costs of the presidential general election races have stabilized. This situation is due to the new campaign finance laws. But while the cost of the races of the principal contenders had fallen by 1963, the totals for the election year continued to increase. Herbert E. Alexander, the director of the Citizens' Research Foundation and the most prominent student of campaign finance, has estimated that the money spent in the 1980 election came to over $1.2 billion (Table 6.1). This figure represented a better than doubling of the cost of four years earlier. This occurred despite the newly inaugurated federal funding of (and limits on) presidential races. The 1980 costs are an 850 percent increase over those for the first of the modern presidential campaigns in 1952 and an increase of 350 percent in less than a decade (1972–1980).

As Table 6.2 shows, the sums spent by Carter and Reagan are misleading. Overall, the federal government made over $103 million available to the presidential candidates. This sum includes the money spent by the two nominees, Carter and Reagan, in the general election, as well as the payments to the national committees of the Republican and Democratic parties to subsidize their nominating conventions ($4.4 million to each party) and subsidies to the ten candidates who ran in the primaries and qualified for assistance (four as Democrats, six as Republicans). Among the latter group, Ronald Reagan received the most ($7.3 million in matching funds). George Bush received the next highest total ($5.7 million). On the Democratic side, Carter qualified for $5.1 million, and Edward Kennedy $4.3 million in matching funds in the primary.

Despite what appear to be major costs, the federal subsidies of elections seem popular. The money comes from tax dollars made available directly by the taxpayer who can check off on her or his

TABLE 6.1
Campaign Costs, All Levels of Elections, 1952–80 (in millions of dollars)

1952	1956	1960	1964	1968	1972	1976	1980
$140	$155	$175	$200	$300	$425	$500	$1200

Source: Herbert E. Alexander, Citizens' Research Foundation.

TABLE 6.2

Federal Funding of the 1980 Presidential Primary and General Election Campaigns

Candidate	Number of submissions	Number of contributions submitted	Average amount submitted	Total amount submitted	Percentage of total request matched	Total amount certified	Amount originally rejected	Percentage of request matched prior to resubmission of rejected amount	Amount resubmitted	Final amount rejected
Brown	15	15,276	65	996,149	89.57	892,249	112,890	88.67	8,892	101,036
Carter	28	63,336	87	5,490,089	93.22	5,117,854	398,763	92.74	26,515	372,241
Kennedy	29	80,138	55	4,447,022	92.95	4,134,815	343,047	92.29	29,754	313,287
LaRouche	14	10,063	56	567,747	92.69	526,253	56,231	90.10	14,730	41,499
Anderson	7	80,744	36	2,895,480	92.57	2,680,347	215,136	92.57	0	201,383
Baker	14	67,490	40	2,699,556	97.61	2,635,042	64,521	97.61	0	68,912
Bush	12	86,612	74	6,373,491	89.69	5,716,246	657,251	89.69	0	696,941
Crane	17	69,695	31	2,140,546	88.71	1,899,631	241,715	88.71	0	206,210
Dole	5	3,752	124	467,113	95.53	446,226	23,767	94.91	2,876	21,313
Reagan	9	213,103	38	8,203,645	88.92	7,294,461	909,188	88.92	0	913,636
Subtotal	150	690,209	61	34,280,838	92.15%	31,343,124	3,022,509	91.62%	82,767	2,936,458
Democratic National Committee convention payments				4,416,000		4,416,000				
Republican National Committee convention payments				4,416,000		4,416,000				
Subtotal				8,832,000		8,832,000				
General Election payments:										
Carter				29,400,000		29,400,000				
Reagan				29,400,000		29,400,000				
Anderson				4,242,304		4,242,304				
Subtotal				63,122,304		63,122,304				
Total						103,297,430				

Source: Federal Election Commission

119

tax returns whether one dollar of her or his tax payment (two for joint returns) can go into a special fund to subsidize presidential contests. The program got off to a rocky start (the Nixon Administration actively discouraged it during its early years) but has proven durable since.

The federal funding of presidential elections is an attempt to contain campaign costs within reasonable limits, while still providing enough leeway for a challenger to make a competitive bid for the nation's highest office. It is also an effort to introduce serious public scrutiny into presidential campaigns and to minimize the influence of single-issue groups, PACs, and wealthy individuals or contenders.[2]

The revelations as to where the money comes from in elections — and the implicit quid pro quo — are factors of consequence in making the public funding of campaigns so attractive. There are no public subsidies for congressional or state-level races. There are also no controls over total expenditures. One consequence is that costs have soared. The 1982 congressional elections were the most expensive in history. Each new off-year election sets a campaign spending record. In the 1982 congressional races, for example, candidates for seats in the U.S. Senate spent 69 percent more than had been spent two years earlier (1980), and candidates for House seats spent 48 percent more than two years earlier.

The *median* expenditure (one-half were above this number, one-half were below) rose from 1980 to 1982 from $1,031,277 to $1,746,230 in 1982 for Senate contests and from $145,292 to $214,767 for House races. In 1980 thirty-two candidates for the Senate had spent $1 million or more in their campaigns. By 1982, the number of candidates was thirty-nine. In 1980, twenty-eight people seeking U.S. House seats spent $500,000 or more; in 1982, fifty-five did.[3]

The 1982 expenditures threatened but did not break the all-time highs of $7,460,966 spent in a Senate race, a record held by

[2] Crotty, *Political Reform*, pp. 168–90; and Bruce F. Freed, "Political Money and Campaign Finance Reform, 1971–1976," in Jeff Fishel (ed.), *Parties and Elections in An Anti-Party Age* (Bloomington: Indiana University Press, 1978), pp. 241–55.

[3] Reports are from the Federal Election Commission, as reported in Adam Clymer, "Campaign Costs Up Sharply in 1982," *The New York Times*, April 3, 1983, p. 14. © 1983 by The New York Times Company. Reprinted by permission.

Jesse Helms of North Carolina (Helms was up for reelection in 1984, and the early betting was that he would double his previous expenditures in an effort to hold on to his office); and just under $2 million ($1,937,209) by the incumbent Republican Congressman, Robert K. Dorman of California in 1980. Mark Dayton, a millionaire and the Democratic U.S. Senate candidate in Minnesota, spent $7,167,263, much of it his own money, in losing to incumbent David Durenberger (Table 6.3). Adam K. Levin, a New Jersey Democrat, spent $1,652,845 in his 1982 campaign and lost to an incumbent Republican who spent one-half as much. One record was set in 1982: the total outlay in the California Senate race — $6,965,696 by Pete Wilson, the Republican nominee and eventual winner, and $5,292,443 by Democratic Governor Jerry Brown, attempting to move into the Senate — established a new record of $12,258,139 for a U.S. Senate contest.[4] It is likely that this will be broken in 1984. The early indicators are that the North Carolina Senate contest, pitting Helms against moderate Democratic governor, James Hunt, in a race with national implications and funding from outside (North Carolina) sources may become the most expensive Senate race in American history.

In 1982 House races, in a battle of incumbents, redistricted into the same Massachusetts district, Democrat Barney Frank spent $1,435,222 to defeat Republican Margaret M. Heckler. The total of almost two and one-half million dollars spent to win one House seat could represent another record.

Overall, five candidates in House contests in 1982 spent more than $1 million on their campaigns (3 losing), and another 10 spent over three-quarters of a million dollars (Table 6.3). Seventeen candidates in U.S. Senate races spent over $2 million, and of these, four spent over $5 million (Table 6.3).

All indications are that the costs of running for political office will continue to increase. As one campaign consultant said, he was "shocked, but not surprised" at the high levels of expenditures.[5] Another made the point that candidates "are just now discovering the sophisticated technology that's been available."[6] They and the public are also just discovering how expensive it can be to use it.

[4] *Ibid.*
[5] *Ibid.*
[6] *Ibid.*

TABLE 6.3
Congressional Candidates Who Spent the Most

House		Senate	
Adam K. Levin* D–N.J.	$1,652,845	Mark Dayton* D–Minn.	$7,167,2
Barney Frank D–Mass.	1,435,222	Pete Wilson R–Calif.	6,965,6
Tom Lantos D–Calif.	1,164,373	Edmund G. Brown Jr.* D–Calif.	5,292,4
Johnnie Crean* R–Calif.	1,096,515	Frank R. Lautenberg D–N.J.	5,230,2
Cissy Baker* R–Tenn.	1,087,587	Lloyd Bentsen D–Tex.	4,907,3
John H. Rousselot* R–Calif.	957,089	James M. Collins* R–Tex.	4,112,9
Tom Vandergriff D–Tex.	953,280	David Durenberger R–Minn.	3,901,0
Margaret M. Heckler* R–Mass.	926,769	Orrin G. Hatch R–Utah	3,490,9
Ronald V. Dellums D–Calif.	922,427	Richard G. Lugar R–Ind.	2,936,4
Morris K. Udall D–Ariz.	831,004	Howard M. Metzenbaum D–Ohio	2,751,4
Frank Luke McNamara Jr.* R–Mass.	807,489	Daniel Patrick Moynihan D–N.Y.	2,680,3
Phil Gramm[a] D–Tex.	784,801	John Heinz R–Pa.	2,589,9
Paul Findley* R–Ill.	722,594	Millicent Fenwick* R–N.J.	2,579,4
Richard J. Durbin D–Ill.	758,660	Edward M. Kennedy D–Mass.	2,447,6
Tony Coelho D–Calif.	750,017	Ray Shamie* R–Mass.	2,300,3
Timothy E. Wirth D–Colo.	746,303	Paul S. Trible Jr. R–Va.	2,083,5
Jim Cooper D–Tenn.	739,276	Jim Sasser D–Tenn.	2,047,8
Milton Marks* R–Calif.	712,664	Lowell P. Weicker Jr. R–Conn.	1,974,9
Phillip Burton D–Calif.	704,723	Dennis DeConcini D–Ariz.	1,898,3
Matthew J. Rinaldo R–N.J.	701,483	Paul S. Sarbanes D–Md.	1,892,8
James J. Howard D–N.J.	686,425	John C. Danforth R–Mo.	1,792,7
William Cobey Jr.* R–N.C.	683,917	Robert C. Byrd D–W. Va.	1,746,2
Thomas A. Daschle D–S.D.	667,436	Ted Wilson* D–Utah	1,670,4
Steve Bartlett R–Tex.	657,556	Harrison Schmitt* R–N.M.	1,665,7
Stan Parris R–Va.	655,450	Robin L. Beard* R–Tenn.	1,612,0
Robert H. Michel R–Ill.	652,773	Howard W. Cannon* D–Nev.	1,547,4
James R. Jones D–Okla.	630,421	Donald W. Riegle Jr. D–Mich.	1,532,6
Jack Brooks D–Tex.	623,806	Jeff Bingaman D–N.M.	1,393,2
Ed Zschau R–Calif.	623,307	Henry M. Jackson D–Wash.	1,327,9
Bill Chappell Jr. D–Fla.	588,240	Toby Moffett* D–Conn.	1,287,1

Figures from reports of spending in 1981 and 1982 filed with the Federal Election Commission.

* Defeated in the general election.

[a] Ran as a Democrat, but switched parties after the election.

Source: Federal Election Commission, as reported in *The New York Times*, April 3, 1983, p. 14. © 1983 by The New York Times Company. Reprinted by permission.

With the technology available and money becoming increasingly more accessible through the PACs, there is no end in sight for the spiraling costs of political campaigns.

WHERE THE MONEY COMES FROM: THE CANDIDATES

Figures such as these have led commentators to question whether candidates "should be allowed to buy public office" and whether a plutocracy has not begun to control elective offices in this country. Columnist David Broder referred to Texas's Clements as using his wealth for "political self aggrandizement."[7] The practice is not uncommon. Clements's Democratic predecessor, Dolph Briscoe, overcame his considerable political shortcomings through his personal wealth.

Anthony Lewis, writing in *The New York Times*, calls the rich candidate financing his own campaign "an outstanding phenomenon of American politics these days."[8] For example, Robert Short of Minnesota, who upset Congressman Donald Fraser, the state party's nominee for the United States Senate nomination in 1978, spent $1,421,000, of which $1,280,000 was his own money. John Warner in the same year "lent" (to be repaid by others investing in the campaign) his primary campaign $616,000, two-thirds of his total expenditures. Seith lent $600,000 to his Senate campaign; about four-fifths of his total came from his own pocket.

Spending by individuals on this scale does affect the political process. Short, for example, was able to unseat Congressman Donald Fraser, the favorite and the state party's nominee in the primary. The Democrats lost both Senate seats, the governorship, and an unusually high number of state legislative districts. The Short candidacy introduced discord into Democratic party ranks, and Short's 35 percent of the vote in the general election did not help the party's ticket.

Charles Percy is a millionaire. His money has allowed him to become a force in national politics. He first served as the chairman

[7] David Broder, "Buying Public Office," *Chicago Sun-Times*, November 19, 1978, Views, p. 6.
[8] Anthony Lewis, "The Rise of the Plutocracy," *The New York Times*, November 13, 1978, p. A23.

of a Republican issues group in the late 1950s and later as the chairman of the platform committee of the 1960 Republican National Convention. He ran for governor in Illinois and lost in 1964. Nonetheless, he had the funds to run for Senator two years later, and he won. He ran for reelection in 1972 and won handily. His campaign spent $1.4 million to his opponent's $335,000. In 1978, Percy spent heavily and won, in part, because when the election became close in the final weeks, Percy could dip into his bank account for the $400,000 to $600,000 needed to finance a last-minute television blitz.

As discussed earlier, Alex Seith gave Percy an unexpectedly close challenge. In large part, it was because Seith could finance his own campaign and could invest heavily in media. This was the first time since Percy entered the Senate that an opponent had recourse to such personal wealth.

Jack Eckerd has been a candidate for several major offices in Florida. Win or lose, his ability to personally fund his campaigns has made him a continuing threat in elections. Personal wealth permits this. Eckerd is not alone (Milton Shapp and Howard Metzenbaum are among the many others, as was Nelson Rockefeller).[9] Wealth allows an individual to come from obscurity to fund, and often win, competitive races. H. John Heinz III of Pennsylvania is an example. He lent his campaign for the United States Senate $2.6 million (none of it repaid by 1978) in 1976. Heinz won. There are others. Heinz, for example, once elected, joined a body, the United States Senate, that already boasted forty millionaires.

The only year that the Federal Election Commission has made a study of personal wealth in campaigns was in 1976. At that time, it was found to comprise 12 percent of all funds received by U.S. Senate candidates and 10 percent of the funds received by House candidates. Most of these funds were in the form of personal or bank-secured loans (with the candidate taking responsibility for repayment). Two years later, better than 80 percent of the loans had not been repaid, indicating that these might better be considered direct financial contributions of the candidate for his campaign.[10]

Among contenders for House seats in the year of the study, 159

[9] See Crotty, *Political Behavior*, pp. 126–30.

[10] "Personal Funds: Loans and Gifts," in *Dollar Politics*, 3rd ed. (Washington, D.C.: Congressional Quarterly Press, 1982), p. 104.

had lent their campaigns between $10,000 and $500,000. Better than one-half of these candidates were challenging incumbents and found adequate funding hard to come by.

The attitude of the candidate on investing unlimited personal funds in his own campaign is best summed up by Heinz, who argued that it "had been the law for about 200 years of American history."[11] Heinz's campaign treasurer may have had the more relevant appraisal. Noting that the campaign reform legislation made it more difficult to raise money, he said, "If the challenger is not a millionaire, he has an enormous problem — probably insuperable. In our case, we are lucky because [then] Congressman Heinz was lucky — to be born rich."[12] Heinz outspent his opponent two to one and won the Senate seat.

Personal fortunes appear to be becoming an increasingly important consideration for entering public office. To curb this, and in the effort to better equalize resources, the 1974 Campaign Reform Act limited to $25,000 (for House campaigns) and $35,000 (for Senate campaigns) the amount of money a candidate could spend of his own or his family's money in seeking federal office. On January 30, 1976, the Supreme Court threw the restriction out as an infringement of free speech (which it equated with the ability to spend a person's own funds). It is rare that a group of incumbent congressmen, with proven access to money and often wealthy in their own rights, pass legislation to limit campaign expenditures (whether theirs or anyone else's) or to improve the chances of their opponents' election. It is likely that the present trend toward higher and higher expenditures in congressional and state campaigns will continue and that those with personal wealth will maintain a decided advantage.

WHERE THE MONEY COMES FROM: THE PACs

Increasingly, the funds for political races are coming from Political Action Committees (PACs).[13] These groups are the fastest

[11] *Ibid.*, p. 105.
[12] *Ibid.*
[13] Alexander, *Financing Politics*, pp. 131–68; Crotty, *Political Behavior*, pp. 168–90; and Freed, "Political Money."

growing source of campaign funds. Their influence in campaigns, at the congressional level in particular, and their impact on policy have become matters of controversy. From 1974 to 1976, and beginning with a base of 608 PACs, the number of PACs increased by 88 percent. Since 1976, the annual increase in PACs has averaged over 20 percent (Figure 6.1), to where, by 1983, there were 3,371 active political PACs. The largest increase among PACs were those speaking for business corporations without capital stock (up 51.5 percent in a one year period, 1981–1982), although the most numerous PACs by far remain the corporate and business category PACs.

In each successive election year, PAC spending sets new records. Between 1980 and 1982 alone, PAC spending increased between 17 percent and an impressive 111 percent, depending on the type of PAC (Figure 6.2). The biggest increases were in the money spent by ideological and professional PACs (although in absolute numbers, professional PACs contribute the least amount of money to campaigns). Corporate and business PACs increased their spending by 40 percent in two years, with their overall contributions to federal candidates of $45.5 million remaining well ahead of their closest competitor (labor at $20.6 million).

PAC spending amounted to a then record $131 million in the 1980 elections. Of this total, $55.2 million went to congressional candidates, approximately double the amount of two years earlier. The PACs also contributed $1.8 million to presidential candidates and spent $14.2 million in "independent" expenditures (spending not coordinated with a campaign or candidate). Most of the latter was used in the presidential races to oppose Edward Kennedy in the primaries and Jimmy Carter in the 1980 general election.

The top three PACs in expenditures and six of the top ten were "New Right" ideological PACs. Rounding out the top ten PACs in 1980 spending were PACs representing the National Association of Realtors and the American Medical Association, supporting conservative candidates; and the United Auto Workers and the National Committee for an Effective Congress, which supported liberals and primarily Democrats in 1980.

The nation's biggest single PAC was North Carolina Senator Jesse Helms's National Congressional Club which raised $7.9 million for the 1980 election. It spent $4.6 million in independent expenditures on behalf of Ronald Reagan's candidacy. The second

FIGURE 6.1
PAC Growth

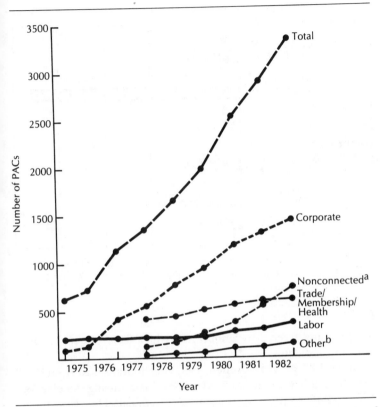

^a For the years 1974 through 1976, the FEC did not identify subcategories of PACs other than corporate and labor PACs. Therefore, numbers are not available for Trade/Membership/Health PACs and Nonconnected PACs.

^b Includes PACs formed by corporations without capital stock and cooperatives. Numbers are not available for these categories of PACs from 1974 through 1976.

Source: Federal Election Commission.

largest PAC, the National Conservative Political Action Committee (NCPAC) directed $3.2 million of its funds into independent campaigns against liberal senators. The ideological PACs prefer to target and spend their money themselves, independent of any direct involvement in individual campaigns, unlike the labor, cor-

FIGURE 6.2
PAC Contributions in 1980 and 1982

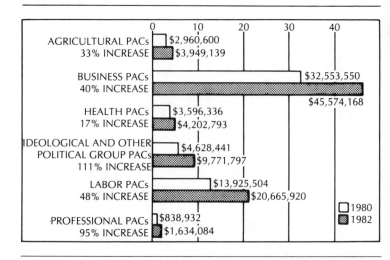

Source: Common Cause, as reported in the *Washington Post*, August 2, 1983, p. A9. Used by permission.

poration, and trade association PACs which favor direct contributions to candidates.

In the 1982 off-year election, PAC contributions had risen by 49 percent to a new record of $183 million spent during the election. The top PAC money-raisers again were dominated by "New Right" groups (Table 6.4). Again the individual leaders were Senator Jesse Helms's National Congressional Club, which spent $9.1 million on the 1982 election, and the National Conservative Political Action Committee which invested $8.9 million. Eight of the top ten were ideological groups, and of these only one, the National Committee for an Effective Congress, was not associated with the New Right. The remaining two groups, the Realtors and AMA PACs, repeated their strong showing of two years earlier and again supported conservative candidates.

Of the top ten PAC spenders among nonideological groups (Table 6.5), the Realtors and AMA were followed by four union PACs (led by the United Automobile Workers and the National Educa-

TABLE 6.4
Top Ten PAC Money Raisers, 1982 Election

Political Action Committee	Amount Raised 1/81–12/82
National Conservative Political Action Committee	$9,990,931
National Congressional Club	9,742,494
Realtors Political Action Committee (National Association of Realtors)	2,991,732
Fund for a Conservative Majority	2,945,874
American Medical Association Political Action Committee (AMA)	2,466,425
National Committee for an Effective Congress	2,430,886
Citizens for the Republic	2,415,720
Committee for the Survival of a Free Congress	2,359,477
Fund for a Democratic Majority	2,307,605
Committee for the Future of America, Inc.	2,190,264

Source: Federal Election Commission.

tion Association) and three trade association PACs (construction, milk producers, bankers, and automobile dealers). Overall, 1,249 corporate PACs donated $41 million to candidates for federal office; 251 labor PACs gave $32 million; 503 trade association PACs contributed $40 million; and 339 ideological groups spent $55 million. Better than 70 percent of the PACs registered with the Federal Election Commission contributed to the 1982 campaign.

Independent spending was again extensive in the 1982 election year, fueled primarily by the ideological and single-issue PACs (Table 6.6). The National Conservative Political Action Committee (NCPAC) led the way with $3.1 million in independent expenditures. Most of these funds were directed against liberal Senate and House members. In fact, one senator, Edward Kennedy, had a PAC dedicated solely to opposing his reelection. Altogether, over $1 million was spent in the effort (Table 6.6). At the lower end of

TABLE 6.5
Top Ten Nonideological PAC Spenders, 1982 Election

Political Action Committee	Amount Contributed 1/81–12/82
Realtors Political Action Committee (National Association of Realtors)	$2,115,135
American Medical Association Political Action Committee (AMA)	1,737,090
UAW Voluntary Community Action Program (United Auto Workers)	1,623,947
Machinists Non-Partisan Political League (International Association of Machinists & Aerospace Workers)	1,444,959
National Education Association PAC (National Education Association)	1,183,215
Build Political Action Committee (National Association of Home Builders)	1,005,628
Committee for Thorough Agricultural Political Education (Associated Milk Producers, Inc.)	962,450
American Bankers Association BANKPAC (American Bankers Association)	947,460
Automobile and Truck Dealers Election Action Committee (Automobile Dealers Association)	917,295
AFL-CIO COPE Political Contributions Committee (AFL-CIO)	906,425

Source: Federal Election Commission.

the list come the conservatives (Hatch and Schmitt in the Senate, for example) against whom independent funds were spent. The amount of independent spending on behalf of candidates was limited. It outweighed the negative campaign expenditures primarily for conservative House candidates (Table 6.6).

The explosive growth in the number of PACs and in their influence can be attributed to a number of factors. The first, and

TABLE 6.6
Independent Expenditures by PACs, 1982 Election

I.   *Committees Reporting Largest Independent Expenditures*

Political Committee	Amount Spent
National Conservative Political Action Committee	$3,177,210
Fund for a Conservative Majority	390,170
Citizens Organized to Replace Kennedy	349,199
Life Amendment Political Action Committee	255,188
NRA Political Victory Fund	234,516
American Medical Association Political Action Committee	211,624
Realtors Political Action Committee	188,060
Progressive Political Action Committee	142,885
Independent Action, Inc.	132,920
League of Conservation Voters	129,163

II.   *Candidates For or Against Whom Most Independent Expenditures Were Made*

Candidate	Spending For	Spending Against
Senate		
Edward Kennedy (D–MA)	$ 1,350	$1,078,434
Paul Sarbanes (D–MD)	30,351	697,763
Robert Byrd (D–WV)	10,034	270,168
John Melcher (D–MT)	40,968	228,011
Lloyd Bentsen (D–TX)		225,119
Lowell Weicker (R–CT)	21,248	200,508
Howard Cannon (D–NV)		192,801
Edmond Brown (D–CA)	9,482	165,176
Orrin Hatch (R–UT)	22,081	85,964
Harrison Schmitt (R–NM)	5,682	79,767

(Continued)

TABLE 6.6 (continued)

Candidate	Spending For	Spending Against
House		
Thomas P. O'Neill (D–MA)		$ 301,055
Jim Wright (D–TX)		217,115
Jim Jones (D–OK)	$13,266	127,029
Dan Rosenkowski (D–IL)		57,507
Bob Edgar (D–PA)	24,762	8,943
Jim Dunn (R–MI)	24,013	8,692
Bill Chappell (D–FL)	30,332	
John Kasich (R–OH)	27,294	
Jim Coyne (R–PA)	25,019	1,681
Edward Weber (R–OH)	17,442	8,692

Source: Federal Election Commission.

foremost, factor has been the changes in the laws governing campaign expenditures. These include the legitimization of PAC activities in the 1971 Federal Election Campaign Act; the elimination of the prohibition of PACs by contractors doing business with the government in the 1974 Amendments to the Federal Election Campaign Act; the Federal Election Commission's decision in the SUN (Oil Company) PAC case, allowing corporations to solicit employees for PAC donations; the recognition by the Supreme Court in the critical 1976 case, *Buckley* v. *Valeo*, of the constitutionality of the use of separate (including PAC) funds in campaigns; and the 1976 Amendments to the Federal Election Campaign Act which established guidelines for corporate and labor union solicitations on behalf of PACs and specifically authorized the formation of PACs by trade associations and other groups.[14]

The PACs concentrate on congressional races. Joseph E. Cantor reports that less than 10 percent of PAC funds go into presidential

[14] These and the other reasons for the growth of PACs are discussed in Joseph E. Cantor, *Political Action Committees: Their Evolution and Growth and Their Implications for the Political System,* rev. ed. (Washington, D.C.: Congressional Research Service, May 7, 1982), pp. 137–47.

races, and the amount that does is put into prenomination contests.[15] Presidential candidates in general election contests are barred from receiving special interest funds.

Another factor funneling money through the PACs into elections has been the $1,000 limit on individual contributions to federal candidates. An individual is allowed to give $5,000 to a multicandidate political committee (such as a PAC), and it appears that many wealthy donors prefer to take this route. If nothing else, the new laws make the source of funding in federal campaigns clearer by identifying its source and funneling it through the better-regulated, more publicized contributions of the PACs. Whether it cuts down on the political access of the wealthy and their impact on the political system is less likely.

There is no limit (similar to the one restricting individuals to a $25,000 maximum in federal campaign contributions in any one calendar year) on how much a PAC can donate to a campaign or a candidate. This situation has its attractions. It is much easier for a candidate to court one or a series of wealthy PACs to acquire the money he or she needs to run an effective race. As the costs of campaigns continue to escalate, there is an attractiveness and economy to fundraising through direct appeals to sympathetic PACs. The PACs, in effect, help minimize one of the most time-consuming and unpleasant aspects of campaigning, raising the money necessary to run for elective office.[16]

The decline of party influence in campaigns has paralleled the surge in importance of the PACs. As the parties have become less cohesive, PACs have become aggressive in funding campaigns, requiring prospective candidates to pledge to support issues critical to the PAC's constituency (from abortion to curbs on foreign trade), and even supplying media consultants and campaign managers for candidates they favor. In some cases, they have gone so far as to recruit their own candidates and then run their campaigns in primaries against the established party candidate, with whom they differed, or in general elections. The proportionate share of funds contributed to House candidates by their respective parties has decreased from roughly 17 percent of the total spent in elections in

[15] *Ibid.*, p. 139.
[16] *Ibid.*, pp. 141–42.

1972 to 2 percent in 1980. Correspondingly, the proportionate PAC share of the money spent has doubled during the same period, going from 14 percent to 29 percent. (The chief source of funds remains individual contributions, although these have been in a steady decline since 1974, falling from about three-fourths of the total to something over one-half by 1980.)

The fragmentation of the party system and the decline in party influence is illustrated by what has taken place in the Congress. In 1970, there were only three informal groups (not recognized in congressional rules or funded by public money) — the Democratic Study Group, the House Wednesday (Republican) Group, and the Members of Congress for Peace Through Law. By 1981, there were more than sixty of these like-minded, policy-focused congressional groups competing with the congressional parties and their leaders for influence over their members and on legislative policy-making. They ranged from The Mushroom Caucus and Solar Coalition to the Rural Caucus, the Textile Caucus, and the Steel Caucus. A single issue (or industry) focus characterizes these groups, much as it does the vast majority of election-oriented PACs. The PACs and policy-oriented caucuses, it is argued, are reflective of a party system and society in disarray.[17]

WHERE DOES THE MONEY GO?

There is a pattern to the PAC giving. More PAC funds are given to incumbents than challengers, and more to Democrats than Republicans (Figure 6.3). Although the gap between the parties has narrowed considerably, the Democrats continued to maintain a slight edge in 1982. PAC money is invested significantly more in the ultimate winners than in those who lose. The point made in an earlier election by an official of Common Cause continues to be relevant: "Newcomers to the House are becoming heavily indebted to interest group PACs, even before they are sworn into office."[18] The same holds true for the Senate, of course (as Figure 6.3, which combines the two, indicates).

[17] *Ibid.*, pp. 145–46.
[18] "Political Groups Reportedly Give $3.3 Million to New Congressmen," *The New York Times*, May 20, 1979, p. 49.

FIGURE 6.3
Campaign Receipts of Congressional (House and Senate Combined) Candidates in General Election, 1982

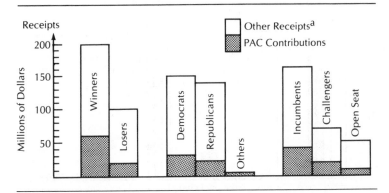

Note: Figure includes receipts for primary and general election campaigns of general election candidates.

[a] Other campaign receipts include, for example, contributions from individuals, contributions from candidates to their own campaigns, contributions from other campaigns, transfers among authorized committees of the same candidate, loans, refunds, and interest income earned on investments.

Among the various types of PACs, corporate PACs give predominantly to Republican candidates, while labor PACs give almost exclusively to Democrats (Figure 6.4). Trade and association PACs donated more to Republicans and the others, who invested significantly less in the 1982 congressional elections, either divided their money evenly or favored the Democrats, who ran the majority of incumbents.

Table 6.7 lists the 50 congressmen who received the most in PAC funds. The sums received from the PACs ranged from lows of $177,000 to a high of $469,000. The latter was given to the Republican leader in the House, Robert H. Michel, whose downstate Illinois seat was under sustained attack by the Democrats. The election had practical and symbolic importance. The Democrats wanted to beat Michel in a Republican district to indicate the lack of support for the Reagan program. Michel had been a down-the-line Reagan supporter and the administration's floor leader in the

FIGURE 6.4
PAC Contributions to Congressional Candidates (House and Senate Combined), 1982 Election, by Type of PAC

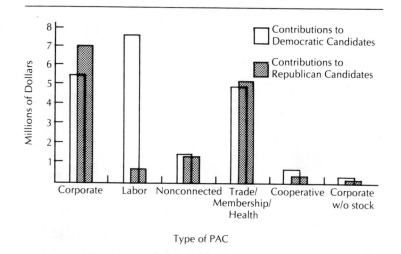

Type of PAC

Source: Federal Election Commission.

House. Republicans wanted to hold the seat for the same reason. Michel won, but in a close and hotly contested race.

The proportion of PAC funds contributed to the races of these candidates accounted for between 14 (Barney Frank, an incumbent Democrat pitted against Margaret M. Heckler, an incumbent Republican in a redrawn district) and 68 percent (Michel) of the money spent. Thirty-three congressmen took 40 percent or better of their campaign budgets from the PACs. Forty-four of the top fifty PAC recipients were incumbents. The highest total for nonincumbents was received by Milton Marks ($258,267), raised mostly from corporate and trade PACs. Marks was opposing the late Philip Burton (who won but died in office, being succeeded in a special election in 1983 by his wife). At the time of the election, Burton chaired the subcommittee on Labor-Management Relations of the House Education and Labor Committee. While disliked by business, Burton was favored by labor, whose PACs gave

TABLE 6.7
Ranking the Top 50 Recipients of PAC Funds

Candidates in 1982 House elections, ranked by the total amount received from political action committees during 1981 and 1982. Thirty-eight were elected; of those elected, 31 are Democrats and seven are Republicans.

Rank	Name	State	District	Party	Total Received From PACs	Pct. of Total Funds From PACs
1	Robert H. Michel	Ill.	18	R	$469,561	68%
2	John H. Rousselot*	Calif.	30	R	410,773	41
3	Philip Burton	Calif.	5	D	382,946	49
4	James J. Howard	N.J.	3	D	330,222	53
5	James R. Jones	Okla.	1	D	301,813	53
6	Dan Rostenkowski	Ill.	8	D	295,120	58
7	Tony Coelho	Calif.	15	D	288,439	40
8	Bill Chappell Jr.	Fla.	4	D	285,396	51
9	Thomas S. Foley	Wash.	5	D	282,735	65
10	Stan Parris	Va.	8	R	269,850	38
11	Milton Marks*[b]	Calif.	5	R	258,267	31
12	Thomas P. O'Neill Jr.	Mass.	8	D	254,917	53
13	Phil Gramm	Tex.	6	D	254,123	31
14	Thomas A. Daschle	S.D.	A.L.	D	248,194	36
15	Les AuCoin	Ore.	1	D	246,284	51
16	Matthew G. Martinez[a]	Calif.	30	D	239,354	60
17	Jack Brooks	Tex.	9	D	238,070	39
18	Jim Wright	Tex.	12	D	235,036	43
19	Cooper Evans	Iowa	3	R	235,015	42
20	Paul Findley*	Ill.	20	R	229,668	30
21	Dante B. Fascell	Fla.	19	D	225,675	43
22	Timothy E. Wirth	Colo.	2	D	221,907	28
23	John L. Napier*	S.C.	6	R	221,057	46
24	Wayne Dowdy[a]	Miss.	4	D	219,798	34
25	Margaret M. Heckler*	Mass.	4	R	218,530	23
26	Lynn Cutler*[b]	Iowa	3	D	216,585	43
27	Barney Frank	Mass.	4	D	216,575	14
28	Thomas B. Evans Jr.*	Del.	A.L.	R	216,338	38
29	Don H. Clausen*	Calif.	1	R	215,849	41
30	Frank R. Wolf	Va.	10	R	215,500	41
31	Clint Roberts*	S.D.	A.L.	R	211,291	38
32	Tom Lantos	Calif.	11	D	206,900	17
33	Peter H. K. Kostmayer[b]	Pa.	8	D	204,791	41

(Continued)

TABLE 6.7 (continued)

Rank	Name	State	District	Party	Total Received From PACs	Pct. of Total Funds From PACs
34	Richard J. Durbin	Ill.	20	D	203,552	27
35	Steny H. Hoyer[a]	Md.	5	D	201,405	36
36	Ray Kogovsek	Colo.	3	D	199,586	62
37	Herb Harris*[b]	Va.	8	D	198,992	49
38	George Sheldon*[b]	Fla.	9	D	196,235	53
39	Jim Coyne*	Pa.	8	R	194,992	41
40	Philip R. Sharp	Ind.	2	D	193,982	51
41	Bill Boner	Tenn.	5	D	186,411	59
42	Bill Hendon*	N.C.	11	R	184,890	37
43	Robert W. Edgar	Pa.	7	D	184,175	38
44	Guy VanderJagt	Mich.	9	R	182,587	53
45	Glenn M. Anderson	Calif.	32	D	180,596	44
46	Jerry M. Patterson	Calif.	38	D	180,100	68
47	Ike Skelton	Mo.	4	D	179,092	42
48	John D. Dingell	Mich.	16	D	178,940	60
49	Richard A. Gephardt	Mo.	3	D	177,650	52
50	John R. Kasich[b]	Ohio	12	R	177,145	48

A.L. = At large.

[a] Two elections, special and general, were held in the 1981–1982 cycle.

[b] Candidate ran in 1982 as nonincumbent.

* Candidate lost the election.

Source: Federal Election Commission, as reported in *The New York Times,* January 19, 1983, p. 8.

him $382,946, approximately one-half of his election budget and the most PAC money received by any Democrat.[19]

The pattern of PAC giving and the "rewarding of friends" psychology used in selecting recipients can be illustrated through an analysis of the donations of PACs associated with the chemical industry. PAC giving in this area provides a clearer illustration of the pattern behind contributions than in some other areas. The chemical industry had entered a period of confrontation with environmental groups over the cleaning up of the environment and

[19] Adam Clymer, "PAC Money's Role in Congress Raises Suspicion," *The New York Times,* January 19, 1983, p. 8.

specifically the use of the Environmental Protection Agency's "Superfund" to locate and clean up hazardous waste dumps. The issue began to receive significant media and political attention in the early 1980s. The chemical industry did not want to take the responsibility for the dumps, to invest the funds in the effort that would be needed to clean them, to locate new areas for dumping or to adhere to new standards for a more sanitary disposal program. Billions of dollars hung in the balance. The Reagan Administration and its appointees in the Environmental Protection Agency (EPA) sided with the corporations, to the point, in fact, that Congress accused the EPA officials of failing to carry out the intent of the law, favoring the chemical companies whose dumping it was supposed to regulate, maintaining conflicts of interest (former chemical industry officials assuming government appointments concerned with supervising their former company's activities), and even perjuring themselves before congressional committees. Eventually, a series of shake-ups in the EPA led to the resignation of many of its chief officials, including the head of the EPA and the director of its "Superfund" toxic waste clean-up program.

On the other side, the dangers of toxic waste dumping had been brought home to many Americans by the "Love Canal" episode near Buffalo, New York, when the persistent illnesses suffered by the population of the community forced its eventual abandonment. A similar situation in New Times Beach, Missouri, had focused media and public attention on a problem that had nationwide implications. It was an emotional issue and a potentially expensive one.

Within this context, U.S. Senators had been asked to vote on four issues in the early 1980s directly related to the controversy (Table 6.8). As Table 6.8 shows, there is a strong association between the chemical industry's PAC giving and the position of senators in opposing increased funding for and regulation of toxic waste dumping. Incumbent senators receiving the most funds cast a total of 89 percent of their votes in favor of the chemical industry's position. Nonincumbents and the few incumbents who wavered occasionally were seen as better risks than their opponents.

"No financial contribution, be it from individuals or PACs, has ever influenced a single vote I have cast in my 16 years in the U.S. Senate," said a press release issued by Senator Charles H. Percy in response to the charge that he had received $88,000 in campaign

TABLE 6.8
Chemical Industry PACs' Contributions to U. S. Senate Candidates, 1982 Election

Top recipients and their votes

Senator	Total 1977-1982	Key votes 1	2	3	4
Pete Wilson (R-Calif.)	$202,622	N	N	N	N
David F. Durenberger (R-Minn.)	165,807	E	E	E	C
Orrin G. Hatch (R-Utah)	158,757	C	C	C	C
Charles E. Grassley (R-Iowa)	134,714	C	C	C	C
Steven D. Symms (R-Ida.)	119,150	C	C	C	C
Richard G. Lugar (R-Ind.)	115,350	C	C	C	C
Russell B. Long (D-La.)	107,050	E	C	E	C
James Abdnor (R-S.D.)	106,350	C	C	C	C
Dan Quayle (R-Ind.)	104,537	C	C	C	C
Paul S. Trible Jr. (R-Va.)	93,407	N	N	N	N
Malcolm Wallop (R-Wyo.)	90,450	C	C	?	C
Charles H. Percy (R-Ill.)	88,699	C	C	C	C
Lloyd Bentsen (D-Tex.)	88,188	C	C	?	E
John C. Danforth (R-Mo.)	80,628	C	C	?	C
Rudy Boschwitz (R-Minn.)	65,252	C	C	E	C
John G. Tower (R-Tex.)	63,323	C	C	C	C
Howard H. Baker Jr. (R-Tenn.)	61,011	C	C	C	C
Robert J. Dole (R-Kan.)	60,535	C	C	C	C
H. John Heinz III (R-Pa.)	56,657	E	C	E	C
William L. Armstrong (R-Colo.)	54,257	C	C	C	C
Frank H. Murkowski (R-Alaska)	53,400	C	C	C	C
Robert W. Kasten Jr. (R-Wis.)	52,300	C	C	C	C
Arlen Specter (R-Pa.)	50,975	C	C	E	C
J. Bennett Johnston (D-La.)	47,430	C	C	E	E
Strom Thurmond (R-S.C.)	43,792	C	C	C	C

Key to votes

1. Budget amendment to allow additional EPA funding for cleanup of hazardous waste sites
2. Budget amendment to allow increased EPA funding for regulation and toxic dump cleanup
3. Motion to kill an amendment providing additional appropriation for EPA research and hazardous wastes cleanup
4. Motion to kill appropriations amendment to provide more funds for EPA and Council on Environmental Quality

TABLE 6.8 (continued)

Key to votes

C: Voted, paired, or announced a "pro-chemical industry" position, for less funding of EPA regulation and enforcement

E: Voted, paired, or announced a "pro-environment" position, for more funding of EPA regulation and enforcement

?: Did not vote or announce a position

N: Not yet in Senate when vote was taken

Source: Common Cause, as reported in *Chicago Sun-Times,* March 28, 1983, p. 4. © Chicago Sun-Times, 1983. Reprinted with permission.

contributions from the chemical industry PACs while voting with them on the four issues in question.[20] Other senators echoed Percy's sentiments. Still, those voting for a Senate amendment to increase EPA funding received average contributions in 1982 from the chemical industry PACs of $18,191; those voting against it were given average contributions of $48,165. The same pattern held in the House. Those voting to exempt hazardous wastes from tighter regulation and those voting against citing former EPA administrator Anne M. Burford for contempt of Congress for withholding subpoenaed materials received average contributions from the chemical industry PACs two and one-half times greater than those voting on the other side of the issue.[21]

Percy is probably right. The corporate, labor, and trade association PACs are unlikely to buy votes. What they choose to do is to invest heavily in those who have supported them on critical issues in the past and/or who are likely to do so in the future. The outcome is the same, only one process is legal and the other (bribery) is not.

[20] Edward Roeder, "Chemical-Firm Aid Flows to Foes of EPA Funding," *Chicago Sun-Times,* March 28, 1983, p. 4.

[21] *Ibid.*

7

Single-Issue
and Ideological PACs

Observers from Walter Cronkite to John Gardner, founder of Common Cause, have commented on the "fragmentation" of American politics and the increasing, in Gardner's words, "paralysis in national policymaking."[1] Many have blamed the development on the rise of single-issue groups. Representatives are judged on their stand on one highly charged issue by groups and voters with the resources and motivation to punish (or reward) their elected officials based on their response to this one concern. Accentuated by the rise of PACs, with ample funding, with an emphasis on media campaigning, and fed by the weakness of the political parties, groups of single-issue voters can often prove decisive in low-turnout primary and general elections. The result is "single-issue government." In such a politically charged and balkanized political atmosphere "no coalition of interests is strong enough to set priorities for the overall public good, to effect re-

[1] John Herbers, "Deep Government Disunity Alarms Many U.S. Leaders," *The New York Times,* November 12, 1978, p. 1. © 1978 by The New York Times Company. Reprinted by permission.

forms that have wide public support, to root out inefficiency and corruption in government programs, and to inspire confidence in political leadership."[2]

The problem has been compounded in recent years by the proliferation of the PACs and the use of a diversity of single-issue lobbies whipsawing legislators. The strength and electoral success of these groups is recent (since the advent of the PACs in 1974). Among the most notable of the single-issue groups in the last several elections have been consumer, environmental, gun (and antigun) control, tax, and abortion groups. Tied in with these developments, and especially with the tax revolt, has been the rise of the "New Right." One of the more vocal of single-interest lobbies, the antiabortionists, feels confident enough to have laid the groundwork for what it hopes will be a new single-interest political party.

CONSUMER GROUPS

The groups with the greatest unrealized political potential are those representing the consumer. Every voter is a consumer, and in an era of high inflation and a decreasing standard of living, consumer consciousness should be at its peak. If so, it should be a relatively easy matter to translate this type of concern into political action.

Such has not been the case. Despite a decade of national concern with consumerism, born in the administration of Lyndon Johnson, and despite the well-publicized appointments of consumer representatives by recent presidents, the gains have been limited. Most states and cities now have some form of consumer complaint agency, and states' attorney generals, and more significantly, private citizens have begun to use the courts more aggressively in pursuing consumer protection issues. These range from cases involving overpricing to efforts to penalize General Motors for substituting inferior Chevrolet engines in higher-priced GM cars. The federal government likes to boast that it has thirty-five separate agencies that deal with the concerns of consumers.

If anything, this diversity reflects the weaknesses of the con-

[2] *Ibid.*

sumer movement. It has proven itself largely incapable of concerted political action to achieve specific and important policy goals. Most of what has occurred in the last decade, though an improvement over the lack of concern that characterized previous years, represents marginal changes with a modest impact.

A 1979 Louis Harris Poll claimed that seven out of ten Americans are potential consumerists. Harris's figures are based on results that excluded those who thought of themselves first as businessmen, farmers, union members, or minority group members.[3] This figure is impressive. Yet in the one battle of the last decade with national political implications, the consumers came in second. For years consumer groups have been attempting to have Congress pass a bill establishing a Federal Consumer Protection Agency. The public supported the idea (58 percent to 28 percent, according to the Harris Poll), and the Carter Administration backed the proposal. But the bill was weakened in the Congress. First its enforcement powers were removed (it became a "Consumer Representation" rather than a "Consumer Protection" Agency), and then in its weakened form it was voted down.

The battle had both practical and symbolic importance. Its practical dimensions are obvious. For the first time, consumers — like farmers, labor, business, and most other politically powerful groups — could count on a government agency to protect and advance their interests at the national level. In symbolic terms, the failure of the consumer groups to mobilize support for such an obviously appealing issue indicated to politicians the weakness of the movement. Few politicians will extend themselves for groups who cannot hold them accountable at the polls.

The Business Roundtable, a group representing the leaders of nationally powerful corporations, the National Association of Manufacturers, and the Chamber of Commerce easily beat such consumer organizations as the Consumer Federation of America, Consumer Union, and the Ralph Nader groups in the climactic battle over the consumer agency. Ironically, they did it by mobilizing grassroots support for their position by playing on public fears over more government regulation and higher taxes.

[3] Arthur Woodstone, "The Consumer Army: Rebels With a Cause," *Parade*, November 12, 1978, p. 10.

Consumer issues have since been paid lip service by politicians, including, many feel, recent administrations. It is a popular issue for campaigners with no penalty for failure to deliver on promises. Until consumer leaders can effectively mobilize their clientele and specifically focus their political muscle on carefully selected, well-publicized congressional (and other) races, the movement's gains will continue to be limited. After the defeat of the federal consumer agency, "we need to regroup," said Esther Peterson, consumer adviser to both Johnson and Carter.[4] "We have to go back to step one — the voting booth," volunteered the executive director of the Consumer Federation of America, an umbrella organization representing 30 million consumers.[5] They are right. At present, the movement is in disarray, its potential far from being realized.

ENVIRONMENTAL GROUPS

The environmentalists are well ahead of the consumerists in many regards. Spearheaded by such groups as Environmental Action and the League of Conservation Voters, they have attempted to defeat legislators whose policy stands they have found the most offensive. Environmental Action, for example, biennially names a "Dirty Dozen" congressional incumbents it then works to depose. It mobilizes nationwide publicity against its targeted legislators and funnels funds and workers into their primary and general election campaigns. Some years it has enjoyed major successes, winning in two-thirds of its targeted contests, and in others it has enjoyed more limited gains. Since beginning its lists in 1970, the group has defeated twenty-four of those in Congress who have appeared on its Dirty Dozen lists. Since lists are chosen on the basis of the individual's voting record on limited matters and his influence within Congress, many of the defeats have involved prominent antienvironmental legislators, including committee chairmen.

---

[4] Ralph Blumenthal, "Consumer Leaders, in Reappraisal, Seek New Initiatives," *The New York Times*, February 15, 1978, p. A21.

[5] *Ibid.*

The League of Conservation Voters pursues a similar strategy. It concentrates more on supporting candidates it believes sympathetic to environmental protection, and it focuses more on competitive races. It contributes funds to campaigns, and its scorecard in the gubernatorial and congressional races in which it endorsed nominees has been good.

The environmental groups have done a good job in publicizing their concerns and in attracting media attention. The Sierra Club and other groups have attempted to educate the public to the need for wilderness conservation and the protection of the natural environment. Other groups have fought for stricter water and air pollution standards, restrictions on industrial waste, and controls on automobile emissions. Among recent concerns have been the fight against nuclear reactors and on behalf of the safer shipment and disposal of radioactive wastes. The "Clamshell Alliance," which protested the nuclear reactors being built in Seabrook, New Hampshire and the successful effort to suspend the opening of a giant dam in Tennessee in order to preserve the three-inch snail darter constitute some of the better-publicized environmental campaigns of recent years. Incidents such as the radioactive clouds let loose by the Three Mile Island nuclear reactor in Pennsylvania and the favorable reception given the movie *The China Syndrome* help keep public attention focused on environmental concerns.

One consequence has been a different type of political offensive, the use of initiative and referenda (later copied by tax revolt groups) to advance environmental causes. Such an approach has its costs. It assumes a public concern of sufficient strength to motivate people to familiarize themselves with an issue and to vote to support the position favored by the environmentalists. It also demands a good deal of funding and well-developed, short-term organizations. Despite its liabilities, environmental groups continue to realize some limited successes from this approach. In recent elections, their gains have been mixed. Among those proposals passed were ones to limit the construction of nuclear plants and several environmentally supported "bottle laws," mandating a deposit on all bottles to encourage their return. In the most publicized contest, a California initiative to ban smoking in all public and work places was voted down. The stakes in such referenda battles can be high; the tobacco industry reportedly spent $5 million to defeat the nonsmoking proposal in California.

The environmental lobby suffered a setback with the election of Ronald Reagan and the appointment of James Watt as Secretary of the Interior. Reversing the trend of recent administrations, Watt was prodevelopment and believed that wilderness and park areas should be opened to oil exploration and private development; that the size and number of federal land holdings should be reduced; and that exploratory and mineral leases sold by the government should be done at rates favorable to the private contractors. At least, these were among the charges leveled at Watt by his opponents in the environmental movement.

With Watt's tenure in the first years of the Reagan Administration, combined with the continuing controversy over the policies and administration of the Environmental Protection Agency, the Reagan Administration managed to alienate every major environmental group. As the Environmental Defense Fund wrote in one of its direct mail appeals, the Reagan Administration and its agencies were "no longer guided by [a] concern for human health or our environment;" and that "problems we thought were solved through hard-won environmental protection regulations are coming back to threaten us."[6]

Faced with this type of opposition and with the 1984 presidential elections on the horizon, the Reagan Administration took action. The top officials of the Environmental Protection Agency were replaced, and the new director, William Ruckelshaus, made an effort to accommodate critics by returning the agency to its original purpose. Watt began a belated, and unsuccessful effort to change his image in the year before the presidential election. He became noticeably less visible and more accommodating, announcing at one point that he really was proenvironment, and when the opportunity offered itself, some time after the 1984 election, and should funds be available, he intended to possibly expand the government's land holdings in park and wilderness areas. However, Watt's liabilities doomed his efforts to recast himself as less of antienvironmentalist. An indiscrete reference to the ethnic, religious and physical characteristics of a commission he had appointed led to a public outcry for his resignation, which he subsequently offered.

---

[6] Mailing of the Environmental Defense Fund, "Warning: The Reagan Administration May be Harmful to Your Health," n.d. [1982], p. 1.

THE GUN LOBBY

One of the perennially most successful political groups is the gun lobby. Led by the National Rifle Association (NRA), the gun lobby has been able to avoid serious restrictions on the use or manufacture of guns. The accomplishment is put in perspective when a number of factors are taken into consideration. First are the deaths by assassination since 1963 of John Kennedy, Martin Luther King, Jr., and Robert Kennedy; the disablement of then presidential candidate George Wallace; the two attacks directed against Gerald Ford and the attempt on the life of Ronald Reagan. No shade of the political spectrum has been immune from attack on the lives of its leaders.

Second, guns contribute directly to urban crime and are the principal weapon used in murders. Several states, though not outlawing guns, have tried to reduce the use of guns in crime by mandating strict automatic sentences (twenty-year minimum in one state) for those convicted of a crime with a gun. Third, most Americans favor some form of handgun control, licensing and/or stricter regulation of their use (Table 7.1).

These seem to be persuasive reasons for enacting gun controls. The political strength, persistence, and financial resources of the NRA have ensured, however, that no major legislation restricting

TABLE 7.1
Attitudes on Gun Control, 1980

A.	*Laws covering the sale of handguns should*	
	Be made more strict	59%
	Be made less strict	6
	Kept as they are now	29
	No opinion	6
B.	*Would you approve or disapprove of having a law in your state requiring that a person who carries a gun outside his home must have a license to do so?*	
	Approve	75%
	Disapprove	20
	No opinion	5

Source: The Gallup Poll, as reported in *The Gallup Opinion Index,* January 1980, pp. 30–31. Used by permission.

access to guns has been enacted. The NRA accomplishes its ends by directly lobbying the Congress and by unremittingly opposing, in his own district, any legislator who supports gun control. The NRA and the progun lobby can be aggressive in their election tactics and in their claims of electoral success. For example, the NRA saw the results of the 1980 election as "a tremendous success for the nation's gun owners and sportsmen. Progun candidates enjoyed widespread victory."[7]

Few politicans are about to dispute the NRA claims. Not only is the organization aggressive and politically successful, it also has a reputation for persistence. The case of former representative Abner Mikva, is an example.

The NRA strongly backed any opponent of Representative Abner Mikva, the chief proponent of gun control in the House. Its support can extend beyond the financial to encompass publicity through NRA organs against its opponents and on behalf of its friends. The NRA will also quietly open offices in a congressman's district and install such things as phone banks to work directly for or against a legislator's election. It did this in Mikva's case, sometimes to the embarrassment of the congressman's opponents, who had not invited the NRA's help. The district favored gun control, although it was not the most important issue facing the voters, and the congressman's opponents did not want to be known as progun candidates (although their stand was more compatible with the NRA's position than Mikva's was). In addition, to save money and resources, the NRA headquarters in the district linked challengers to a number of local candidates whom the NRA favored for state legislature seats (and with whom often Mikva's opponents did not want to be associated). In a very close race (and all of Mikva's races were close) this type of crude support probably hurt the Mikva challenger. Interest group backing can be a mixed blessing.

Later, Mikva was selected for appointment to the federal bench. The NRA announced that it would strongly oppose his nomination. True to its word, the NRA generated a nationwide mailing to senators against approving the Mikva appointment (as Senator Robert Dole told Mikva in the confirmation hearings: "I didn't know so many people knew you in Kansas")[8], and its repre-

---

[7] *The American Rifleman,* January 1981, p. 62.

[8] "Mikva Under Fire for Anti-Gun Crusade," *Chicago Sun-Times,* July 22, 1979, p. 64.

sentatives appeared before the Senate panel considering Mikva's nomination. The gun lobbyists labeled Mikva a "radical" and a "bigot" against firearms owners, and the executive director of the NRA's lobbying arm explained its opposition to Mikva as follows: "If you were a black and I were the imperial wizard of the Ku Klux Klan, then how you would feel about the nomination of the imperial wizard of the Ku Klux Klan is how we feel about Abner Mikva being nominated as a federal judge."[9]

The gun lobby may not have won in the Mikva case, and its lobbying both before the Congress and in the home district may be obvious, but this type of unrelenting opposition causes most politicians to weigh the costs before they oppose the lobbyists' interests.

In 1968, after the assassinations of King and Robert Kennedy, there was a strong national movement for effective gun control. The momentum had been building since 1963, and by 1968 restrictive gun legislation appeared to have the support of the majority of the public and the Congress; it was also backed by the Johnson Administration. Nonetheless, after a long and frustrating national debate, the only legislation the antigun forces were able to enact was a weak ban on imported guns and restrictions on the sale of the "Saturday Night Special," a type of cheap handgun.

An indication of the NRA's legislative muscle is the law restricting the sale of Army surplus ammunition and weapons only to NRA members. These are sold at less than half their retail value. The program has been in existence for seventy-five years. The Army has 700,000 surplus M-1 rifles alone, but since the turmoil of 1968 it has restricted the civilian sale of these. The NRA and Congress were putting pressure on the armed services to expand the scope of their sales to NRA affiliates.

One rationale for the program was that NRA groups could form gun clubs and use the surplus weapons. Any individual, however, can join the NRA by paying fifteen dollars in annual dues. A group opposing the NRA announced a courtsuit to challenge the law limiting the sales of Army guns to NRA members, a case it eventually won. Its intention was to weaken the attractiveness of NRA membership.

The proposed limitation of guns is an emotional one. Those supporting gun control point to murders and crime associated with

---

[9] "Mikva Hit, Praised at Hearing," *Chicago Sun-Times*, July 13, 1979, p. 26.

guns. Those opposing it believe it is a plot to restrict the freedom of gun owners, most of whom, they argue, are sportsmen and hunters. Some go further. They contend that proposals to register guns are efforts to deprive Americans of the right to defend themselves and their property against invaders or tyrants. They argue that the right to keep guns is guaranteed in the Constitution. The executive director of the NRA was asked before a House Judiciary Subcommittee on Crime if he and his organization "would rather allow those convicted felons, mentally deranged people, violently addicted to narcotics . . . to have guns, rather than to have the screening process for honest people like yourself. Is that correct?" "A price we pay for freedom," the NRA representative replied.[10] This pretty much sums up the opposing positions and the lack of common ground between them.

The gun control lobby is a classic example of effective lobbying. Although the majority of voters favors another position, opposition support is diffuse and unorganized. The single-interest gun groups are well organized and financed. Their members may hold a minority position, but they hold it strongly, and they are willing to vote against anyone who opposes them on this one issue.

THE ANTIABORTION LOBBY

"Aren't you glad your mother let you live?" "Babies are sisters, too." "All we are saying is, Give life a chance" (chants of the "prolifers"). "Not the church / Not the state / Women must decide / Our fate" (a cry of the "prochoicers"). These are among the less provocative slogans of the most emotion-laden issue of any of the single-issue groups: the abortion controversy. There is little common ground between the contenders on both sides. The communications of the National Abortion Rights Action League, a Washington-based proabortion group, convey the intensity of the feeling generated by the issue. They also are representative of the type of communication single-issue groups send out. For these reasons it is reproduced in full (see pages 152–155).[11]

---

[10] The quotation is contained in a memorandum (undated) sent out by Nelson T. Shields, III, Chairman of Handgun Control, Inc., p. 1.

[11] Communication from the National Abortion Rights Action League.

The NARAL Foundation is the sister organization of the National Abortion Rights Action League, which is the largest national membership organization solely working to keep abortion legal. The NARAL Foundation supports NARAL's goals through training programs, educational publications, and informational media campaigns.

If you want to learn more about this crucial issue, please write to:

The NARAL Foundation
attn.: Publications
1424 K St., N.W.
Washington, D.C. 20005

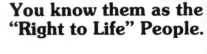

You know them as the "Right to Life" People.

They oppose abortion.

But did you know . . .

They Mean Business. . . . .

Ask any Senator or Member of Congress who's just received a dozen roses before a crucial vote. Ask the family planning agencies whose federal funding is threatened due to 'Right to Life' lobbying efforts. Ask the March of Dimes, target of a 'Right to Life' boycott because of its research on birth defects. They'll all tell you that the 'Right to Life' people are a strong, well-organized, and well-financed lobbying force that will stop at nothing until it has reached its goal. . . **An amendment to the Constitution banning abortions under any circumstances.**

The 'Right to Life' people call themselves "Pro-life." Yet they don't concern themselves with the issues of capital punishment, nuclear proliferation or disarmament. So whose "life" are they "pro"? Certainly not the life of the mother. Certainly not the life of a child born defective, fatally ill, destitute, or simply unwanted. The "pro-life" people are merely "anti-abortion."

The End Justifies The Means

Neither truth nor logic has ever hindered the 'Right to Life' people. They'll say or do just about anything to further their cause. Their literature portrays abortion as "cosmetic surgery" used by careless, wanton women as casually as birth control. They indoctrinate children in the schools with propaganda disguised as "textbooks," and often use these children in their marches and publicity stunts. They claim the availability of birth control is responsible for the rising teenage birth rate, and that, if we simply do away with birth control education, the problem will miraculously disappear. They quote the lowering birth rate, and claim that abortion is never necessary, that unwanted babies are quickly adopted. . . while thousands of these unwanted children are institutionalized each year.

One Answer For Everything

To the 'Right to Lifers' the answer is the same, no matter what the circumstances are: **"You must have that baby, whether you like it or not!"**

"But I'm only 12 years old."
"We have seven children already."
"I was raped."
"We'll have to go on welfare."
"The doctor says it will die before it's two."
"I'm 50. I thought I couldn't get pregnant any more."

Their answer is the same: "You **must** have that baby!"

But Isn't It Still Legal To Choose An Abortion?

Yes, but that choice is under attack. For some people, the choice has already been revoked.

After intense 'Right to Life' lobbying, Congress passed in 1977 the Hyde Amendment, which denies Medicaid funds for abortion. This forces poor women either to bear unwanted children, or face the trauma of illegal or self-induced abortions.

Congress has also approved legislation to restrict access to abortion. Military health care programs no longer cover abortion for military personnel and dependents. Health programs for Peace Corps Volunteers' now cover no abortions whatsoever. Attempts have even been made to prohibit all federal employees' health insurance from covering abortion services.

Of course, the ultimate goal of all "Right to Life" groups is to make abortion illegal for all women for all time, and to give the fetus, from the moment the sperm fertilizes the egg, all the rights now given to born persons. Many constitutional amendments and bills to prohibit abortion have already been introduced in Congress and their passage is close to a reality.

They Like To Call Us Pro-Abortion

If you believe that you, not the government, should decide when you will or won't have a child, then you are what the 'Right to Lifers' call "Pro-Abortion."

Frankly, we at NARAL, don't know **anyone** who is "pro-abortion." But all birth control methods can fail, and unwanted pregnancies do occur.

Some people feel abortion is immoral. Others feel it is immoral for a government to force a woman to bear a child or to force her to risk illness and death with a back-alley butcher.

An unwanted pregnancy is a situation faced by thousands of Americans every day. It's a situation where there are no good answers, only rational decisions. The 'Right to Life' people are winning in their campaign to make your decision for you. And they won't stop without a fight.

It's your choice. Keep it.

...that they are against contraception?

...that they actively oppose sex education in the schools?

...that they are working to stop research in amniocentesis, the science of detecting prenatal birth defects?

...that they helped persuade Congress to deny poor women access to abortions?

The 'Right to Lifers' are sincere and dedicated in what they're trying to do. But what they're trying to do is turn their personal beliefs into law. And they're succeeding.

If you believe they should make your moral, ethical, and religious decisions for you, and for all Americans, you needn't read any further.

Source: The NARAL Foundation. Reprinted by permission.

The direct mail letters from the National Abortion Rights Action League are accompanied by such material as a memo documenting incidents of "Violence against the Right to Choose" in communities across the United States; a pledge that the group was "Dedicated to Guaranteeing and Implementing a Woman's Constitutional Right to a Safe and Legal Abortion"; and a request to fill out a membership card and pledge a contribution of from $15 to $500 or better.

The slogan and tactics of the antiabortionists (or "prolife" groups) are at least as inflammatory as their prochoice opponents and considerably more politically effective. The National Right to Life antiabortion group claimed a membership of 11 million associated with its 1800 chapters and expects a membership of 25 million in the 1980s.

The extreme emotional overtones associated with the issue are considerable. As an illustration, at one convention of the National Right to Life movement, and to the applause of the delegates, one speaker compared abortions in America to the Nazis' extermination of the Jews in Germany in the 1940s. He felt that the news media in America played a role analagous to that in Hitler's Germany "in concealing the facts and the public's right to know."[12] Doctors who performed abortions were the "executioners"; bureaucrats who provided financial and support services were the "medical mercenaries"; and the Upjohn Company, a major pharmaceutical concern that manufactured abortion devices, the I. G. Farben of the proabortionists.[13] I. G. Farben, among other things, manufactured the chemicals used to exterminate the Jews in the death camps.

Annual rallies of 50,000 to 100,000 people are held by prolife action adults and children to mark the anniversaries of the Supreme Court decision striking down restrictive state laws on abortion (*Roe* v. *Wade,* January 22, 1973.) The march past the White House and to the Capitol has become an annual event. The movement's symbol is a rose and its slogan "the American Holocaust — Six Million Exterminated by Abortion." Speakers claimed that 1.3 million lives a year are lost to abortion.[14]

[12] John Herbers, "Anger and Optimism Mixed at Parley of Abortion Foes," *The New York Times,* June 24, 1979, p. 16. © 1979 by The New York Times Company. Reprinted by permission.

[13] *Ibid.*

[14] "Anti-Abortion March Hits 'American Holocaust,' " *Chicago Tribune,* January 23, 1979, Sec. 1, p. 2.

The abortion debate, though volatile enough on its own, touches on other concerns that have disturbed many Americans. These include gay rights and homosexuality; the pro- and anti-ERA debate; permissiveness in society; anticrime, anti-moral decay and profamily concerns; and the value and propriety of sex education in schools. To further inflame passions, there is an undercurrent of questions relating to church-state relations in the controversy. Specifically, the Catholic Church through the leadership of the National Conference of Catholic Bishops has been an active proponent of the prolife position. The Catholic bishops have created a lay lobby arm for its position, the National Committee for a Human Life [Constitutional] Amendment which it funds at approximately $300,000 a year. The contributions come from dioceses around the country. The Catholic Church itself has taken a direct role in making its position on abortion known to its communicants and in relating this to the political events of the time. Catholic clergy have actively represented the antiabortion position in public forums. For them and many others, it is a theological and moral issue as much as a political one. A priest writing in a Chicago newspaper, for example, in answering a prochoice columnist exemplified the tendency. His letter indicated how deeply much of the clergy felt about the issue and its implications: "She [the columnist, Ellen Goodman] sees the Catholic Church as merely a political 'structure,' and not as the unequivocal defender of human life and dignity that it is and has always been. Its protective arm embraces those waiting to be born and the retarded, the deformed and the senile aged. To do any less would be an insult to Him who made us all."[15]

There has been a reaction among other religious groups to the Catholic Church's militant support of the antiabortion forces. A class action suit has been brought by the Women's Division of the United Methodist Church in cooperation with Planned Parenthood and a number of doctors and poor women, challenging the present restrictions on Medicaid abortions. The suit is supported by fifteen other national religious interest groups including the American Jewish Congress, the synagogue unions of Conservative and Reform Judaism, the United Presbyterian Church, the United Church of Christ, and the Disciples of Christ.

[15] Father Arthur LaPorte in "Letters: Abortion So Important It Deserves 'One Issue' Victory," *Chicago Sun-Times*, June 29, p. 50. Reprinted with permission. © Chicago Sun-Times, 1979.

The case in question is called *McRae* v. *Califano*. It is presently in the federal courts, and may well end up in the Supreme Court. Basically, the plaintiffs argue that the present law (as refined by Congress in the Hyde Amendment of 1976) represents an unconstitutional "establishment of religion" because it implicitly accepts the teachings of one religious group (the Catholic Church) on abortion. The prochoice side argues that, practically speaking, Catholic dogma is advanced by federal law.[16] This is not quite accurate: the Catholic Church's views are far more restrictive than the present law. Nonetheless, supporters of abortion have argued that the Church's aggressive lobbying seriously impinges on religious freedom.[17]

A number of Catholics, in turn, many of whom do not support the Church's position, are alarmed by the reaction. Some fear the beginning of a serious challenge to the constitutional right of American Catholics comparable to the 1850s Nativist campaign.[18] This concern seems exaggerated. Protestant groups, most notably the National Council of Churches, do not fault the attempt to make society responsive to ethical considerations, based on religious beliefs.[19] The introduction of such issues touches a sensitive strain in American history with roots that go well into the past.

Because of the emotionalism and the broad ramifications that surround the debate, compromise appears impossible. The president of the National Organization of Women (NOW), fearing that the "extreme climate of the crusade against abortion is taking on the overtones of a religious war," invited groups on both sides to a meeting. The intention was "to seek ways to lessen the need for abortion, to reduce the incidence of unwanted pregnancy, and to end the polarization and violence that surround the abortion issue."[20] One congressman, a leader in the antiabortion movement, refused to sit down and negotiate "what respect for life means" until there was a moratorium on all abortions. The president of the March for Life organization responded, "I do not sit and negotiate with baby-killers."[21]

---

[16] "Ecumenical War Over Abortion," *Time*, January 29, 1979, p. 62.
[17] *Ibid.*
[18] *Ibid.*
[19] *Ibid.*, pp. 62–63.
[20] "Anti-Abortion March."
[21] *Ibid.*

Nonetheless, the meeting was held, and it was attended by eight antiabortion and twenty proabortion groups. Three women interrupted the conference. They marched before the television cameras covering the session and opened the blankets they carried, revealing two human fetuses.[22] The incident had the expected shock effects. It had been planned and carried out by the People Expressing a Concern for Everyone, an offshoot of the Right to Life Committee. Although many were appalled, the act was applauded by the National Right to Life Committee.[23] In such an atmosphere, little is likely to be accomplished through direct talks and negotiations.

Before discussing the political and other tactics of the prochoice and prolife single-issue groups, it is advisable to map the public attitudes on abortion. Most adults favor abortion in some form. According to polls, 25 percent feel abortion should be "legal under all circumstances" and 18 percent believe it should be "illegal under all circumstances." These are the polar extremes. Most people fall somewhere in between in a complex mix of positions. The results of several polls on the issue are shown in Table 7.2. Although the hierarchy of the Catholic Church has played a forceful role in fighting abortions, the position of most Catholics is close to that of Protestants. The position of the public on abortion parallels that found in earlier, related surveys during the 1970s.

The tactics of the prolifers can be extreme (as the showing of the fetuses indicates). They do attract attention, and they do include everything from sit-ins and disruptions to political campaigning.

Many consider the antiabortionists the politically most successful single-issue group. Most of the groups that form the antiabortionist coalition were established between 1971 and 1973, the latter the date of the Supreme Court decision striking down many legislative restrictions on abortion. Since then, the prolife groups have moved from a position of little strength or visibility to one of remarkable achievements. The years since 1976 have been particularly fruitful for them.

In 1976 the antiabortionists decided to contest in primaries for the Democratic presidential nomination. Their candidate was Ellen McCormack, a fifty-year-old Long Island housewife and

[22] "Birth Control Parley Shaken as Protesters Display Two Fetuses," *The New York Times*, February 16, 1979, p. B7.
[23] *Ibid.*

TABLE 7.2
Attitudes on Abortion, 1980

A. *Abortion should be*	
Legal under any circumstances	25%
Legal under certain circumstances	53
Illegal under all circumstances	18
No opinion	4
B. *Abortion should be legal if*	
Woman's health is seriously endangered	90%
Woman is unmarried/does not want to marry	48
Woman is married and does not want more children	47

Sources: A. The Gallup Poll, as reported in *The Gallup Opinion Index,* July 1980, p. 7. B. The National Opinion Research Center, General Social Surveys, as reported in *Public Opinion,* August/September 1980, p. 39. Reprinted with permission.

mother of four. McCormack entered presidential primaries in eighteen (of thirty) states — in itself an accomplishment of note. She received few votes however: only 238,027, or 1.5 percent of the total 16 million cast in the primary. From such a modest beginning, impressive results were to flow. First, McCormack generated a good deal of publicity and media attention. She was not a legitimate contender for the Democratic nomination. She ran simply to draw attention to the antiabortionists' position. This she succeeded very well in doing. The media exposure was free, which suggests an approach many single-issue groups with nationwide constituencies might follow in the future.

Second, she forced politicians generally, and the Democrats specifically, to deal seriously with the abortion issue. It became necessary for the presidential contenders to address the issue, and McCormack and the antiabortionists managed to bring it to the forefront of the nation's political agenda.

Third, her candidacy helped to unite the proliferating antiabortion groups and give them a common focus. Since 1973 the number of groups that have sprung up is enormous. As an example, in Illinois alone there are 162 antiabortion groups. Despite the political successes since 1976, one of the movement's chief weaknesses continues to be the diversity and independence of its many groups.

Fourth, despite McCormack's small-to-negligible vote (she averaged only slightly over 13,000 votes in the states where she contested), she and the prolifers demonstrated that there was a small, fiercely committed constituency who would vote solely on a candidate's stand on this particular issue. In a close race, such a highly motivated vote can make the difference. It is a small but potent constituency that a candidate cannot ignore. Also, siding with the antiabortionists invokes few risks. Although the majority of voters may favor the prochoice position, abortionist groups are not as well organized or as electorally sophisticated as their opponents. And, of course, the bulk of voters do not feel strongly on the issue and will not commit themselves to a candidate based on his abortion position alone. Five percent of the electorate in a CBS poll said they would vote for or against a candidate solely on the basis of their feelings against abortion.[24]

Finally, the success of McCormack has encouraged the antiabortionists to exploit this approach further. In 1978 another Long Island housewife and ally of McCormack's, Mary Jane Tobin, ran for governor of New York. She received few votes (120,000), but to the surprise of political experts she received more than one of the nation's longest established and most influential third parties, the Liberals, could deliver for the candidate they endorsed, Governor Hugh Carey. As a consequence, the antiabortionist Right to Life Party has won status as a regular party with an established line on the New York state ballot. As with its national counterpart in 1976, the purpose of the party is not to win office but to force all candidates, from tax assessor to governor, to take a public stand on abortion. "The issue is overriding," according to Tobin. "Disqualifying," is the way McCormack puts it.[25]

The antiabortionists (and, to a lesser extent up to the present, the proabortionists) have begun to employ a tactic favored by the environmentalists. Building on their successes from 1976, they have begun to enter congressional races, supporting favored candidates with PAC funds and volunteers. To maximize the media value of their efforts, and to bring home their message to legislators, the prolifers have developed a "hit list" of candidates they

[24] Anthony Lewis, "A Singular Issue," *The New York Times*, November 16, 1978, p. A27.
[25] Maurice Carroll, "The Unlikely Beginning of the Right to Life Party," *The New York Times*, November 25, 1978, p. 25.

feel it imperative to defeat. Whenever one of these candidates loses, the antiabortionists have been quick to claim credit.

Without question, they are active in congressional races. In targeted states they invest funds and they establish Pro-Life Action Councils, or their equivalent, to supervise and coordinate their campaign activities. The results may be less persuasive than the antiabortionists would have us believe, however.

The campaign against Dick Clark in Iowa in 1978 provides a case study of the antiabortionists' approach. Clark had been selected by the national right to life organizations as their number one target. Clark was vulnerable; a Democrat, he had been elected in an upset six years earlier when his boss (then a congressman, and later senator, John Culver) refused to run in a contest he believed unwinnable. Clark had aroused the ire of the prolifers by voting for a bill permitting the federal government to support abortions for indigent women. He had also announced publicly that his conscience would not let him support a constitutional amendment to outlaw abortions.

The antiabortionists were already effectively organized in Iowa and had shown their political muscle by successfully working against a favored woman candidate who sought the Democratic nomination for lieutenant governor. The woman did not share the prolife views on abortion. The state contingent, "Iowans for Life," thus provided an experienced nucleus with which to oppose Clark. The senator was vulnerable regardless of what the antiabortionists did. He was the perfect target. He had voted wrong on abortion, and the antiabortionist opposition at the state level to his reelection was already organized.

It is the state group's contention that the national right to life groups made only marginal contributions to Clark's defeat. The state group, however, was very active on behalf of Clark's opponent, conservative Republican Roger Jepsen. Jepsen was a former lieutenant governor who took a strong antiabortion stand. Despite his liabilities, Clark was favored in the race and led in the polls by never less than 10 percentage points. Nonetheless, he lost in a close race to Jepsen by 26,000 votes. A poll by the *Des Moines Register* on election day found that 25,000 people voted for Jepsen on the abortion issue alone. This could be taken as evidence that the antiabortion vote put Jepsen over the top or that he would have won, barely, without it. The same voters, if they had swung in any numbers to Clark, would have made a difference in his behalf.

As in any other race, attributing the outcome solely to the pro-life vote is simplistic. A number of factors were at work. Clark was a liberal (according to the *Congressional Quarterly's* computations, the most liberal senator in Congress the previous year), and Iowa is a conservative state. A number of single-issue groups — in addition to the antiabortionists — opposed his reelection. These included New Right opponents of the Panama Canal treaties, antilabor supporters of right-to-work laws, and the gun lobby. Also, and many thought this decisive, anger with the indecision and vagueness of the Democratic administration's farm program alienated many farmers, undergoing one of their periodic down cycles, from the Democratic party.

The Republican party's candidate for governor, incumbent Robert Ray, was popular and won handsomely, eclipsing Jepsen's vote by 67,000. The Republican party was organized as well as it has been in its history, and its leaders felt that its professionalized get-out-the-vote efforts made the difference in its campaigns. Republicans won both houses of the state legislature for the first time in four years. Clark's loss, in such circumstances, may not have been such an upset.

Nonetheless, analysts in Washington, the antiabortionists, and Clark himself seemed to believe that the opposition of the prolifers was critical in his loss. One particular tactic many believed to have swung the election: On the Sunday preceding the Tuesday vote, the antiabortionists distributed 300,000 pamphlets attacking the senator's stand on abortion. These were given out at churches, primarily in urban areas and principally (although not exclusively) to Catholics. The Clark forces could not answer these effectively in the short time remaining before election day. They believed this tipped the scales.

Finally, the entire effort cost the prolife groups only $10,000.[26] For this amount they defeated Clark, gained nationwide media exposure, and impressed congressmen with the potential costs of opposing them on legislation.

Right to life groups did not always fare so well. In fact, they lose

---

[26] Douglas E. Kneeland, "Clark's Defeat in Iowa Laid to Single Issue," *The New York Times*, November 13, 1978, p. A18.

many more races than they win, but their losses seem to go unnoticed. The political impact of highly publicized victories in key races during an election year can be enormous. As the *New York Times* editorialized:

> In a careful reading of the evidence, the foes of abortion do not appear to have won big this fall. They did, however, score an important psychological victory merely by winning small. For this is the first general election in which they have demonstrated even a modicum of strength at the ballot box. They have, thereby, tossed a challenge to the majority of voters in this country who, according to repeated polls, still favor free choice for abortion early in pregnancy.[27]

The appearance of victory is often more important than the reality. It is this that the antiabortionists counted on and are building from for the future.[28]

The antiabortionists have been unusually effective in translating their demands into legislative successes. In fact, this is where the movement's greatest strength lies. Because of the relatively small numbers involved in the prolife movement, their success in the Congress says much for the potential influence of single-issue groups on the totality of American life. The policy-making process is particularly vulnerable to organized pressure of this nature.

Antiabortionists have used the Congress to limit the implications of the Supreme Court's 1973 decision. The assault began in earnest in 1976. In that year Representative Henry J. Hyde (R–Ill.) introduced what has come to be called the "Hyde Amendment." It resulted in the first successful legislative effort to limit the applicability of the Court's action. Hyde was able to attach to an appropriations bill funding the departments of Labor and Health, Education, and Welfare a prohibition against the use of any federal Medicaid money for abortions "except where the life of the mother would be endangered if the fetus were carried to term." In both 1977 and 1978 efforts were made to liberalize the provision. Modifications have been introduced, and the law presently reads that federal funds cannot be spent for Medicaid abor-

[27] Soma Golden, "Abortion's Morning After," *The New York Times,* December 4, 1978, p. A20. © 1978 by The New York Times Company. Reprinted by permission.
[28] "6 Senators Top Abortion Foes' Election 'Hit List,' " *Chicago Sun-Times,* December 3, 1978, p. 74.

tions except when the life of the mother is endangered or "for victims of rape or incest, where such rape or incest has been reported promptly to a law enforcement agency or public health service" or when "severe and long-lasting physical damage to the mother would result if the pregnancy were carried to term when so determined by two physicians."[29] Overall, the present prohibitions on the use of federal funds for abortions represent significant victories for the foes of abortion.

In the twenty-two states with restrictions on abortions similar to those contained in the Hyde Amendment, figures provided by the Alan Guttmacher Institute, the research arm of Planned Parenthood, show a decline in Medicaid abortions of between 96.8 and 99.2 percent. The director of the National Committee for a Human Life Amendment, the lobbying representative of the National Conference of Catholic Bishops, estimates, "We've been able to cut the public-funded abortions from 300,000 a year to 2800."[30]

In 1978 Congress adopted a provision that would apply the Hyde Amendment to the Defense Department, thus limiting public funding for military personnel and their dependents. There were 26,000 abortions that this provision could apply to in the fiscal year preceding its adoption. In addition, Congress in its pregnancy disability bill required private employers to include coverage of pregnancy in their health care plans. Abortion coverage was not required. Finally, Congress placed a restriction on the United States Civil Rights Commission, prohibiting it from studying or gathering any facts concerning abortion policies in this country.

The proabortionists are naturally disheartened. There have been some successes, but these have been mostly negative efforts — attempts to stop prolifers' actions. There have been repeated attempts in the House and Senate to bring out an amendment to the United States Constitution prohibiting abortion. The efforts have gotten nowhere because of the continuing opposition of the chairs who head the respective subcommittees that must pass on the necessary legislation.

[29] Ellen Warren, "The Politics of Abortion — A Big Business," *Chicago Sun-Times,* November 27, 1978, p. 6.
[30] *Ibid.*

Thirteen state legislatures have called for a constitutional convention to enact the antiabortion amendment to the Constitution. Twenty-one more states are needed; securing this backing is at best difficult and more than likely impossible.

If these are successes for the prochoice coalition, they do not discourage the antiabortionists. The prolifers believe that the actions of the states to date can be placed in a more favorable perspective. To their way of thinking, these actions place increased pressure on the Congress to consider seriously the human life amendment. Furthermore, they believe the battle on the state level is far from lost. More recently, the antiabortionists have turned their attention to state legislative races. They believe that relatively modest levels of funding in these races can go a long way in getting what they want.

In the immediate future the antiabortionists intend to continue contesting elections at all levels and to force candidates to take a stand on the abortion issue; to restrict further the availability of state and federal funds for abortions; to push the needed state legislatures to pass resolutions calling for a constitutional convention; and to force Congress to consider their demands for enacting a human life amendment to the Constitution. If anything, their visibility should continue to increase over the next few years. The proabortionists, on the other hand, have yet to begin to counter such initiatives effectively.

THE NEW RIGHT, SINGLE-INTEREST POLITICS AND THE CONSERVATIVE REVIVAL

Many political observers believe the antiabortionists to be the most successful of the new single-issue groups, and without question they have accomplished much more than anyone would have predicted. Yet, despite the emotionalism involved, the media attention given the movement and the significance of the concerns being debated, abortion is a relatively narrow issue that directly concerns few. The rise of what has been called the "New Right" and the success of conservatism in the late seventies and early eighties involves a far greater number of people. The New Right and its conservative policies on taxation, inflation, a balanced budget and cutbacks in government-sponsored social services have far broader implications. The New Right is a label given to a broad coalition of conservative groups that have assumed increasing importance in American elections. The development is new and has grown since Watergate. It has been spurred by the new campaign laws and it takes advantage of the new technology of politics. It makes use of the issue politics of the contemporary period and it moves into the void created by the decline of the political parties. The New Right has benefited from the concern with single-issue politics and, in fact, attempts to build coalitions in elections of groups from anti-ERA'ers to those protesting taxes. The strategy has been successful. Its goals are nothing less than the capture and redirection of the entire American policymaking apparatus.

A number of factors have favored the New Right's surge. These range from a spiritual exhaustion of both traditional liberalism and conservatism to a receptive political climate in the late 1970s and early 1980s. The New Right has evolved to fill the vacuum created by the political decline and intellectual bankruptcy of the old conservatism, associated for generations with the Republican party and with such issues as protection of the free enterprise system, a balanced budget, New Deal opposition, and a primitive economic competition of all against all. Interestingly, the New Right does not reject these positions; it simply does not emphasize them. It is concerned with winning elections. The belief is that the old-fashioned Republican conservatives of the 1950s did not "understand the politics of the average person" and could not relate to his concerns. The old-time conservatives were left to argue their cause; they were a "stuffy, boring lot" with little concern for electoral victory, according to one New Right leader.[31]

Traditional liberalism is also in a period of confusion. In effect, it is a victim of its own success on domestic issues. The programs of government economic regulation and social services associated with the New Deal have been largely enacted. They are popular with voters, a point the New Right (unlike the traditional conservatives) accepts. With its domestic goals basically realized, traditional liberalism has fallen into disarray. The New Deal coalition

[31] Gary McMillan, "What Is the New Right Up To?" *Boston Globe*, December 17, 1978, Section A, p. 1. Reprinted courtesy of The Boston Globe.

was shaken by the Vietnam War. Now it is in a period of flux with no clear leadership, value assumptions, or policy positions. The New Right has been quick to take advantage of the vacuum.

The new conservatives want to win. This alone, they believe, distinguishes their approach from the electorally disastrous one of their predecessors. Perhaps more than anything else they want to win and force American politics to move along the lines they believe it should. Many (but not all) on the New Right would argue that a majority of Americans actually support their position. Their contention would be that this support has simply never been adequately focused on politics. The argument is not new. The supporters of Robert Taft in 1952 and Barry Goldwater in 1964 made the same points, with terrible electoral consequences. The difference is that the New Right of contemporary politics has had visible success in translating their potential support into political reality.

To win, the New Right attempts to build coalitions of primarily middle-class Americans into an effective political force. It is not concerned that the coalition agree on all (or even most) points; it is willing to tolerate diversity for the sake of winning. "The secret is to be able to put together the right kind of coalition that will supersede the point of view on other issues," as one New Right strategist has maintained.[32]

The coalitions are built from single-issue groups such as those supporting prolife, anti-ERA, and antigun control positions. They have benefited enormously from the economic issues of the late 1970s and early 1980s and from the rise of single issue groups to contest property taxes, inflation, a decreasing standard of living, and the energy squeeze. As a leader of the Committee for the Survival of a Free Congress, a New Right group, described it, the coalition is held together by a concern with "family, right-to-life, schools, [and] neighborhoods."[33]

Overall, its policy positions fall somewhere between those of the neoconservatives, the disgruntled New Deal Democrats symbolized by Senator Daniel Moynihan and Ben Wattenberg, former campaign manager for Senator Henry Jackson's presidential bid and coauthor (with Richard Scammon) of the influential *The Real*

[32] *Ibid.*
[33] *Ibid.*

Majority (1970),[34] and the Far Right of anticommunist fanatics. On social issues, and in its choice of candidates to support, many moderates in the Republican party see it as close to, and possibly interchangeable with, the Far Right. It is by any measure among the most conservative influences in American politics.

The New Right is also far more pragmatic than its conservative predecessors, It principally, but *not* exclusively, supports Republican candidates and the Republican party. But the New Right's primary commitment is to policy positions and to winning office. Consequently, the New Right makes a point of backing conservative Democrats who identify with its causes. It goes further than this. In an approach that has alienated other conservatives, the New Right will enter Republican nomination battles to back candidates it favors. It will even field its own candidates to run against incumbent Republican moderates. These efforts have infuriated Republican officeholders.

Strategy

The tactics of the New Right are modeled after those of the left. The inspiration for the single-issue groups of the late 1970s and 1980s was the anti-Vietnam lobby of the 1960s. The electoral approach of the New Right was pioneered by the National Committee for an Effective Congress (NCEC), a bipartisan liberal group that channeled funds and campaign services to congressional candidates it supported, and Common Cause, a public citizen lobby concerned with securing the public financing of elections. Both the NCEC and Common Cause used direct mail techniques to acquire funds and to develop a following. They, like the Vietnam lobby, employed the media as best they could to publicize their cause and develop a public awareness of their concerns. Common Cause has been successful. It has a membership of 15 million nationwide, and it has been instrumental in the congressional adoption of presidential funding and campaign ethics bills. The NCEC is a more modest operation. Although it has been operating for three decades, it has a small staff, centered on an executive director, and a low overhead. Its only concern is with

[34] Richard M. Scammon and Ben J. Wattenberg, *The Real Majority* (New York: Coward, McCann & Geoghegan, 1970).

congressional races. Its activities hardly compare with those of the New Right.

The major New Right groups are the National Conservative Political Action Committee (NCPAC), one of the most generous funders of conservative candidates; the Committee for the Survival of a Free Congress (CSFC); Citizens for the Republic (CFTR), begun by Ronald Reagan with a $1 million surplus from his unsuccessful 1976 presidential campaign, the Fund for a Conservative Majority (FCM), an outgrowth of the Young Americans for Freedom, an extremely conservative youth group within the Republican party; Gun Owners of America (GOA); Committee for a Responsible Youth Politics (CRYP); the Conservative Victory Fund (CVF), affiliated with the American Conservative Union; Senator Jesse Helms's National Congressional Club; and the Conservative Caucus, headed by Howard Phillips. President Nixon appointed Phillips to head the Office of Economic Opportunity with the explicit charge of dismantling this symbol of the Johnson era's commitment to social programs. Phillips left the Nixon Administration in 1973 because he felt it was not conservative enough.

The New Right groups are well funded (Table 7.3). Most of these funds have been raised by direct mail solicitations and much of them by groups directly associated with one of the technological gurus of the New Right, Richard Viguerie. Direct mail solicitation has proved a bonanza for right-wing groups, and Viguerie has mastered this art of fund raising. To avoid the $5000 limitation PACs can contribute to a candidate for each primary or general election race, Viguerie also hires out to individual conservative candidates to institute direct fund raising for them that is not subject to the PAC limitations.

Viguerie also claims to have direct mail lists estimated to contain from between 0.5 or 2 million up to 15 million names (hyperbole is not uncommon in the business) of proven contributors to conservative causes (compared to the NCEC's 80,000). Viguerie has proven to be a prodigious fund raiser, but the cost of his services comes high. Ninety-one cents of every dollar collected can go to in-house costs. Only nine cents from the dollar may reach the candidate. Other conservative groups, all of whom depend on direct mail, claim costs as low as forty to fifty cents on the dollar. The liberal NCEC says its costs are less than thirty-two cents on the dollar with the remainder going directly to candidates.[35] Viguerie has become a multimillionaire through his work on behalf of conservative causes.

Viguerie does make a point that is well taken. He argues that direct mail techniques publicize causes and candidates as well as raise funds; that these are an excellent way of reaching the voter, and thus in themselves are a form of campaigning. "Direct mail is an unbelievably successful advertising medium when properly used," he claims.[36] He is right.

Direct mail not only can publicize a cause; it also can motivate a large number of people to involve themselves directly in an issue. Their willingness to contribute funds to a campaign is one gauge. Another is the massive letter-writing campaigns these conservative groups have been able to institute to influence the Congress on legislation they favor. For example, the NCPAC claims it can stimulate a million letters to Congress on any given issue or like numbers to the White House in support of the Reagan program. The New Right also points out that the direct mail strategies of opposition they employ have been refined by Common Cause, the moderately liberal "citizens' lobby."

It is not difficult to understand the ability of direct mail letters to motivate recipients. First, the refined lists contain the names of people sympathetic to the cause being promoted. Second, the messages tend to be extreme; they present the worst possible case; and they aim to polarize and anger their audience. A classic example was NCPAC's letter asking recipients to "send $5 or $10 contributions today to help defeat liberal senators who want to give our Panama Canal away."[37] The solicitation was marked "Urgent" in red letters and went on to identify sixteen Democratic and Republican senators who "will decide if a Marxist dictator will take both our canal and our money, and then open the canal to Russian warships — while our Navy is blocked from going through."[38] Such exaggeration is not unusual. When the national chairman of the Democratic National Committee attacked the New Right for its "shrillness, stridency and superficiality," the leader of the FCM

---

[35] Buchanan, "New Right," p. 2652.
[36] *Ibid.*, p. 2651.
[37] *Ibid.*
[38] *Ibid.*

countered: "In some cases, the shriller you are the more success you have in raising funds."[39] This does appear to be the case. Nonetheless, some conservatives are concerned. The editor of *Policy Review,* a conservative journal, fears that "the New Right will position conservatives too far out."[40] If so, and despite its present position as the one reasonably cohesive political and intellectual force in American politics, it will destroy its credibility and with it that of conservatives generally.

Increasingly, the New Right is moving beyond the funding of selected candidates to provide a variety of campaign services. The larger New Right groups, particularly NCPAC and CSFC, believe that by providing campaign consultants, media advice, polls, voter targeting services, and precinct organizers they can be both more effective and exercise more control over the candidates and campaigns they fund. Consequently, these groups (like the NCEC) have begun to take a more direct role in campaigns. The CSFC, as an example, will provide the salary of one full-time precinct organizer. If the organizer undertakes anything other than the precinct voter mobilization plan the CSFC believes so central to electoral success, his salary will be discontinued. As the director says, "If they want our help, they do it our way."[41]

NCPAC runs training seminars for candidates and prospective campaign organizers on ways to set up a campaign structure, to use telephone banks and mail contacts, to follow up on prospective voters, and to take polls. Several successful campaigns have been built around trainees from these seminars.

There is a problem, however. Many conservative groups teach not only standard campaign techniques but the election strategy they favor and want implemented. First, they dictate the organizational arrangement. Second, they insist on developing special interest coalitions. The anti-ERAers, antiabortionists, and so on are cultivated. "Very seldom does a candidate win in his own right. More often he gets votes from those dissatisfied with the status quo," according to the director of the Conservative Caucus.[42] Finally, the candidate must present a clear conservative (New Right) alternative to his opponent. "Victories don't count unless you can

[39] *Ibid.*
[40] McMillan, "What is the New Right Up To?"
[41] *Ibid.*
[42] *Ibid.*

influence public policy."[43] Both the left and right could probably agree on this. Those in the middle, where practicing politicians tend to be, feel the pressure.

There are a number of difficulties with the approach. One is that the candidate may have very little control over his own campaign. This appears to occur. If the candidate is totally in sympathy with the groups dictating his strategy, problems are minimal. If not, the candidate may have a campaign direction and a set of legislative commitments he did not bargain on.

The New Right has gone one step beyond dictating campaign strategy. It has entered its own candidates into prenomination races to contest incumbents of whom it disapproves. One example that was to have national implications will illustrate the point. Conservatives had long been disillusioned with the moderate policies of Representative John Anderson of Illinois, the third-ranking Republican leader in the House. In 1978 they decided to challenge him. The Committee for the Survival of a Free Congress recruited a fundamentalist minister, the Reverend Don Lyon, to make the race. The CSFC, the Conservative Victory Fund (representing the American Conservative Union), and the Gun Owners of America sent funds and workers into the district. They instigated an active media campaign and managed to give Anderson what he considered to be his closest race. In a high-turnout race (70 percent voted in the district's primary), the congressman won with 58 percent of the vote. Anderson was, nonetheless, upset over the closeness of the vote: "There is a real danger that they [the New Right] can so totally focus on relatively narrow issues and dominate the political dialogue. There is an entirely legitimate conservative force, but I don't want to see it contaminated by a virulent anti-right that will provoke a backlash in other directions."[44] In 1980 Anderson gave up any chance for reelection to risk a long-shot bid for the Republican party's presidential nomination, and when this failed, ran as an independent candidate for president.

The influence of the New Right is probably overstated. These groups cultivate publicity, as do all single-issue groups, and their claims of success are often exaggerated. They do receive a good

[43] *Ibid.*
[44] *Ibid.*

deal of political attention, and they can be effective. There are no cohesive, well-funded alternatives on the left, and the political parties offer little in the way of competition. The Republicans, unlike the Democrats, have made an effort to invest in state legislative and congressional races. A vacuum does exist, however, and it invites the attention of the New Right and increases the odds of their success.

The threat of the New Right may be as effective as its actual clout. An infuriated Senator Charles Mathias of Maryland, and eight other targets of the New Right, once complained to the Republican National Chair about the movement's funding of extremely conservative candidates to contest incumbent Republicans. It "is not the kind of healthy competition we should encourage within the Republican party. It is cannibalism."[45] Such complaints, of course, have done nothing to deter New Right opposition. Its activists have even expanded their operations to include supporting candidates for Republican leadership positions in the Congress.

Issue Tests of the New Right

The ideological PACs have extensive funding available to them (Table 7.3). They enjoyed higher receipts during the 1982 off-year election cycle than any other category of PACs. They also, as Table 7.3 shows, invested heavily in the 1982 congressional elections. Interestingly, the liberal National Committee for an Effective Congress ranked among the more lavish funders of candidates, as did Walter Mondale's candidate-PAC, an indication of Mondale's seriousness in positioning himself for the run for his party's presidential nomination.

The issues of concern to the New Right have not changed, although their tactics and appeals have been modified somewhat by having a New Right candidate in the White House. While the New Right has been impatient with the Reagan Administration over its support for constitutional amendments (if necessary) for school prayer and outlawing abortion, and while it has been uneasy about the historic budget deficits run up by the administration's economic policies, it still has put much of its effort into publicizing

---

[45] Buchanan, "New Right," p. 2650.

TABLE 7.3
Ideological PAC Funding in the 1982 Election

▨ Contributions to Federal candidates

Total receipts: $64.7

| $11.1 | $53.6 | IDEOLOGICAL ORGANIZATIONS |

Total receipts: $47.2

| $29.3 | $17.9 | CORPORATE |

Total receipts: $43.2

| $22.8 | $20.4 | TRADE, MEMBERSHIP AND HEALTH |

Total receipts: $37.4

| $20.8 | $16.6 | LABOR |

	Receipts	Contributions	Pct. of Receipts Donated
National Conservative Political Action Committee	$9,990,931	$263,171	2.6%
National Congressional Club	9,742,494	135,264	1.4
Fund for a Conservative Majority	2,945,874	119,595	4.1
National Committe for an Effective Congress	2,430,886	368,443	15.2
Citizens for the Republic	2,415,720	471,367	19.5
Committee for the Survival of a Free Congress	2,359,477	156,123	6.6
Fund for a Democratic Majority	2,307,605	175,959	7.6
Committee for the Future of America (Mondale PAC)	2,190,264	228,562	10.4
Republican Majority Fund	1,967,119	455,547	23.2
Independent Action Inc.	1,189,059	109,840	9.2

Contribution figures do not include totals for independent expenditures for or against candidates, which totaled $3,177,210 for the National Conservative Political Action Committee; $388,399 for the Fund for a Conservative Majority, and $132,920 for Independent Action Inc.

Source: Federal Election Commission, as reported in *The New York Times*, April 29, 1983, p. 11. © 1983 by The New York Times Company. Reprinted by permission.

Reagan's policy positions and in attempting to mobilize support for these positions. For example, the nuclear freeze movement proved to be a strong issue and one that the candidates for the Democratic party's presidential nomination immediately seized upon (and, in fact, Senator Alan Cranston of California made it a cornerstone of his campaign). One response was for the Rev. Jerry Falwell, a founder of the "Moral Majority" and a ranking figure in the New Right hierarchy to begin a direct mail appeal. He took out full page advertisements in major newspapers nationwide, asking readers to show their support for a president "who wants to build our military strength" but who is being attached by "freeze-niks," "ultra libs," and "unilateral disarmers." "I don't want the American people, especially our children, to be cremated in a nuclear explosion" (see the reproduction of Falwell's letter).[46] This type of appeal in support of the Reagan Administration was to become common in the early 1980s. Reagan could not accomplish all that the New Right wanted. Nonetheless, he was infinitely better than the choices offered by the opposition. As the vice-president for communications of the Moral Majority put it: "The liberals have blown it in every area. The other side offers perversion, immorality, rampant venereal disease, [and] AIDS. Their only issue is the nuclear freeze and that's not going to win them the election [the presidency in 1984]."[47] Given the alternatives as the Moral Majority sees them, and if its views substantially reflect those of others on the New Right, it is not difficult to see why it chooses to stick with Reagan, however much it feels he might have failed the organization once he was in office.

Has the influence of the New Right crested? Its connections with, and at times ambivalent attitudes toward, the Reagan presidency has muted some of its stridency. Perhaps also it is running up against the political realities of a democratic process. There is only so much it can achieve, and it has experienced a string of successes since the mid to late 1970s that are impressive. Maybe the tide is turning. It did not do well in the 1982 off-year elections. Paul Weyrich of the Free Congress Foundation, a leader of the

---

[46] Rev. Jerry Falwell, "An Open Letter From Jerry Falwell on the Nuclear Freeze," *Chicago Tribune*, March 23, 1983, p. 12.

[47] Bruce Buursma, "Moral Majority Tells Its Side of Story," *Chicago Tribune*, June 18, 1983, p. 6.

FIGURE 7.1
An Open Letter from Jerry Falwell on the Nuclear Freeze

Fellow Americans:

War in any form is abominable. We all know that. But there is something at least as abominable, and that is life without liberty — life without the freedom to write and speak and pray.

I don't want the American people, especially our children, to be cremated in a nuclear explosion.

What I do want for them is to have the chance to love life and truth and God.

Our national task and challenge, therefore, is both to prevent a nuclear war and to insure peace with freedom.

I for one refuse to sit back and wait for the Soviets to enslave us or to destroy us in a rain of nuclear warheads.

And that is why I'm writing you this letter today. I feel that I must speak out on our alarming national defense situation.

This message is for every American who wants to make sure our country has the military strength to prevent war and keep us free.

We cannot afford to be number two in defense! But, sadly enough, that's where we are today. Number two.

And fading!

So, I urge you to cast your ballot today for Peace Through Strength and to preserve freedom.

I promise you I will publish the result of this poll all over America. Here are the questions:

1. *Are you willing to trust the survival of America to a nuclear freeze agreement with the Soviet Union, a nation which rejects on-site inspection of military facilities to insure compliance?*

   Yes ☐   **No** ☐

2. *Are you for stopping those U.S. strategic weapons programs aimed at restoring nuclear parity with the Soviet Union?*

   Yes ☐   **No** ☐

3. *Do you believe our NATO partners should be outnumbered in "theater" (intermediate range) nuclear weapons?*

   Yes ☐   **No** ☐

There they are: three burning issues. Three straightforward, uncomplicated questions.

Here are three additional issues you might think about:

1. *Is the Soviet regime likely to permit freedom of thought and religion under Uri Andropov, the former head of the KGB?*

2. *What would happen if Moscow and Peking patched up their quarrel?*

3. *What would be the effect on the nuclear balance if we cancelled the MX and the B-1 programs, while the Soviets went ahead with their programs to build two new ICBMs and two heavy bombers?*

And, you might also ask yourself: what would happen if the President of the United States received a call on the "hotline" some day, and the Soviet President said: "Give up or be destroyed?"

If our President said no, it could mean that more than half our people would be incinerated in a nuclear attack. If he said yes, the United States would no longer be the land of the free and home of the brave.

(Continued)

FIGURE 7.1 (continued)

But right now — at this very moment — it is not too late to rebuild our defenses.

What is needed is a loud and clear call from the American people.

Now, I can predict what will happen when this letter goes out. The "anti's" and the "ultra's" will start screaming: "There goes that war-monger again. He won't be satisfied until we have a nuclear showdown."

I've endured that kind of abuse before. And I will now.

It is incredible, but those of us who believe in peace with freedom, who believe that peace can best be insured through strength — which means moral as well as military strength — have to put up with this kind of abuse. So be it.

Let's review the basic points: war in any form is abominable.

The lesson of history is that weak nations cannot "buy" peace with treaties. "Deals" with tyrants don't work.

There is only one sure formula for peace with freedom and that is through strength.

Therefore, unless the leaders of this country have military strength at least equal to that available to the Kremlin tyrants, we can in time expect either an attack or nuclear blackmail.

Do we have such strength? These are the facts:

1. *The Soviets have almost a two-to-one advantage in nuclear weapons. And type for type, theirs are bigger than ours and newer.*

2. *The Soviets are building new strategic bombers and submarines, and testing new missiles. All we* *have in production is the new Trident submarine.*

3. *The Soviets have a nationwide civil defense program to protect their people, a massive bomber defense network, and anti-ballistic missles to protect Moscow. We have no civil defense program to protect the American people, a tiny air-defense network, and no missile defense at all.*

4. *In conventional weapons, the Soviets have four times as many tanks and artillery pieces and over twice as many men in uniform ready for war.*

While the Soviets have been building up during the last decade, we have:

1. *Cut our Navy in half.*

2. *Cancelled the production of Minute-man missiles.*

3. *Delayed the Trident program.*

4. *Cancelled the original B-1 program.*

5. *Spent years debating the best ways to protect MX Missiles, while building none.*

So, if you fear for the safety of your children and your friends, cast your ballot today for Peace Through Strength.

All of us must rally at this critical time and make our voice heard.

We have a President who wants to build up our military strength. But he is catching it from all sides. The "Freeze-niks," "ultra libs," and "unilateral disarmers" are after him.

He and the loyal members of Congress need to know that you are with them.

FIGURE 7.1 (continued)

Do send in your ballot right away.

This letter is being printed in major newspapers and mailed to millions of Americans.

We will tabulate your ballot and thousands of others and send the results to President Reagan and the Members of Congress.

It is time for patriotic, God-fearing Americans to speak up and let the nation's leaders know where you stand on the critical issues of national defense.

No matter how you look at it, the peace of the future is going to be decided by strength. Is it going to be American strength or Soviet strength? Vote now for Peace Through Strength. I promise you, your voice will be heard.

Sincerely,

Reverend Jerry Falwell

■ ■ ■ ■ Peace Through Strength Ballot ■ ■ ■ ■ ■

Please cast your vote on each of these questions:

1. Are you willing to trust the survival of America to a nuclear freeze agreement with the Soviet Union, a nation which rejects on-site inspection of military facilities to insure compliance?
   ☐ Yes   ☐ No

2. Are you for stopping those U.S. strategic weapons programs aimed at restoring nuclear parity with the Soviet Union?
   ☐ Yes   ☐ No

3. Do you believe our NATO partners should be outnumbered in "theater" (intermediate range) nuclear weapons?
   ☐ Yes   ☐ No

Dear Jerry,

Here is where I stand on the critical issues of national defense. Please carry the results of this balloting to our national leaders:

Name

Address

City _____ State _____ Zip _____

Mail To: Jerry Falwell
499 South Capitol Street, Suite 101
Washington, D.C. 20003

Source: Reprinted by permission of The Moral Majority.

New Right, called the results "a disaster, a rout."[48] NCPAC, as an example, did poorly in the 1982 elections. Only one of the fourteen or seventeen or twenty senators (the number seems to vary in the aftermath of the election) it endorsed and campaigned for won. In the House, 40 percent of the most conservative House members lost as against only 2 percent of the more liberal.[49] These results may be signs of a coming reaction. They may also be explained by the fact that the New Right has few left on its enemies' list who are well known, easy to focus attention on, and whose voting record is

[48] Morton Kondracke, "Hard Times for the New Right," *The New Republic,* December 20, 1982, p. 20.

[49] *Ibid.*

unrepresentative of a more conservative electorate. In this regard, success may have taken its toll.

The ability of the policy-making institutions to respond to the broad demands made on it and to act in the best interests of the public-at-large is in question. A strong and cohesive party system could build broad coalitions and advance the policy concerns of the major groups in its coalition. It could also command a degree of loyalty to ensure that the programs it advanced were given serious legislative attention. The American party system has had difficulty in executing its responsibilities in these regards and, in comparison with those in other democracies, has appeared weak and disorganized.[50] Nonetheless, the old party system, if it can be called this, was considerably better than the single-issue, polarized politics of the present slick party era. The real problems may just be beginning. The stronger the ideological and single-issue PACs are, the weaker and more fragmented the party system is likely to become.

CAMPAIGN REFORM

There is a movement afoot to correct some of the worst abuses in the electoral process. There are limits presently on PAC contributions (Tables 7.4 and 7.5). Many believe these limits to be ineffective. Changes in the law have been proposed to limit expenditures in congressional campaigns, reduce by one-half (or so) the amount individual PACs can donate to a candidate; or limit the total amount of PAC money that could be used by a candidate in a campaign (a ceiling of $70,000 is the most often heard figure). The most far-reaching of the alternatives has received little media or public attention, and it may be among the least popular with congressmen. The PACs, of course, strongly oppose it. It is the movement to equalize resources for elective office and to remove some of the worst abuses of the single-issue, corporate, and labor PACs through the public funding of Senate and House campaigns.

[50] Kenneth Janda, *Comparative Political Parties: A Cross-National Survey* (New York: Free Press, 1980); and Janda, "A Comparative Analysis of Party Organizations: the United States, Europe, and the World," in William Crotty (ed.), *The Party Symbol* (San Francisco: W. H. Freeman, 1980).

There are a number of proposals before the Congress. One of those most favored by reformers in the House would be voluntary (candidates could opt in or out). For those accepting public financing, there would be a spending limit of $150,000 in general election campaigns, plus an additional $30,000 allowed for fund raising and $15,000 for one mailing within the district. A cost-of-living escalator has been proposed, but its specific provisions have yet to be worked out. Candidates would have individual contributions to their campaigns of $100 or less matched in $10,000 increments up to $60,000. Also, the amount an officeholder could contribute to his own campaign would be limited to $25,000.

Problems confront the House bill. At present its provisions apply only to general elections. When opponents, in a legislative maneuver designed to weaken its support, managed to expand it to include primaries, the bill was killed in committee. Others want (1) to increase awards made directly to the national parties, having the parties in turn distribute the funds to prospective candidates; (2) to reduce or eliminate altogether the role of the Federal Election Commission in administering the bill's regulations; and (3) to raise the threshold of funds needed to qualify for the program from the presently specified $1000 to $10,000 to make public funding more selective.

There is a danger, as some opponents argue, that the spending ceilings may be too low to allow a challenger a real opportunity to unseat an incumbent and that the program may be too restrictive in its qualifying procedures (thus discouraging competition). Also the potential cost of the public financing of congressional elections in a period of economic uncertainty has been criticized. The House bill would cost between $22.2 million and $29.7 million, according to the most recent estimates of the Federal Election Commission.[51] The bill is open to compromise, and its final form has yet to be decided.

The Senate public financing proposal would also be voluntary and would apply only to general elections. For those who accepted public money, a spending ceiling of $250,000 plus ten cents for every voting-age citizen of their state would be instituted. Population projections indicate that the ceilings for individual states could

[51] "New Numbers on Public Financing," *Congressional Quarterly*, April 28, 1979, p. 779.

TABLE 7.4
Federal Election Commission Rules Governing PACs: Contribution Lists

Contributions from	To Candidate or His/Her Authorized Committee	To National Party Committee[a] Per Calendar Year[b]	To Any Other Committee Per Calendar Year	Total Contributions Per Calendar Year
Individual	$1,000 Per election[c]	$20,000	$5,000	$25,000
Multicandidate Committee[d]	$5,000 Per election	$15,000	$5,000	No Limit
Party Committee	$1,000 or $5,000[e] Per election	No Limit	$5,000	No Limit
Republican or Democratic Senatorial Campaign Committee,[f] or the National Party Committee, or a Combination of Both	$17,500 to Senate candidate per calendar year in which candidate seeks election	Not applicable	Not applicable	Not applicable
Any Other Committee or Group[g]	$1,000 Per election	$20,000	$5,000	No Limit

a For purposes of this limit, each of the following is considered a national party committee: a party's national committee, the Senate Campaign committees, and the National Congressional committees, provided they are not authorized by any candidate.

b Calendar year extends from January 1 through December 31. Individual contributions made or earmarked to influence a specific election of a clearly identified candidate are counted as if made during the year in which the election is held.

c Each of the following elections is considered a separate election: primary election, general election, run-off election, special election, and party caucus or convention which has authority to select the nominee.

d A multicandidate committee is any committee with more than 50 contributors which has been registered for at least six months and, with the exception of State party committees, has made contributions to five or more Federal candidates. An SSF may qualify as a multicandidate committee.

e Limit depends on whether or not party committee is a multicandidate committee.

f Republican and Democratic Senatorial Campaign committees are subject to all other limits applicable to a multicandidate committee.

g Other Committee may include an SSF not qualified as a multicandidate committee; group includes an organization, partnership, or group of persons.

Source: Federal Election Commission.

TABLE 7.5
Federal Election Commission Rules Governing PACs: Who May Be Solicited

Who May Be Solicited	By Corporation	By Labor Organization	By Incorporated Membership Organization [a]	By Incorporated Trade Association
Anytime	• Executive and administrative personnel and families • Stockholders and families	• Members and families	• Noncorporate members [b] • Executive and administrative personnel and families	• Noncorporate members • Executive and administrative personnel and families • With prior approval, corporate members' executive and administrative personnel, stockholders and the families of both

Twice Yearly[c]

• Nonexecutive and nonadministrative personnel and families

• Nonmember employees and families

• In corporations that employ members of the labor organization, corporate nonmember employees, stockholders and the families of both

• Nonexecutive and nonadministrative personnel and families

Source: Federal Election Commission.

[a] These rules apply, as appropriate, to corporations without capital stock and incorporated cooperatives.

[b] If a membership organization has stockholders as well as members, it may also solicit its stockholders and their families.

[c] Individuals who may be solicited at any time may also be included in a twice-yearly solicitation.

range from about $275,000 in Alaska to approximately $2 million in California. To qualify for federal funds, candidates would first have to raise $100,000 or 10 percent of their state's spending quota, whichever was lower. They would be required to do this in contributions of $100 or less.

The Senate has traditionally proven to be more receptive than the House on matters of public financing. But overall, politicians, and especially the incumbents that must vote such bills out, prefer to retain a system heavily weighted to their advantage. The Republican party has been consistent in its opposition to such measures, and the corporate, single-issue, and ideological PACs strongly oppose any effort to undermine their influence. Nonetheless, there is a precedent for such a program. Public financing of presidential prenomination and general election races was introduced in 1976, and it has worked well. It was passed by the Congress in the backlash created by the revelations of Watergate and under heavy public pressure. Conservatives, centrists, and liberals all appear pleased with the program, and there is no effort presently underway to rescind it.

The cost of congressional campaigns keeps escalating. A major contributing factor to the escalation has been the abundance of funds made available by PACs. The public, at least, seems disillusioned. A majority of the American people (57 percent), as reported by a Gallup poll, favor the public funding of congressional races. Support is strong among Democrats (57 percent), Republicans (54 percent), and independents (60 percent).[52]

The case for public funding has been well put by former Vice-President Walter Mondale. The vice-president warned that the dependence of congressional candidates on massive amounts of financing, supplied in increasing abundance by the PACs, has reached "extremely dangerous proportions." He cautioned, "This nation is not for sale. It belongs to our people. . . . We should have a new system of comprehensive public financing."[53] It should not require another Watergate to bring about a needed reform.

---

[52] American Institute of Public Opinion (Gallup Poll), "Federal Campaign Funding Has Strong Support," *Chicago Sun-Times,* April 1, 1979, p. 24.

[53] Jon Margolis, "Mondale Urges Public Financing to Elect Congress," *Chicago Tribune,* December 9, 1978, p. 2.

8

The Parties Respond

The changes documented in the earlier sections of this part
(and others) have threatened the operations and very existence of
the political parties. Both political parties are aware, in varying
degrees, of their problems. And both have made efforts to correct
them and better prepare themselves for the demands of the late
twentieth century. Most notable in these regards have been the
reform movements of the last decade.

The Democrats were forced to reform after their unhappy experiences in 1968. The Democratic National Convention of that year,
held in Chicago, turned out to be a bloody and bitter confrontation, the most violent in either party's history. It capped a debilitating series of battles between insurgents, backing Eugene
McCarthy and Robert Kennedy (assassinated on the night of the
California primary), and regulars, supporting Vice-President
Hubert Humphrey. The nominating rules of each of the state parties were found to be antiquated and, in most cases, not open to
influence from grassroots party members. The unruly Chicago
convention with its volatile confrontations among party leaders,
delegates, city officials, the media, street demonstrators, and the
police ensured that something of consequence would have to be

done about the abuses encountered in party procedures. The eventual result, however, was unexpected — a decade of reform that transformed the Democratic party.[1]

PRESIDENTIAL NOMINATIONS

The tone of the new reform movement was set by the first and most aggressive of the reform committees, the McGovern-Fraser Commission. The commission was created to assess the party's nominating practices (its most important duty) and to recommend changes. It held nationwide hearings, allowing both insurgents and regulars to voice their feelings. The hearings generated substantial media coverage and helped create a broad constituency for change. At the end of its first year of operation, the commission formulated seventeen "guidelines" intended to ensure "all Democratic voters . . . a full, meaningful and timely opportunity to participate" in the selection of national convention delegates, in influencing convention deliberations, and ultimately in choosing the party's presidential nominee.[2]

The commission made its position, and the intent of its proposals, clear: "We believe that popular control of the Democratic Party is necessary for its survival."[3] It did not find that popular

---

[1] Accounts of the process can be found in: William Crotty, *Party Reform* (New York: Longman, 1983); William Crotty, *Decision for the Democrats* (Baltimore: Johns Hopkins Press, 1978); Austin Ranney, *Curbing the Mischiefs of Faction* (Berkeley: University of California Press, 1975); William Crotty, *Political Reform and the American Electorate* (New York: Crowell, 1977); Austin Ranney, "The Democratic Party's Delegate Selection Reforms, 1968–1976," in Allan P. Sindler (ed.), *America in the Seventies: Problems, Policies, and Politics* (Boston: Little, Brown, 1977), pp. 160–206; Austin Ranney, "The Political Parties: Reform and Decline," in Anthony King (ed.), *The New American Political System* (Washington, D.C.: American Enterprise Institute, 1978), pp. 213–47; Robert T. Nakamura and Denis G. Sullivan, "Party Democracy and Democratic Control," in Walter Dean Burnham and Martha Wagner Weinberg (eds.), *American Politics and Public Policy* (Cambridge: MIT Press, 1978), pp. 26–40; Kenneth Janda, "Primrose Paths to Political Reform: 'Reforming' v. Strengthening American Parties," in W. Crotty (ed.), *Paths to Political Reform* (Lexington, Mass.: D. C. Heath-Lexington, 1980); and William Crotty, "Assessing a Decade of Reform" (Washington, D.C.: A Paper Presented at the 1979 Annual Meeting of the American Political Science Association).

[2] Crotty, *Decision,* pp. 59–103.

[3] Commission on Party Structure and Delegate Selection, *Mandate for Reform* (Washington, D.C.: Democratic National Committee, 1970), p. 49; and Crotty, "Building a 'Philosophy,' " p. 24.

control evident in the party procedures it examined. Its seventeen guidelines were meant to ensure such responsiveness in presidential nominations. Later reform commissions, most notably the Sanford, or Party Charter Commission (1972–74), attempted to extend the same concerns and safeguards to all aspects of party affairs.[4]

The McGovern-Fraser Commission made other notable contributions to the reform effort. In fact, without it, reform would have remained unrealized. After adopting its guidelines, it went on to *require* the state parties to enact them. It is this last point that reshaped the face of American party politics. Prior to this, national party committees were considered advisory: they had few sanctions over state parties and no real power to force a transformation of state party practices on the scale advocated by the McGovern-Fraser Commission. Nonetheless, through a clever use of the political resources available to it, with the backing of many groups influential in party deliberations and feeding on the public mood of discontent, the commission was able to force the individual state parties to conform to its standards. By the 1972 Democratic National Convention, the reformers could claim a 97 percent compliance with its guidelines.[5].

In effect, the reform battle was won here. There were later (successful) attempts to refine the guidelines to make them more accommodating to the interests of party regulars (while still preserving their integrity) and to expand the reform initiatives into other areas of party operations (beyond presidential nominations). National convention procedures were modernized, and a party charter, roughly analogous to the federal Constitution, was adopted to ensure fair and open party procedures.[6] By 1976, reform had largely run its course. After that, attention was directed toward making the 1980 and 1984 nominating rules more accommodating to the wishes of the party regulars.

Overall, the results were impressive. Reform had fundamentally reshaped party politics, especially presidential nominating

[4] Crotty, *Decision*, pp. 240–50; and Crotty, *Political Reform*, pp. 247–55.

[5] Crotty, *Decision*, pp. 104–47. There were substantial costs, however. See William Crotty, "Anatomy of a Challenge: The Chicago Delegation to the Democratic National Convention," in R. Peabody (ed.), *Cases in American Politics* (New York: Praeger, 1976), pp. 111–58.

[6] Crotty, *Political Reform*, pp. 252–55; Charles Longley, "Party Nationalization in America," in Crotty, *Paths*; and Denis G. Sullivan, Jeffrey L. Pressman, and F. Christopher Arterton, *Explorations in Convention Decision Making* (San Francisco: W. H. Freeman, 1976).

practices. Presidential nominations (and, to a lesser extent, all party agencies) had been opened to greater popular participation. Dominant influence within party circles had shifted from the elites and interest group leaders that had decided presidential nominations prior to 1972 to the individual party members who chose to participate in the local caucuses and primaries. As a consequence, more people than ever before have participated in party decision making. Party nominations had become more competitive within both major parties, and more contenders, representing all shades of political opinion, were competing for their party's nomination.[7] All of these had been objectives of the reform movement.

REFORMING THE PARTY STRUCTURE

Reform of the national party organization was intended to be part of the overall reform thrust after 1968. The earlier reform commissions, however, devoted all of their time and energies to restructuring the presidential nominating system and to modernizing national conventions. Little energy was left over for attacking the problems associated with the manner in which the national party operated or the representativeness of its institutions. As a consequence the 1972 Democratic National Convention created the Party Charter Commission to deal with this area of concern. The new commission was led by Duke University president and former North Carolina governor, Terry Sanford. A moderate, Sanford was acceptable to all party factions.

The commission was the last of the creative reform exercises. Its report of 1974 attempted to spell out new directions that the party could follow. It attempted to institutionalize the party structure, open it to influence from Democrats at all levels, and provide party members with the basic procedural safeguards implicit in presidential selection (as a result of the McGovern-Fraser Commission's work). The new party charter was intended to govern all aspects of party affairs.

Some aspects of the party charter were clearly visionary: a judicial council, resembling the Supreme Court, to resolve all intraparty disputes, and a National Education and Training Council,

[7] Crotty, "Assessing a Decade."

intended to expand the party's influence to new areas of social concern. As adopted in December of 1974, the party charter:[8]

Requested the national party to take stands on policy issues that represented the views of its rank and file.

Recognized the national convention as the party's supreme governing body and asked the state parties "to take provable positive steps" to adjust their forms and policies to the national party and party charter requirements.

Reaffirmed the new (McGovern-Fraser and succeeding reform commissions') delegate selection rules for national conventions.

Enlarged the national committee to 350 members.

Made the national committee's executive committee more responsive to and dependent on the national committee's membership.

Allowed for midterm conferences to be held.

Established a judicial council to arbitrate party disputes.

Created a national finance council to fund national party operations.

Provided for a National Education and Training Council to conduct "education and training programs for the Democratic Party."

Banned discrimination and supported affirmative action programs in party affairs.

Encouraged "full participation by all Democrats, with particular concern for minority groups, native Americans, women and youth" in all party activities.

Required that all meetings of the national committee, its executive committee and those of all party commissions be open to the public and that all votes be public.

Required an annual report of the national party, to include an accounting of its finances.

Required written rules of all state parties for the conduct of all party business.

Because of the lax organizational structure that characterized the Democratic party, the party charter signified a potentially evolving interest in developing a cohesive organization style. A restructured and more democratically representative party could

[8] See Crotty, *Political Reform*, pp. 247–55; and Crotty, "Assessing a Decade."

result in an organization more responsive to contemporary political and social concerns.

One of the more significant steps in this direction was the introduction of a midterm conference to consider policy alternatives and update the party's platform. The main objective of the first midterm convention was the debate over, and ratification of, the party charter. With a few modifications, party regulars found it acceptable, and they and the reformers combined to pass it.

The 1978 and 1982 midterm conventions faced many restrictions on topics for debate. Delegate selection (as in 1974) was tightly controlled. The midterm conference's agenda and delegate selection procedures were determined by the national chairman. In addition, the national chairman and a select committee of the national committee served as gatekeepers for the convention. Virtually all proposals for discussion had to be cleared in advance with them.

The midterm conferences as operated in 1974, 1978, and 1982 represented a considerable departure from what the reformers had envisioned. Nonetheless, the midterm conference has considerable potential for members to debate policy issues and address the concerns of the party's grassroots constituency. Party regulars appear to be increasingly comfortable with the idea. The midterm convention, if handled properly, could provide an instrument for evolving a policy-oriented party, in touch with contemporary concerns, much as the reformers had wanted.

Beyond the introduction of the midterm conference, the party charter has had a limited impact on the party. The national committee was tripled in membership, in an effort to make it more inclusive and reflective of the party's rank and file. As Charles Longley has shown, the changes have had negligible consequences. The national committee can be slightly more independent of a national chairperson, but its composition has not been greatly affected by the reforms.[9] The role of the national committee in American politics is as undistinguished now as it was before the reform movement.[10] It would be hard to distinguish, in any

[9] Charles Longley, "Party Nationalization in America," in William Crotty (ed.), *Paths to Political Reform* (Lexington, Mass.: D. C. Heath-Lexington, 1980).

[10] William Crotty, "The National Committees as Grassroots Vehicles of Representation," in William Crotty (ed.), *The Party Symbol* (San Francisco: W. H. Freeman, 1980).

positive sense, national committee operations in the 1980s from those of the 1960s. Overall, to this point the party charter's impact has not been notable.

REFORM IN THE REPUBLICAN PARTY

The Republican party has also attempted reform. It created two reform commissions, the Delegates and Organization (DO) Commission in the period 1969–72 and the Rule 29 Commission during 1972–74. These groups were intended to deal with the type of issue that occupied the McGovern-Fraser Commission, in particular, a recasting of the party's presidential nominating procedures to make them more equitable, open, and reflective of the party's grassroots base; and the problem of adequate minority group representation in party processes. Both commissions came up with a series of broad recommendations, generally reminiscent of those put forward by the McGovern-Fraser Commission. However, where the McGovern-Fraser Commission's guidelines revolutionized the Democratic party's presidential nominating practices, the corresponding proposals advanced within the Republican party have had little impact.[11]

The reasons for this are many. First, there was little support for fundamental change within the Republican party. In effect, reform had no constituency. Despite their problems, Republicans are well satisfied with their party, whom it represents, and the way in which it operates. Second, the national Republican party perceives itself as a coordinating and servicing agent for fifty basically independent state parties. It takes what could be called a "states' rights" approach to party affairs. It prefers emphasizing how little power it has to force its state affiliates to follow any course of action specified by the national party. As a consequence, Republican reform proposals — or those which were finally endorsed by the national committee and the national convention, a process that adds years to the consideration of reform questions — are essentially advisory. They are exhortations to the states to allow for

[11] On Republican reform, see Crotty, *Political Reform*, pp. 255–60; and Charles Longley, "Party Reform and the Republican Party" (New York: A Paper Presented at the 1978 Annual Meeting of the American Political Science Association); and Crotty, *Party Reform, op. cit.*

greater participation, but they carry few penalties. Such an approach is guaranteed to produce little change.

Republican reform efforts did not proceed beyond presidential nominating processes. There was not, for example, any equivalent of the party charter or any effort to recast and make more representative such bodies as the national committee. Again, there was no significant group within the Republican coalition that felt such change was needed to ensure a party more responsive to its contemporary political environment.

Nonetheless, some change has come to the Republican party nationally. In an important work, Cornelius P. Cotter and John F. Bibby have traced the evolution of national party operations in broad historical perspective. It is their argument that, in comparison with the past, the national parties, "are more heavily engaged in rule enforcement, campaign and organizational services, and administrative activities. In addition, they are exerting greater discipline over their respective state and local organizations and influencing those organizations through the services provided by the national party."[12]

Cotter and Bibby's analysis has particular applicability for the Republican party. They make the point that Republican reform has not followed the participant-oriented, structural-change path taken within the Democratic party. Rather, the Republican party has emphasized increased nationalization and institutionalization of the party by, in effect, making the national party more relevant in politically traditional ways: providing new services and support.

The authors' intensive examination of the operations of the Republican National Committee lends substance to their point. For example, the Republican National Committee's 1978 budget of $9.7 million is quantum leaps above its 1965 budget of $125,000. Its budget supported a paid staff of 220 (in 1977) and a series of activities from public relations promotions to candidate recruitment and campaign counseling that was impressive (and that contrasted markedly with those provided by the far smaller Democratic National Committee with its limited budget and staff).[13]

---

[12] Cornelius P. Cotter and John F. Bibby, "The Impact of Reform on the National Party Organizations: The Long-Term Determinants of Party Reform" (Washington, D.C.: A Paper Presented at the 1979 Annual Meeting of the American Political Science Association), p. 5.

[13] *Ibid.*, pp. 17–19.

The Republican party, then, has experienced changes. The national party has expanded its activities and services. The party's presidential nominating procedures have also been affected (perhaps against its will) by the reform spirit. When one party in the American two-party system changes extensively, it cannot help but affect the other. The emphasis on the increasing number of primaries and the shifting in the balance of national convention from caucus selection to primary election has taken place in both parties. In part, it results from modifications in state party laws for both parties. In part also, it is a concession to a changing age and the emphasis on media coverage that primaries encourage.

The spirit of competition over presidential nominations has also influenced both parties. An incumbent president is no longer guaranteed renomination. Serious intraparty opposition to the renomination of a party's incumbent president is a recent occurrence, dating back to 1968. Since that year the Democrats have had two incumbents — Lyndon Johnson and Jimmy Carter — challenged from within their own ranks. The Republican party has not escaped the changing mood. Gerald Ford, a sitting president in 1976, was barely able to withstand the challenge of Ronald Reagan for his party's nomination.

There have been changes then in both parties in form and approach and, in many respects, they are formidable. The party system of the 1980s is not the party system of the 1960s or even the 1970s.

CONCLUSION

The question remaining is, Has enough been accomplished? The McGovern-Fraser Commission, the most influential of the reform bodies, put the matter bluntly:

> If we are not an open party; if we do not represent the demands of change, then the danger is not that people will go to the Republican Party; it is that there will no longer be a way for people committed to orderly change to fulfill their needs and desires within our traditional political system. It is that they will turn to third or fourth party politics or the anti-politics of the street.[14]

[14] Commission on Party Structure, *Mandate,* p. 49.

Party reform is just a beginning. Where the parties will go from here is, at the moment, uncertain. In broad terms, political parties have adjusted poorly to the political and social demands of the last quarter of the twentieth century. They have found themselves in a changing, and basically hostile, climate. To date they have not made the new technologies and the evolving political climate work to their advantage. Change has been resisted, and adaptation to change is (as, for example in the reform efforts) often bitterly opposed.

III

THE DECLINE OF THE PARTY IN CONGRESS

Introduction

A confusing mix of conflict and cooperation now occurs between the president and Congress, between the president and his party in Congress, and between congressional party leaders and followers. It is not unusual, historically, for the president and Congress to be at odds or for party discipline in Congress to dissolve on a particular issue. What is unusual is the degree to which this has become the norm. The roots of the problem reach far deeper than one president or one election. They are found in broad, long-term changes in American society as well as in specific events of recent political history. Put most simply, party and presidential leadership suffers from the effects of more than a decade of intense social and political strain. But other, less obvious forces have also been at work.

The aim in this part is to explore how the congressional parties — and the task of leading them — have evolved in response to broad changes in the political climate and to specific political events. Chapter 9 focuses on electoral politics. In an important sense, the loosening of party ties in Congress is no more than a natural consequence of the decline in party loyalty among citizens. In this and other ways, relations between members and constituents have been developing in directions that increasingly limit the relevance of parties to both.

The consequences for congressional party leadership are traced out in Chapter 10. Adjustments within the congressional parties to the changing needs and perspectives of members have substantially altered many aspects of congressional organization and procedure. A few have strengthened the hand of party leaders; most have had the opposite effect. As will be apparent, these conflicting tendencies arise from the contrary demands of electoral and legislative performance.

Since every president depends to some degree on party leaders to enact his legislative programs, any important change in their capacity to lead bears implications for presidential power. Presidents rely heavily on their party's leaders in Congress. The legislative party leaders' problems are frequently the president's also. The relationship has been compounded by the acts of recent presidents, and the congressional responses to these. In Chapter 11 we will consider these problems. In a final chapter we will then present some speculation about the future of the congressional parties and of party and presidential leadership.

9
Parties in Congressional Elections

THE ELECTORAL INCENTIVE

Perhaps the simplest way to begin untangling the complex combination of circumstances that has progressively undermined the authority of party leaders is to consider the motives and goals of individual members of Congress. Nearly all of them want to be effective legislators. They seek to win influence and respect in Washington and to put their imprint on public policy. But this means winning election and reelection. And the demands of effective policy making and of winning elections may pull members in opposite directions. When they do, party loyalty suffers.

Parties are most valuable to members of Congress when those members act as legislators, writing and passing laws. Legislating is a collective activity. At minimum, majority coalitions must be arranged at various stages of the legislative process. Normally, much more than this minimum cooperation is necessary. The party is the basic mechanism for arranging cooperative action in pursuit of legislative goals. The details of how the congressional parties do this will be taken up later. Insofar as members are concerned with writing and passing effective legislation — and in gaining influence and respect through that achievement — the importance of parties is enhanced.

But for most members, winning elections comes first. Logically, of course, winning office is only a means to the achievement of other goals. The real point is not to get elected, but to do the things getting elected allows you to do. But you have to be in Congress to pursue a congressional career. So the need to get elected takes precedence. "All members of Congress," said a former congressman, "have a primary interest in being reelected. Some members have no other interest."[1] Although the electoral incentive is not the only one, it is so prevalent that David R. Mayhew, a political scientist, could make a convincing case that most of what goes on in Congress is best explained by the simple assumption that its members are "single-minded seekers of reelection."[2]

According to this argument, party loyalty, deference to the wishes of a president, or conscientious attention to legislative work will prevail only if they do not hinder reelection. In recent years, a growing number of members have evidently decided that they do. And they may well be right. The crucial question is: how do members win and hold congressional seats? And, in particular, what difference do parties and partisanship make in this endeavor?

PARTY ORGANIZATIONS IN CONGRESSIONAL ELECTIONS

As *campaign organizations*, parties have been relatively unimportant to congressional candidates for many years. Even in localities where party organizations have remained comparatively robust and active, congressional candidates are hardly the main attraction. Local party activists are much more interested in state and local offices — and in the patronage they bring. Often House districts do not coincide with the locally more important divisions, the counties or cities; congressional campaigns therefore do not fit

---

[1] Quoted in David R. Mayhew, *Congress: The Electoral Connection* (New Haven: Yale University Press, 1974), p. 16.

[2] Mayhew, *Congress*, p. 5.

neatly into the party's regular campaign operations. Congressional candidates fall, as it were, between two or more organizational stools. Of necessity, they therefore put together their own campaigns. "If we depended on the party organizations to get elected," observed one congressman in the late 1950s, "none of us would be here."[3]

The general irrelevance of local party organizations is apparent from Richard Fenno's recent study of how eighteen different House members work to retain their seats. According to Professor Fenno,

> Only two of the eighteen members studied were originally recruited by the local party organization. And eight began their careers by challenging the party organization. Most of the eighteen coexist with the party — because of party indifference to the congressional office or because the party leaders value the proven independent strength of the congressman as a resource. Most primary constituencies consist of people whose loyalties are to the congressman rather than to the party. And in only two or three cases is there an integrated working relationship between the congressman's personal organization and the local party organization. That is exactly the way most of our House members want it — separate organizations pursuing separate tasks. The task of the congressman's personal organization is to keep him in Congress. The task of the local party organization is to keep the party in control of local offices.[4]

FINANCING CONGRESSIONAL ELECTIONS

Furthermore, party organizations have never provided much financial assistance to congressional candidates. On occasion, the parties have even expected contributions *from* the candidates.[5] The problem of financing campaigns has become more formidable over the past two decades with the growth in campaign costs. Campaigning has become more and more costly, in part because party organizations have decayed; they provided little help before;

---

[3] Quoted in Charles L. Clapp, *The Congressman: His Work as He Sees It* (Washington, D.C.: Brookings Institution, 1963), p. 397.

[4] Richard F. Fenno, Jr., *Home Style: House Members in Their Districts* (Boston: Little, Brown and Company, 1978), p. 113.

[5] Clapp, *The Congressman*, pp. 398–99.

they provide even less now. Individual campaigning is naturally more expensive. The economies to scale that parties could supply by combining several campaigns are lost. And, apart from other changes, the development of new kinds of campaign technology has driven up the cost of campaigning quite dramatically. Congressional candidates must now be prepared to wage *expensive* individual campaigns.

The most obvious change in campaign technology has been the advent of television as a campaign medium, but it is by no means the only one. In many places, professional campaign managers have supplanted parties as conductors of campaigns. The professionals rely on modern techniques of advertising (especially broadcast advertising), market research, and personnel management. They employ professionally conducted polls, individualized direct mail advertising, and computerized data processing as part of the campaign arsenal. Campaign expenses have as a consequence increased sharply. The entire package of campaign techniques — not just television — is expensive.[6]

Congressional candidates who wish to run competitive races — challengers trying to unseat incumbents, incumbents facing attractive and well-heeled challengers, candidates scrambling for open seats — normally have to raise a great deal of money. And how much they raise and spend clearly does make a difference in the outcome. The vote won by nonincumbent candidates — challengers to incumbents or candidates for open seats — depends directly on how much they spend on the campaign. The more they spend, if other things are equal, the larger their share of the vote. This is not true of incumbent members of Congress, however. The more they spend, the *smaller* their share of the vote. The paradox is only apparent. Campaign expenditures do not cost them votes. What happens is that incumbents feel compelled to raise and spend more money when they face a serious challenge, and a serious challenge *does* cost them votes. The result is that close, competitive congressional elections are characterized by heavy spending by *both* candidates.[7]

A conservative estimate would place the cost of a competitive

[6] For an extended account of these developments, see Robert Agranoff (ed.), *The New Style in Election Campaigns* (Boston: Holbrook Press, 1972).

[7] See Gary C. Jacobson, "The Effects of Campaign Spending in Congressional Elections," *American Political Science Review* 72 (June 1978): 469–91.

House campaign at close to $200,000; Senate campaigns are even more expensive. Candidates with weak, underfinanced opponents may get by with much less than this amount. Indeed, wise incumbents work to discourage strong opponents; we will see more on that later. But serious opposition requires a major financial effort. Candidates who wish to enter and remain in Congress must therefore be able to raise large campaign kitties. And so they are likely to be sensitive to the wishes, interests, and expectations of those who supply campaign funds.

It is important to recognize, then, that parties normally supply a conspicuously *small* proportion of the needed campaign funds. And this proportion has been decreasing over the last few elections. The greatest share of campaign money — about two-thirds — comes from donations by private individuals. The second most important source of funds is nonparty political action committees (PACs). Political parties now supply much less money than either of these sources.

As shown in Chapter 7, PACs represent a variety of economic and ideological interests. Some are organized by individual firms and labor unions. Others represent industries (banking or shipbuilding, for example), occupational interests (doctors, lawyers, teachers), or agricultural sectors (milk producers, tobacco growers). Collectively, they supply a growing share of congressional campaign funds.

If members of Congress are at all attuned to the concerns of those who finance their campaigns — or who might, if aroused, finance their opponents' campaigns — they will be more attentive to individual donors and to organized interests than to their parties. They will be most sensitive to the wishes of individual donors *if* they can determine what those wishes are. But it is often difficult to do so. People give money to candidates for a great variety of reasons, many of them irrelevant to what the candidate does in office. Although personal services and attention to the financial "constituency" are obviously prudent, it may well be impossible for a member to estimate the collective preferences of individual contributors on policy questions. They therefore can hardly circumscribe his actions.

With political action committees it is quite otherwise. As the second most important source of campaign funds, they cannot lightly be ignored. And they often have strong and conspicuous preferences on legislation and other matters before Congress. This does not imply that members must invariably dance to the tunes called by groups that help finance their campaigns. It does mean that their preferences will be taken into account as members decide what to do. This is the minimal payoff that contributing groups expect.

MOTIVES AND STRATEGIES OF PACs

A closer inspection of the motives and strategies of organized campaign contributors will provide some insights into how current campaign finance practices weaken the bonds of party loyalty in Congress. Many PACs openly contribute most heavily to members who are in a position to do them the most good — or harm — regardless of party. Dairy industry committees, for example, give most of their money to incumbents of both parties who sit on congressional committees dealing with agriculture. They give seven dollars to incumbents to every dollar they give to challengers, but they do not shrink from giving to *both* candidates if each has a chance to win. And they are entirely indifferent as to whether or not the candidate actually needs the money; even unopposed candidates may get contributions. Although their declared intention is "to keep our friends in office and elect those who are our friends,"[8] it is perhaps more accurate to say that they aim to make certain that those in office remain friendly.

Similarly, the American Medical Association's AMPAC gives money disproportionately to sponsors of the AMA's health care proposals and to agreeable members of committees dealing with health policy; party is scarcely a factor.[9] The banking industry's BankPAC funds campaigns of members of committees handling banking legislation.[10] And maritime industry groups give mainly to members who support laws that would require American ships and crews to be used for the delivery of various products.[11]

---

[8] *Congressional Quarterly Weekly Report* 31 (March 17, 1973): 569.

[9] *Congressional Quarterly Weekly Report* 30 (October 21, 1972): 2720–21; *Congressional Quarterly Weekly Report* 31 (March 17, 1973): 570.

[10] *Congressional Quarterly Weekly Report* 31 (March 17, 1973): 570.

[11] *Dollar Politics*, vol. 2 (Washington, D.C.: Congressional Quarterly, October 1974), p. 54.

For many groups, the strategy of contributing to members of Congress who are best situated to help or harm their interests is simply good business. When the Congress's decisions have a substantial impact on profits and losses, it is a sound business policy to deploy financial resources to promote the friendliest possible relations with its members. Campaign contributions are one approach among many. It should come as no surprise, then, that business associations contribute almost as much to Democrats as to Republicans, despite the ideological differences that continue to exist between the business community and the Democratic party.[12] Democrats will continue to enjoy a sizable share of business' bounty as long as they control the Congress.

Other economic interests are more definitely partisan. The leaders of organized labor have traditionally claimed independence from any party, preferring to "reward friends and punish enemies" wherever they are found. But in fact labor has become the major organizational source of funds for Democratic congressional candidates. More than 95 percent of the money given by labor groups goes to Democrats. Friendly Republicans are more often helped by labor's lack of support for their opponents than by any direct assistance.

Recently, labor has been less than delighted by the return on its political investments. Almost every major item on labor's agenda for recent Congresses has failed to pass. Most galling must have been the antilabor votes of many Democrats who had received large labor contributions. The alternative sources of funds — including business PACs — readily accessible to agreeable incumbents are no doubt partly to blame. But there are other, stronger reasons. The inability of organized labor, traditional mainstay of the Democratic party, to get its way with a Congress roughly two-thirds Democratic is by itself a clear signal that parties are not what they used to be.

DISCOURAGING CHALLENGERS

Shrewd incumbents are as sensitive to the effects of their actions on potential challengers (and their financial backers) as

---

[12] *Congressional Quarterly Weekly Report* 36 (January 21, 1978): 119.

they are to the effects on their own supporters. The reason is that the ease with which they can win reelection depends on the vigor of the challenge they face. If the opponent is an inexperienced campaigner who conducts a modest, shoestring campaign, the incumbent is certain to win. An experienced, amply funded opponent means a much harder campaign. More time and energy must be invested, and more money must be raised. Members may sometimes enjoy campaigning, but by all accounts they hate raising money. The late Senator Hubert Humphrey once called it a "disgusting, degrading, demeaning experience,"[13] to which the great majority of his colleagues would reply, "Amen."

Even though they raise and spend large sums of money and mount full-scale campaigns, members suffer their closest calls — and defeats — when opposed by attractive, well-financed challengers. It is much safer to discourage vigorous opposition before the campaign starts. Indeed, because of the way money works in congressional elections — helping nonincumbents much more than incumbents — it is more important for members to prevent campaign resources from being mobilized against them than it is to mobilize their own campaign resources. Members serve themselves best by denying their potential opponents financial support. This has the complementary benefit of keeping more experienced and ambitious politicians from making the challenge. They recognize that without adequate resources, the chance of winning is slight.[14]

Members of Congress therefore have a real incentive to avoid actions that might excite opposition from groups not already actively committed against them. Among other things, they are likely to be conscious of the potential reactions of groups, such as the gun lobby or the antiabortionists or the environmentalists, which specifically target prominent "enemies" for electoral attack. They are also well advised to keep in visible touch with their districts. A high profile back home prevents any impression from developing that a member is losing his grip on the district and is therefore vulnerable.

[13] Quoted in David Adamany and George E. Agree, *Political Money: A Strategy for Campaign Finance in America* (Baltimore and London: Johns Hopkins University Press, 1975), p. 8.

[14] See Gary C. Jacobson, *Money in Congressional Elections* (New Haven: Yale University Press, 1980), pp. 106–107.

MEMBERS AND THEIR CONSTITUENTS

Congressional candidates run individual, personal campaigns in part because they must; party resources are much too thin to carry them. But they also do so because this approach to campaigning pays off on election day. Members of the House must run for reelection every two years. Their campaigns never really end. They pursue reelection throughout the term, so their campaign strategy is visible in all their dealings with constituents. It is important to emphasize, then, that within their constituencies, members typically cultivate personal images surprisingly empty of partisan or even programmatic content. They present themselves to people in the district as trustworthy, hardworking individuals who merit support on the basis of personal qualities rather than political beliefs or goals.

Richard Fenno, who traveled extensively with eighteen House members as they made the rounds of their districts, found that each member projected a personal "home style" that defined his relationship to the groups he relied on for political support. Home styles varied among members according to the character of the district and the personality of the individual member. But in one way or another, all members basically sought to inspire *trust* among their constituents.[15] They did this by emphasizing their personal qualifications, including moral character, by identifying with their constituents ("I am one of you," they implied, "so you can trust me to make the right decisions"), and by working to develop bonds of empathy with the groups and individuals they met.

For most of them, issues, policy, and partisanship were *not* prominent objects of discussion with constituents and were not used to elicit support. Even members who did display an issue-oriented home style used issues primarily to cement ties of trust: "Issues are not as important as the treatment of issues."[16] Members used issues to present themselves as the kind of people constituents would want in Washington; the issues themselves were secondary.

Fenno's House members agreed that representation could ba-

[15] Fenno, *Home Style*, p. 55.
[16] *Ibid.*, p. 241.

sically be defined as accessibility. Constituents were continually reminded that the lines of communication were open and that they had access to the member whenever they needed it. And this was done most effectively through a steady flow of services to the district.

> Many activities can be incorporated under the rubric of "district service," or "constituency service," but the core activity is providing help to individuals, groups, and localities in coping with the federal government. Individuals need someone to intercede with the bureaucracies handling veterans benefits, social security checks, military status, civil service pensions, immigration proceedings, and the like. Private groups and local governments need assistance in pursuing federal funds, for water and sewer projects, highways, dams, buildings, planning, research and development, small business loans, and so forth.[17]

VOTING IN CONGRESSIONAL ELECTIONS

Members of Congress believe that their personal standing, maintained through individual attention to constituents and emphasis on district services, is what discourages opposition, wins votes, and keeps them in office. Studies of the congressional electorate indicate that they are right, even though, paradoxically, most voters base their voting decision on the candidate's party. One veteran House member recently complained that "party loyalty has really withered away. It shouldn't be that way. They didn't get elected on their own. A lot of these guys wouldn't have been elected if they didn't have Democrat behind their name."[18] In a way, he is right. The basic determinant of voting in congressional elections is the party identification of the voter. Voters most often vote for the candidate of their preferred party. But, in a broader sense, he is quite wrong. Members do not win reelection on the basis of their loyalty to the party.

For one thing, there is no evidence that people who vote for members on the basis of party affiliation expect candidates to vote with their parties once they are in office. Voters' perceptions and evaluations of congressional candidates are almost empty of policy

[17] *Ibid.*, p. 101.
[18] *Congressional Quarterly Weekly Report* 36 (May 27, 1978), p. 1302.

content. Only a tiny minority usually has any knowledge of how a member voted on any particular bill, let alone how loyal the member has been to party leaders. The basic reason so many voters use party cues in deciding how to vote is that they have no other information about the candidates. In a study made of the 1958 House elections, for example, Donald F. Stokes and Warren E. Miller found that 59 percent of the people they surveyed had neither read nor heard anything about either House candidate; fewer than one in five knew something about both candidates. Forty-six percent cast their ballots without having received any information about either candidate.[19] With no other information, voters simply go by their party preference.

When voters do have additional information about candidates, party loyalty is not nearly so automatic. The evidence for this is in Table 9.1. Table 9.1 shows the impact of one piece of information — the name of the candidate — on party loyalty among congressional voters. Voters who remember the name of their own party's candidate only are the most consistent party line voters; they remain loyal in more than 90 percent of the cases. Voters who remember only the name of the other party's candidate have actually defected to the opposition in a majority of cases since 1966. Any recall of the other party's candidate increases the likelihood of partisan defection.

There is, to be sure, more to it than merely recalling the name of the candidate. Voters' *evaluations* of candidates are even more important. A survey of voters' attitudes toward 1974 Senate candidates found that about 80 percent of those who remembered a candidate's name could also remember something they liked or disliked about the candidate. Interestingly, about one-third of those who could *not* remember the candidate's name were still willing to offer evaluative comments. Most comments — 51 percent — referred to the candidate's personal qualities. Only 15 percent referred strictly to partisan characteristics. These were, not surprisingly, more common among voters who could not recall the candidate's name. The other 34 percent combined these and other miscellaneous criteria in specifying their likes and dislikes.[20]

---

[19] Donald E. Stokes and Warren E. Miller, "Party Government and the Saliency of Congress," in *Elections and the Political Order* (New York: John Wiley and Sons, 1966), p. 204.

[20] Jacobson, "Effects of Campaign Spending," p. 488.

TABLE 9.1

The Effects of Candidate Recall on Partisan Defection in House and Senate Elections

Percentage Who Defected in:	Voter Recalled Name of:			
	Both Candidates	Own Candidate	Other Candidate	Neither Candidate
House Elections				
1958	17 (196)[a]	2 (166)	40 (68)	8 (368)
1966	19 (198)	4 (98)	66 (41)	14 (231)
1968	23 (303)	5 (97)	51 (57)	19 (267)
1970	24 (152)	1 (148)	57 (37)	13 (256)
1972	23 (151)	7 (100)	62 (26)	21 (242)
1974	29 (281)	1 (154)	58 (79)	15 (374)
Senate Elections				
1974	25 (317)	2 (138)	62 (87)	10 (205)
1978	32 (343)	6 (165)	61 (97)	10 (432)

[a] Number of cases from which percentages were computed. The 1974 and 1978 samples were weighted.

Source: Information for the years 1958–1970, reprinted by permission from Robert B. Arsenau and Raymond E. Wolfinger, "Voting Behavior in Congressional Elections." Paper presented to the Annual Meeting of the American Political Science Association, New Orleans, Louisiana, September 4–8, 1973, p. 14; 1972, 1974, and 1978 figures are from the Center for Political Studies.

Assessments of the candidates had a strong impact on how people voted. This is shown in Table 9.2. Partisan voters who evaluated the other party's candidate positively and their own negatively were most likely to defect to the opponent. Voters who

TABLE 9.2
Evaluation of Senate Candidates and Partisan Voting Behavior in 1974
(Percentage of Partisan Voters Defecting)

Evaluation of Other Party's Candidate:	Evaluation of Own Party's Candidate:			
	Positive	Positive and Negative	Negative	Marginal Totals
Positive	28.6 (21)[a]	77.1 (35)	77.1 (35)	65.9 (91)
Positive and Negative	4.5 (139)	31.1 (45)	56.0 (25)	16.3 (209)
Negative	4.2 (167)	3.4 (59)	40.0 (5)	4.8 (231)
Marginal Totals	5.8 (327)	30.9 (139)	66.2 (65)	19.8 (531)
No Evaluation	16.5 (115)			

[a] Number of cases from which percentages were computed. The sample is weighted.
Source: 1974 CPS Survey.

had positive things to say about their own party's candidate and negative comments about the other party's candidate were most loyal.

Comparable studies of voting for House candidates support the same conclusions: personal judgments of candidates predominate, and they affect the vote.[21] Thomas E. Mann's research on the 1976 elections actually suggested that evaluations of House candidates were more important than party identification in determining how people voted that year. He carefully explored the connection between a candidate's familiarity to voters — measured by whether voters could either *recall* his name or *recognize* it once it was

[21] See Stokes and Miller, "Party Government," pp. 205–207; Thomas E. Mann, *Unsafe at Any Margin: Interpreting Congressional Elections* (Washington, D.C.: American Enterprise Institute for Public Policy Research, 1978), pp. 60–74; Alan J. Abramowitz, "Name Familiarity, Reputation, and the Incumbency Effect in a Congressional Election," *Western Political Quarterly* 28 (1975): 678.

mentioned — and their evaluations and support. He discovered that "visibility does not insure popularity, but it is an essential prerequisite. Voters who fail to *recognize* a challenger's name . . . invariably move disproportionately into the incumbent's camp. . . . Among those who did not recognize them, the challengers lost an average of 38 percent of their own partisans."[22]

The importance of visibility explains why money works as it does in congressional elections. Incumbents are already known by voters at the beginning of the campaign; most have spent a good portion of the previous two years keeping constituents aware of them. Challengers are rarely as well known; victory is possible only if they can grab the attention of voters during the campaign. The campaign is crucial, and a vigorous campaign costs money. Challengers do better the more they spend because they become better known the more they spend.[23] Spending an ample amount of money does not guarantee them victory (any more than it would the incumbent). The kind of person who is presented by all that campaigning is by no means irrelevant. But without the money, even a very good candidate will not get very far. Voters will remain unaware of his virtues, and they will therefore ignore him on election day. This is why it is so valuable to incumbents to face obscure and poorly funded opponents.

THE DECLINE OF PARTISANSHIP IN CONGRESSIONAL ELECTIONS

Returning for a moment to the figures in Table 9.1, notice that partisan defections appear to be much more common in the 1960s and 1970s than they were in 1958. Other data show the trend away from party loyalty even more clearly. Table 9.3 lists the proportion of loyal, defecting, and independent voters in congressional electorates from 1956 through 1976. The proportion of voters casting ballots for candidates of the opposite party more than doubled between 1956 and 1976.

The decline in party line voting for Congress is part of a wider decrease in the electoral importance of party. Voting behavior at

[22] Mann, *Unsafe at Any Margin,* p. 59.
[23] Jacobson, "Effects of Campaign Spending," pp. 479–85.

TABLE 9.3
Party Line Voting in House Elections, 1956–78 (in percentages)

Year	Party Line Voters	Defectors	Independents	Total
1956	82	9	9	100
1958	84	11	5	100
1960	80	12	8	100
1962	83	12	5	100
1964	79	15	5	99
1966	76	16	8	100
1968	74	19	7	100
1970	76	16	8	100
1972	73	17	10	100
1974	74	18	8	100
1976	72	19	9	100
1978	75	13	13	101

Note: Party line voters are those who voted for the party with which they identified. (Independents leaning toward a party are treated as partisans, not independents.) Defectors are those who voted for the party other than the one they claimed as their own. Data may not sum to 100 because of rounding.

Source: Reprinted by permission from Thomas E. Mann, *Unsafe at Any Margin: Interpreting Congressional Elections* (Washington, D.C.: American Enterprise Institute for Public Policy Research, 1978), p. 14. Data are originally from SRC/CPS National Election Studies. 1978 figures are taken from the Center for Political Studies SRC/CPS National Election Studies.

all levels has undergone significant changes in this direction since the early 1960s. Not only do an increasing number of voters refuse to identify themselves as Republicans or Democrats, preferring to be called independents, but even the self-designated partisans are less loyal to their party's candidates than they once were. And public attitudes toward the parties as institutions have grown increasingly negative.[24]

The weakening of party loyalty has had profound consequences for the electoral side of congressional politics. Partisan defections are by no means randomly distributed among candidates. Voters are much more likely to defect to *incumbents* than to nonincum-

[24] See Jack Dennis, "Trends in Public Support for the American Political Party System." Paper presented at the Annual Meeting of the American Political Science Association, Chicago, Illinois, August 29–September 2, 1974.

TABLE 9.4

Partisan Defections to Incumbents and Challengers, 1958–78 (in percentages)

Year	Incumbent Partisans		Challenger Partisans	
1958	8.9	(406)[a]	16.2	(291)
1960	7.7	(534)	19.3	(394)
1962	—[b]		—[b]	
1964	10.9	(430)	25.1	(311)
1966	9.1	(296)	32.5	(200)
1968	13.5	(355)	32.5	(286)
1970	4.7	(253)	32.1	(190)
1972	5.9	(323)	56.0	(168)
1974	12.9	(255)	48.6	(181)
1978	9.8	(452)	42.7	(243)

[a] Number of cases from which percentages were computed.
[b] Data not available.

Source: From Albert D. Cover, "One Good Term Deserves Another: The Advantage of Incumbency in Congressional Elections," *American Journal of Political Science,* Vol. 21 (August 1977), p. 535, Table 4. Reprinted by permission of the publisher, The University of Texas Press. The 1978 figures are from the Center for Political Studies.

bents of the opposing party. And the increase in defections is composed almost entirely of more frequent defections to incumbents. The figures in Table 9.4 make these points very clearly. Defection rates of voters identifying with the incumbent's party have fluctuated; no trend is apparent. In sharp contrast, voters of the challenger's party defect much more frequently in recent elections. Albert Cover, who collected these data, emphasizes the crucial point: *"Since 1972 about half of those identifying with the challenger's party have deserted their party's congressional candidate in contested elections involving an incumbent."*[25]

THE ADVANTAGES OF INCUMBENCY

Why have voters consistently defected more often to incumbents than to challengers? And why do they now defect more

[25] Albert D. Cover, "One Good Term Deserves Another: The Advantage of Incumbency in Congressional Elections," *American Journal of Political Science* 21 (1977): 535.

frequently than in the past? The first question can be answered with relative confidence. Partisan defection is clearly related to the amount of information voters have about candidates. Table 9.1 established that point. And voters normally have much more information about incumbents than about nonincumbents. Using recall of the candidate's name as a simple indicator of information, Table 9.5 shows this to be the case. Incumbents are invariably recalled more frequently than nonincumbents; their advantage here is unmistakable. Its effect is even more telling — in light of the data in Table 9.1 — because when the contest is between an incumbent and a challenger and only one of the candidates is recalled (the two middle columns of Table 9.1), that candidate is almost always the incumbent. This is true in more than 96 percent of the cases in the 1972 and 1974 surveys, for example.

But the second question is not answered so easily. The information in Table 9.5 indicates that the relative advantage of incumbents in voter recall has *not* increased over the years during which defections to incumbents *have* increased. In fact, partisan voters are more likely to defect to incumbents even when they cannot recall their names.[26] This has led some scholars to conclude that the growing value of incumbency cannot be attributed to more successful self-promotion by officeholders (though more *extensive* self-promotion cannot be doubted; these efforts will be reviewed shortly). But name recall is not a perfect measure of candidate information. Voters need only recognize the name of the candidate when they see it (e.g., on a ballot in the voting booth) for the effects of candidate familiarity to operate. And name recognition is much more common than name recall.[27] If voters consistently preferred incumbents to challengers without recognizing *or* recalling either one, the phenomenon would defy rational explanation. So the question of whether or not incumbents are merely reaping the benefits of more extensive self-advertising is still open.

This and the other explanations that have been offered for the increase in voter support for incumbents more often reinforce than contradict one another, but clear differences at least in emphasis are evident. One straightforward explanation is that as voters have progressively detached themselves from party ties, they have merely replaced one simple voting cue — party — with

[26] John A. Ferejohn, "On the Decline of Competition in Congressional Elections," *American Political Science Review* 71 (1977): 171.

[27] Mann, *Unsafe at Any Margin*, p. 32.

TABLE 9.5
Percentages of Voters Recalling Names of Candidates in Contested Congressional Elections

	Incumbents		Nonincumbents	
House Elections				
1958	57.6	(738)[a]	38.0	(947)
1964	63.0	(856)	39.8	(920)
1966	55.9	(583)	37.6	(703)
1968	63.7	(703)	46.5	(861)
1970	54.7	(548)	31.3	(630)
1972	50.0	(498)	30.9	(718)
1974	57.2	(856)	32.2	(1230)
1978	61.2	(656)	38.4	(1648)
Senate Elections				
1974	72.7	(595)	48.3	(1023)

[a] Number of cases from which percentages were computed.

Source: From John A. Ferejohn, "On the Decline of Competition in Congressional Elections," *American Political Science Review* 77 (1977), p. 170. Reprinted by permission. The 1978 sample was weighted. Figures for 1978 are from Center for Political Studies.

another — incumbency. Incumbents are simply enjoying the windfall from the general decline in partisanship among voters.

An alternative view is that members of Congress are responsible for their own increased electoral success. Although they have always worked hard to win reelection, they now have access to — and exploit — vastly greater resources for keeping themselves in office. The quantity, variety, and dollar-value of the resources available to members of Congress through their offices have grown dramatically since 1960. Recent estimates place the value of salary, staff, travel, communications, and office allowances at about $400,000 *per year* for a United States representative;[28] even more is provided to senators, with the amount scaled to the size of the state. Staff allowances alone may come to more than $900,000.[29]

[28] Cover, "One Good Term," p. 537.
[29] *Congressional Quarterly Weekly Report* 34 (July 3, 1976): 1700.

Back in 1960, each member of the House could hire up to nine staff employees; today, the number is eighteen. House members were permitted three reimbursed round-trips to the district in the early 1960s. The number was subsequently increased to five (1966), twelve (1968), eighteen (1973), twenty-six (1975), and to thirty-two (1977).[30]

And the growth of other official resources has kept pace. The most important congressional prerequisite is no doubt the franking privilege — the right of members to use the mails free of charge for "official business," which is broadly interpreted to include most kinds of communications to constituents. Franked mail increased by more than 600 percent between 1954 and 1970. One estimate put the total cost of congressional mail for a twelve-month period at $62,736,438, which averages out to more than $117,000 per member.[31] Other media have not been ignored. Facilities for preparing radio and television tapes and films are available to members free of charge. And members have voted themselves an unlimited WATS line for long distance telephone calls.[32]

The centrality of the electoral incentive guarantees that members will use whatever resources their office provides to pursue reelection. And the uses to which this growing array of assets have been put are instructive. Self-promotion through publicity and communication directly to constituents is only one important example. Morris P. Fiorina has published some equally revealing data about congressional staffing. They are presented in Table 9.6. Notice that in 1960, 14 percent of congressional staff personnel were assigned to district offices; by 1974, when staff sizes had doubled, 34 percent worked in district offices. The percentage of congressmen whose district offices close when they are not in town has fallen to nearly zero. And almost half the members now maintain more than one district office. A disproportionate share of the additional personnel available to members has been used to augment their capacity to provide services to constituents.

Fiorina contends that this is the basic source of greater incumbent security. His argument is subtle. Decisions taken by the

[30] Morris P. Fiorina, *Congress: Keystone of the Washington Establishment* (New Haven: Yale University Press, 1977), p. 61.

[31] *Hartford Courant*, March 28, 1977, p. 6.

[32] Lewis Perdue, "The Million Dollar Advantage of Incumbency," *Washington Monthly* 9 (March 1977): 51.

TABLE 9.6
Growth of Personal Staffs of Congressmen, 1960–74

	1960	1967	1974
Total Staff	2344	3276	5109
Percentage of total staff assigned to district offices	14	26	34
Percentage of congressmen whose district offices open only when congressman is home or after adjournment	29	11	2
Percentage of congressmen listing multiple district offices	4	18	47

Source: From Morris P. Fiorina, *Congress: Keystone of the Washington Establishment,* p. 58. Copyright © 1977 by Yale University. Reprinted by permission of Yale University Press.

Congress have increased the size of the federal government and the scope of federal authority tremendously. This, in turn, has greatly increased the demands for help from members to cope with the bureaucratic maze or to take advantage of federal programs. Members have, at the same time, continually added to their capacity to deliver services. The greater demand for such services generates more opportunities for building credit with constituents, and "the nice thing about case work is that it is mostly profit; one makes many more friends than enemies."[33]

It is also nonpartisan. The party of the member delivering the service — or of the constituent receiving it — is beside the point. What matters is a member's ability to deliver services, which increases with his tenure in Washington and his consequent seniority and mastery of the administrative apparatus. It therefore makes perfect sense for voters to prefer candidates on the basis of their incumbency rather than on their party or policy stands. And it makes equally perfect sense for incumbent members to focus on

[33] Morris P. Fiorina, "The Case of the Vanishing Marginals: The Bureaucracy Did It," *American Political Science Review* 71 (1977): 180.

providing services rather than on making national policy as a means for staying in office.

Fiorina's theory admittedly rests more on reason than on evidence at this point, but there is little question that attention to constituency services commands a greatly enlarged share of members' and their staffs' time. And there is no question that incumbents have become more secure. By this argument, voting behavior has changed in response to changes in the behavior of members of Congress. But the causal link might just as well work in the opposite direction: members may have exploited the weakening of party ties to solidify their position by more intense cultivation of the district. When voters vote as partisans, attention to the district makes little difference; incumbents may still be swept out by national tides favoring one party or the other. They may still be punished for the perceived failings of their party or its leaders. But if voters are detached from parties, members will be able to ride out contrary political tides on the cushion of their personal esteem and popularity. It then makes good strategic sense to cultivate a highly personal connection with the district.

THE DISAPPEARING MARGINALS

Whatever its true causes, an obvious consequence of this change in congressional voting behavior is that incumbent members are winning reelection more easily than in the past. They are not winning any more *frequently,* however; their success rate was already so high that it left little room for improvement. In House elections from 1956 through 1982, over 90 percent of the candidates running were incumbents. Of these, less than 2 percent lost primary election contests; less than 10 percent were defeated in general elections; over 90 percent won reelection. The smallest percentage of incumbent victories in general elections in any of these years was 86.9 percent; the largest was 96.8 percent.[34] By the criterion of reelection, House incumbents have been quite safe for years.

[34] William J. Keefe, *Parties, Politics, and Public Policy in America,* 2nd ed. (Hinsdale, Ill.: Dryden Press, 1976), p. 39; *Congressional Quarterly Weekly Report* 34 (November 6, 1976): 3119–22.

But by another standard — the ease with which they are reelected — incumbents have enjoyed a measurable increase in security since the mid-1960s. Political scientists designate congressional seats that are won with less than a specific percentage of the two-party vote as "marginal" seats. By either of the usual thresholds, 55 or 60 percent, the number of close elections, and hence marginal seats, has fallen off significantly. In the decade prior to 1966, about two-thirds of incumbent House candidates won with more than 60 percent of the vote. Since 1966, 75 percent have won by at least this margin. In contrast, elections for open seats, when neither candidate is an incumbent, remain thoroughly competitive and fall frequently into the marginal range.[35]

Additional evidence of the enhanced electoral value of incumbency is found in data on elections involving first term incumbents and on elections in districts where incumbents have voluntarily retired. The average gain in the percentage of the vote between a member's first and second election (adjusted for national trends) was + 2.7 percent from 1962 through 1966, + 6.6 percent from 1968 through 1974. Similarly, the fall off in the vote for a retiring incumbent's party averaged − 2.2 percent in the earlier period and − 7.7 percent more recently.[36] These data also indicate that House seats are safe for specific incumbents, not for their parties. When a safe incumbent retires, the seat is likely to become marginal — candidates of either party have a chance to win.

INCUMBENCY IN SENATE ELECTIONS

It is important to note that the sharp increase in incumbent security is confined largely to the House. Incumbent senators remain much more vulnerable. In the four decades between 1920 and 1960, from 75.0 to 78.6 percent of Senate incumbents contesting general elections won. In the 1960s, their success rate jumped

[35] Albert D. Cover and David R. Mayhew, "Congressional Dynamics and the Decline of Competitive Congressional Elections," in Lawrence C. Dodd and Bruce I. Oppenheimer (eds.), *Congress Reconsidered* (New York: Praeger, 1977), pp. 55–56; David R. Mayhew, "Congressional Elections: The Case of the Vanishing Marginals," *Polity* 6 (1974): 298–301.

[36] Cover and Mayhew, "Congressional Dynamics," p. 60.

to 92.2 percent; but for the 1970s, it fell back to 76.6 percent.[37] Senate seats are much more likely to be marginal. Most are won with less than 60 percent of the vote. Party loyalty has evidently declined as a force in Senate elections, too, relative to incumbency, but not to a point where incumbent senators are significantly more difficult to defeat.[38]

This difference between the two houses needs explaining. Senate elections have not been very thoroughly studied, but plausible explanations are not difficult to imagine. Senators are not nearly so well situated to build and maintain bipartisan support through personal services to their constituents. States are, with six exceptions, more populous than congressional districts, often very much so. The opportunities for personal contact with constituents and attention to individual problems are proportionately fewer. Even the larger Senate staffs cannot make up the difference.

Nor is it certain that voters expect senators to act as their ombudsmen and errand boys. They may expect senators to take more prominent policy stands, which are controversial and divisive in a way that district services are not. Action in the Senate is more visible; it has fewer members, and they are given more attention by the news media. And normally they must try to represent much more socially and politically diverse constituencies — whole states rather than congressional districts.

Senators also do not have the pressure of a two-year election cycle to keep them attuned to the folks back home. Electoral coalitions may fall out of repair, and a careless senator may discover that he must begin almost from scratch when reelection time rolls around. Senate incumbents are much more likely to face prominent, well-funded opponents; Senate races attract stronger candidates and larger amounts of campaign money than House races.

For whatever combination of reasons, incumbent senators remain twice as vulnerable as House members. The evident loosen-

[37] From data in *Congressional Quarterly's Guide to U.S. Elections* (Washington, D.C., 1975), pp. 457–509, and *Congressional Quarterly's Guide to the 1976 Elections: A Supplement to CQ's Guide to U.S. Elections* (Washington, D.C., 1977), pp. 36–44; the 1978 data were compiled by the author.

[38] Warren Lee Kostroski, "Party and Incumbency in Postwar Senate Elections: Trends, Patterns, and Models," *American Political Science Review* 67 (1973): 1213–34.

ing of party ties has not benefitted them so directly. Yet incumbency is still to their advantage, and most incumbents win. The 1974 survey found that partisan voters defected to Senate incumbents at a rate of 32.9 percent; the defection rate to challengers was only 12.2 percent. Recall from Table 9.3 that the comparable defection rates for House voters were 48.6 percent and 12.9 percent that year.

THE DECLINE OF PRESIDENTIAL COATTAILS

The growing security of incumbent members of Congress (at least those in the House) has, among other things, greatly diminished the electoral relevance of presidents and presidential candidates. Although the performance of presidents and presidential aspirants may influence the vote received by other candidates of their parties,[39] most incumbents now enjoy a sufficient electoral cushion to survive even in the face of a disaster at the top of the party ticket. Richard Nixon's landslide victory over George McGovern in 1972 (he won more than 60 percent of the vote) resulted in a Republican gain of only 13 seats in the House. Republicans suffered a net *loss* of two seats in the Senate. The aggregate vote for Republican candidates was very high by historical standards. But the distribution of those votes, strongly affected by incumbency, was such that they scarcely helped where it matters, in election victories.[40]

The detachment of presidential from congressional voting is most readily apparent in Walter Dean Burnham's data on the percentage of congressional districts that delivered split results — majorities for the congressional candidate of one party and the presidential candidate of the other. These data are reported in Table 9.7. In 1972 no less than 44.1 percent of the House districts

[39] See Edward R. Tufte, "Determinants of the Outcomes of Midterm Congressional Elections," *American Political Science Review* 69 (1975): 812–26; Samuel Kernell, "Presidential Popularity and Negative Voting: An Alternative Explanation of the Midterm Congressional Decline of the President's Party," *American Political Science Review* 71 (1977): 44–66; Gary C. Jacobson, "Presidential Coattails in 1972," *Public Opinion Quarterly* 40 (1976): 194–200.

[40] Jacobson, "Coattails," pp. 197–99.

TABLE 9.7
Proportion of Split Results: Congress and President, 1940–76

Year	Number of Districts Analyzed	Percentage of Split Results
1940	362	14.6
1944	367	11.2
1948	422	22.5
1952	435	19.3
1956	435	29.9
1960	437	26.1
1964	435	33.3
1968	435	31.7
1972	435	44.1
1976	435	28.5

Source: 1940–1972, from *The American Party Systems: Stages of Political Development*, Second Edition, by William Nisbet Chambers and Walter Dean Burnham. Copyright © 1967, 1976 by Oxford University Press, Inc. Reprinted by permission. 1976 from Charles M. Tidmarch, "Congressmen and the Electorate, 1976: A Halt to the Onward March of Party Decomposition?" Prepared for delivery at the Annual Meeting of the Northeastern Political Science Association, 1978. Used by permission.

voted for a president and a congressman of opposite parties. Richard Nixon actually carried 77.4 percent of the districts that elected Democrats to the House in 1972.[41]

In 1976 the number of split results dropped back to 28.5 percent, but there is no evidence that Jimmy Carter's coattails had anything to do with it. Of the 292 Democrats elected to the House that year only 22 received a smaller share of the vote in the district than Carter. Few members of the Ninety-fifth Congress had reason to think that his performance in the election had anything to do with getting them elected.[42] Research has shown that members of Congress are more loyal to presidents who have run ahead of them

[41] Walter Dean Burnham, "Party Systems and the Political Process," in William Nisbet Chambers and Walter Dean Burnham (eds.), *The American Party Systems*, 2nd ed. (New York: Oxford University Press, 1975), p. 321.

[42] *Congressional Quarterly Weekly Report* 36 (April 22, 1978): 971–74.

in their districts, so this is not a trivial point. [43] In recent elections (1976, 1980), presidential candidates have hurt more than helped their party's candidates.

WINNING AGAINST THE TIDE

The 1974 and 1976 elections gave striking evidence of the capacity of incumbents to hold onto their jobs in the face of contrary electoral tides. And they reinforce another critical point: the value of incumbency does not appear magically or automatically; it depends on what the incumbent does with the resources available to him.

The 1974 election, following Watergate, Nixon's resignation and pardon by President Ford, and a period of distressful economic conditions, was generally a disaster for Republicans. The party took its worst electoral beating in many years; thirty-six of the Republican House incumbents were defeated. But Burnham made the surprising discovery that "first generation of 'new-incumbent' Republicans as a group actually *improved* their position very slightly in the face of an exceptionally large national shift towards the Democrats."[44] And in 1976, no fewer than forty-eight of the forty-nine Democrats elected to formerly Republican seats in 1974 won a second term; seventy-two of the total seventy-four freshman Democrats who sought reelection won.

In both instances, new members resisted a trend against their party more successfully than older members. The best explanation for this is that they behaved differently. Legislative activity and status and power accumulated in Congress through seniority obviously had little to do with their success. Rather, they made energetic use of the perquisites of office to solidify their position back home. The younger Democrats in particular "exhibited great ingenuity and phenomenal tenacity in 'cultivating' their districts."[45]

[43] See George C. Edwards III, "Presidential Electoral Performance as a Source of Presidential Power," *American Journal of Political Science* 22 (1978): 152–68.

[44] Walter Dean Burnham, "Insulation and Responsiveness in Congressional Elections," *Political Science Quarterly* 90 (1975): 419.

[45] Charles M. Tidmarch, "The Second Time Around: Freshman Democratic House Members' 1976 Reelection Experiences." Paper presented at the Annual Meeting of the American Political Science Association, Washington, D.C., September 1–4, 1977, p. 27.

The general point has been ably argued by Thomas E. Mann. He found that the district-level shifts in the vote from one election to the next show a much wider range of variation than could be accounted for by the national shifts from one party to the other. The difference from district to district depends largely on differences in the use incumbents make of their opportunities and resources. Members who use both to cultivate the district make themselves "safe." Those who do not can and will be successfully challenged.[46] This is the clear message of the last few elections. The lesson has been learned especially well by members first elected in the 1970s. Members who do not heed it are indeed likely to be weeded out by a sort of natural selection.

Constituency services and attention do pay off at the polls. But they may well detract from the job members do in Washington. The time, energy, and staff resources that members use to pursue their separate reelection strategies back home in the district are taken from legislative chores on Capitol Hill. By concentrating on their individual electoral pursuits, members of Congress necessarily slight their collective policy-related activities. This naturally lessens the importance of the congressional parties. Another consequence is that the institutional performance of Congress declines as the electoral performance of its members improves. And this explains the otherwise surprising conjunction of strongly *negative* popular evaluations of Congress with quite *positive* assessments of individual members — and their monotonous reelection. As Fenno discovered, members appeal to constituents by disassociating themselves from the institution; they run *for* Congress by running *against* Congress.[47] The implications of this pattern of activity for what goes on in the House and Senate, and particularly for the willingness of members to follow party and presidential leadership, are traced out in greater detail later.

THE CHANGING GENERATIONS

Since members of Congress have become harder to turn out of office since the mid-1960s, we might expect the turnover in

---

[46] Mann, *Unsafe at Any Margin,* pp. 101–106.
[47] Fenno, *Home Style,* pp. 163–68.

congressional seats to be decreasing. Congress would be composed of an aging group of increasingly senior legislators. But that has not happened; quite the opposite. Although incumbents who run for reelection are winning more handily, fewer of them are choosing to run. Consider the data in Table 9.8. They are quite remarkable. The table lists the number of members retiring voluntarily from the House at the end of each session of Congress from 1966 through 1978. The increase in the number of voluntary retirees is striking. Of course some members "retire" to run for another office or to accept political appointment. But the proportion of "pure" retirements — members choosing to leave without aiming at another office — has remained steady at about 56 percent. Thus the number of pure retirements has gone up just as sharply.

The combination of greater electoral security and less inclination to seek reelection is only apparently paradoxical. They are actually explained by the same circumstances, for what has made incumbents more secure has also made the job less appealing to many members.

Constant cultivation of the district provides the margin of electoral safety. But it is an endless, time-consuming chore. Fenno points out that the trust members try to inspire in their constituents is not something that can be achieved once and for all. It must be built up, and *maintained,* by constant attention to the

TABLE 9.8
Voluntary Retirements from the House of Representatives, 1966–78

1966	(after Eighty–Ninth Congress)	12
1968	(after Ninetieth Congress)	13
1970	(after Ninety–first Congress)	7
1972	(after Ninety–second Congress)	28
1974	(after Ninety–third Congress)	30
1976	(after Ninety–fourth Congress)	47
1978	(after Ninety–fifth Congress)	49

Source: This table drawn from "Opting Out: Retirement from the House of Representatives 1966-1974," by Stephen E. Frantzich, is reprinted from *American Politics Quarterly* Vol. 6, No. 3 (July 1978), pp. 251–73, by permission of the publisher, Sage Publications, Inc.; 1976 and 1978, *Congressional Quarterly Weekly Report.*

district. Service-oriented members must continue to deliver the services if they are to continue winning by comfortable margins.

But attention to the district detracts from work in Washington. Reelection is a means, not an end in itself, for most members. Congressional careers involve more than merely hanging on to the office. Success on the Hill means influencing policy, writing and passing legislation, and gaining the respect of one's colleagues. All of these things require attention to legislative and other duties that can be given only in Washington. The longer an individual is in Congress, the more opportunities there are open to pursue legislative and other policy-related goals. But they demand a different allocation of resources — of time, energy, and staff — than does the maximal pursuit of reelection. The contradictory demands of district and Washington service generate a tension that increases the longer a member remains in office.

Members are safe only as long as they continue to do what they have been doing. They may lose their security if they do not continue to use their resources to maintain constituency support. When, in time, they do more in Washington and less at home, they are likely to face increasingly serious electoral challenges. The campaign may become tougher and the struggle for reelection more arduous, if no less certain, statistically, rather than easier after the first few terms. An increasing number appear to be deciding that the game is not worth the candle.

These are not the only pressures retiring members mention. The pace and volume of work has grown enormously in recent years. Changes in rules and procedures intended to strengthen the legislative branch and to "reform" its operations (these will be discussed at length later) have made work on Capitol Hill more burdensome at the same time that constituency demands have grown. The issues Congress now faces are extraordinarily difficult and complex. The general public is in a surly mood, skeptical and suspicious of political institutions and politicians. And measures designed to bolster public confidence in members of Congress may have encouraged some to leave. The amount of money members may earn by outside activities is now limited to 15 percent of their salary; they are required to report yearly on their financial status and sources of income. Many can make much more money — with less work — elsewhere. And finally, more generous pensions enacted a few years ago may have made retirement more inviting than before.[48]

The growing number of retirements has meant a larger influx of new members into the most recent congresses. This trend was magnified among the Democrats by the Democratic sweep in the 1974 elections. The impact of this new generation of legislators has been extraordinary, for its members are by no means carbon copies of their predecessors.

Table 9.9 displays the trend toward an increasingly junior, inexperienced Democratic contingent in the House. Listed are the number of Democrats elected to the Ninetieth through Ninety-sixth Congresses and the proportion of each group composed of freshman and freshman and sophomore members. In the most recently completed congress, the Ninety-fifth, a full 43 percent of the Democrats were in their first or second term.

The average House member at the start of the Ninety-sixth Congress was 48.8 years old — the youngest since World War II.[49] A majority of all House members elected to the Ninety-sixth Congress in the fall of 1978 entered Congress no earlier than January 1975. The same is true of a majority of House Democrats; 152 of 277 were not in office when Richard Nixon was president. And the Senate is not immune from the same trend; forty-eight of its hundred members were serving their first term in the Ninety-sixth Congress.

The influx of new members is important because, to put it simply, they are quite different from their elders. This is hardly surprising. They are mostly people who came of political age during a decade of assassination, riot, protest, the Vietnam War, environmental crisis, energy shortages, political scandal, and a decline in respect for authority of all kinds — especially that of political institutions and leaders. If the Congress reflects, however imperfectly, American society, it would be strange indeed if all this turmoil left the institution and its members unchanged. It has not.

The newer members tend to differ from their elders in political goals and strategies, expectations of themselves, standards of behavior, and attitudes toward parties, party leaders, and presidents.

[48] Richard E. Cohen, "Retiring from Congress — The Job Ain't What It Used to Be," *National Journal* 10 (March 11, 1978): 391–93.

[49] *Congressional Quarterly Weekly Report* 37 (January 27, 1979): 154.

TABLE 9.9
First- and Second-Term Democrats in the House of Representatives, 1967–79

Year and Congress	Number of Democrats	Percentage First Term	Percentage First and Second Term
1967 (90)	248	7	23
1969 (91)	243	7	16
1971 (92)	255	11	20
1973 (93)	248	10	20
1975 (94)	291	26	35
1977 (95)	290	16	43
1979 (96)	276	15	31

Source: After Table 4.5 (p. 82) in *Stability and Change in Congress* by Barbara Hinckley. Copyright © 1978 by Barbara Hinckley. Reprinted by permission of Harper & Row, Publishers, Inc.

They have contributed heavily to transformations in the way Congress operates, with important consequences for the distribution of power among its members. Their aggressiveness and independence has indeed changed the entire tone of congressional life; retiring members often complain of it. The result has been new headaches — and new opportunities — for congressional party leaders. These developments are the subject of the next chapter.

10

The Congressional Parties: Leaders and (Sometimes) Followers

PARTIES IN CONGRESS

The changing electoral environment — and the influx of new congressmen adept at carving out secure niches in it — has left few aspects of congressional life untouched. The impact on the congressional parties has been complex and profound. Any change that alters the effectiveness of the parties carries important institutional implications, for it is largely through the parties that Congress generates whatever *coherent* policy making it can muster. Parties are crucial to the collective legislative activities of Congress.

The House and Senate are highly decentralized bodies. Power and influence are widely distributed. Most important legislative activity and all administrative oversight — the major institutional functions of Congress — take place in separate committees or subcommittees.

Activity and authority in Congress are decentralized in order to allow *specialization*. The volume and complexity of matters that come before Congress require that members develop specialized knowledge of specific policy areas. This in turn requires a division of labor among members. Each needs to focus his legislative attention narrowly, since none has the time or energy to develop a thorough grasp of more than a few complex issues and questions. The alternative to developing specialized expertise in Congress is surrender of power to the experts in the White House, the administrative agencies, or the private sector. A decentralized system of standing committees with fixed jurisdictions is Congress's organizational strategy for survival as a significant policymaking institution. And largely because of its committee system, Congress has been able to maintain its authority far more successfully than most legislatures in other advanced democracies.

The decentralized and specialized committee system cannot work effectively without some regular means for coordinating the activities of the diverse parts. Although most important decisions are made in committee or subcommittee, bills and resolutions can be passed only by a majority of each house. The fragmented activity must be brought into some sort of harmony and the diverse membership welded together from time to time into majority coalitions if Congress is to play its policymaking role. This is what the congressional parties are for. They operate to counteract the centrifugal tendencies of the committee system.

CONGRESSIONAL PARTY STRUCTURES

Members of Congress elect their own party leaders and run their own party organizations. The congressional parties are entirely their instruments and necessarily reflect their purposes. National party leaders, even presidents, are expected to keep their hands off, and they do. The main components of both parties in the House and Senate are quite similar, with one important exception. The head of the majority party in the House of Representatives is the Speaker, who is also the chief presiding officer of that body. Party leadership and House leadership are therefore formally united. The Speaker is assisted by the majority leader and the majority whip; these three run the party — and the House — machinery on a day-to-day basis.

The Senate has no direct counterpart to the Speaker. The vice-president is its constitutionally designated presiding officer, and his duties, other than breaking tie votes, are largely ceremonial. So the majority leader is the head of the majority party in the Senate. He is also the principal leader of the whole Senate insofar as it ever allows itself to be led.

In both houses, the minority is led by a minority leader, aided by the minority whip and his assistants. Each congressional party also maintains an organization composed of all members of the party as a body. The House Democrats call theirs a caucus; both the Senate Democrats and the Republicans in both houses call it a conference. The elected chairman of the caucus (or conference) is also an important party leader (the majority leader retains this position in the Senate Democratic Conference). The business of these groups is often conducted by smaller executive committees, variously called policy, steering, or policy and steering commit- tees, which normally work in tandem with the elected party leaders.

On paper, the caucus or conference has the final say in all party decisions, but their actual power varies from party to party, house to house, and time to time. Until a few years ago, they had been somnolent for a long time, content to ratify decisions made by party leaders. This is no longer true; the Democratic caucus has played a major part in bringing about far-reaching changes in House procedures, as we shall see.

MAJORITY PARTY LEADERSHIP IN THE HOUSE

Members of Congress have traditionally preferred party leaders who focus on the legislative process, giving little attention to the content of legislation. Party leaders of the majority in the House set the agenda, organize the distribution of work, and plan and execute legislative strategy. They operate at the center of a network that gathers information on the progress of legislation through committees, schedules the workload (no small matter when so many members head for home, at government expense, every chance they get), and tries to keep count of the supporters and opponents of pending legislation. They are thus strategically situated to take a hand in the negotiations, compromises, bargains, and persuasive arguments through which legislative coalitions are pieced together.

The leaders are also well situated to put their own imprint on legislation, but they rarely exploit the opportunity. They are usually more interested in coming up with bills that can command majorities than with enacting specific measures. Party leaders normally formulate no independent "party policy" or "party program." If the president and the majority are of the same party, his proposals become the party program, and leaders take responsibility for passing the president's agenda (though rarely without modification). When the president's party is a minority in Congress, congressional majorities may enact alternatives to the president's proposals, but these are most often created in committee. The party program, such as it is, is merely a collection of measures churned out by the fragmented committee system.

Reflecting their role, party leaders are usually legislative pragmatists with moderate ideological commitments (within, of course, the context of their respective parties). But they are also party and institutional loyalists, and consider the effectiveness of the party and the Congress as policymaking entities to be their responsibility. They therefore take pains to line up party (and opposition) support for the measures they adopt as the party's programs regardless of origin.

Congressional party leaders control some resources that help them to gather the support of party members, but not nearly enough to permit them to keep a tight rein on party members should they wish to do so. Control over the scheduling of legislation, for example, allows leaders to do favors for members. They may facilitate bills for members' pet projects or arrange for votes to be postponed when members are out of town. Such favors are useful bargaining chips for coalition building.

Party leaders are also influential in assigning members to committees. This is potentially the most valuable chip they hold. Committee assignments are very important to members. Many gravitate toward those committees which handle matters of interest to their constituents. Those representing farm areas want seats on Agriculture; westerners prefer Interior; members from coastal areas go after Merchant Marine and Fisheries. Appointment to the right committee can help ensure reelection by giving members additional means for serving their districts. Members also seek power over legislation and policy; this too is apportioned by the committee system. A good committee assignment can help where it counts in either case.

Traditional congressional wisdom held that control over committee assignments gave the party leaders special clout with junior members, who had yet to acquire choice committee seats. But this particular source of leadership influence has gradually dried up over the last two decades. Irwin Gertzog has shown that freshman committee assignments have become thoroughly routinized. They are much more automatic than discretionary and so not very amenable to manipulation by party leaders. His figures on freshman assignments to "semiexclusive" committees for three ten-year periods are presented in Table 10.1.[1] Between 1947 and 1955, only 38 percent of the House freshmen won seats on these relatively desirable committees. Between 1967 and 1975, the figure was 94 percent. Louis P. Westefield's work explains what has happened. Over the years, party leaders have increased the size of the desirable committees in order to control more rewards for encouraging loyalty and cooperation. They increased the supply of assignments to meet the demand. But scarcity determines the value of this as of any other currency. As the supply increases, scarcity decreases. In time, the currency loses its value. When nearly everyone can count on a desirable committee assignment, influence over committee assignments provides leaders little leverage.[2] Ironically, a potentially valuable resource for rewarding loyalty among junior members had withered away just as a horde of new members was entering the House.

[1] The distinction between "exclusive," "semiexclusive," and "nonexclusive" committees was made in the Legislative Reorganization Act of 1946. Exclusive committees are the most desirable; they are exclusive because House members who sit on them have no other committee assignments. Least desirable are the nonexclusive committees; semiexclusive committees are the best to which freshmen can aspire.

[2] Louis P. Westefield, "Majority Party Leadership and the Committee System in the House of Representatives," *American Political Science Review* 68 (1974): 1593–1604.

TABLE 10.1
Freshman Assignments to Semiexclusive Committees, 1947-75

Years	Congresses	Number	Percentage	Total Freshmen
1947–1955	80–84	143	38	378
1957–1965	85–89	227	69	329
1967–1975	90–94	289	94	306

Note: These figures do not take into account transfers made during the first term. Moreover, if a freshman was initially assigned to two semiexclusive committees, both were included in these summary figures.

Source: From Irwin N. Gertzog, "The Routinization of Committee Assignments in the House of Representatives," *American Journal of Political Science,* Vol. 20 (1976), p. 700. Reprinted by permission of the publisher, The University of Texas Press.

THE DEMOCRATIC CAUCUS

Without question the most important party-related change to hit Congress in the 1970s was the emergence of the Democratic caucus as a powerful party agency. An increasingly assertive caucus has effected major changes in the way House business is conducted, and these have had a decisive impact on the distribution of power and influence in that body. House party leaders have both gained and lost power as a result, the net effect being important changes in the way that leadership is exercised.

The revival of the Democratic caucus as a major party institution was inspired by the Democratic Study Group. The DSG was originally founded in 1959 by frustrated junior liberal Democrats. They hoped by pooling their numbers to provide a counterweight to the conservative southern Democrats who dominated the House leadership. The DSG has since grown to include more than two-thirds of all House Democrats, many of whom have now advanced through the seniority system to important committee and party leadership positions. It now constitutes the core of the Democratic party in the House. The DSG is chiefly responsible for all of the procedural reforms intended to "democratize" the workings of the House.

The DSG's first important success came in 1969 when it overrode Speaker John McCormack's objections to initiate regular meetings of the caucus. Before, meetings had been called at the Speaker's discretion, which meant rarely. Members were also accorded the right to place items on the agenda for the caucus to consider, which had also been the Speaker's prerogative. In 1971, the newly revived caucus enacted a rule that permitted debate on nominations made by the Committee on Committees. Up to that time, the caucus could only vote on them — a vote that was a mere formality. It passed another rule that forbade members to chair more than one subcommittee (though members already holding multiple chairmanships could keep them). The passage of this rule opened a number of subcommittee chairmanships to junior members.

Procedural reforms continued in 1973. The most important change was to make committee chairmen subject to election by secret ballot in the caucus if at least 20 percent of the caucus members requested it. This was a direct blow at the sacrosanct seniority system, through which members had been elevated to committee chairmanships — powerful positions in a body that is organized as the House is — by the criteria of reelection and longevity. The caucus also reduced the power of committee chairmen by giving the Democratic members on each committee the right to select subcommittee chairmen, set subcommittee budgets, guarantee each member a good subcommittee assignment, and set party ratios on subcommittees that reflected party ratios in the full House. Chairmen could no longer run their committees like independent despots.

The caucus reform movement reached its peak in 1975. The DSG contingent was bolstered by the votes of seventy-five freshmen Democrats, who gave nearly unanimous support to DSG-sponsored motions. Three committee chairmen who under the old rules would have held their positions automatically as senior Democrats in years of service on their committees were deposed. A fourth would have been voted out had he not voluntarily resigned his chairmanship. The formal authority to make committee assignments was taken away from the Democratic membership of the Ways and Means Committee and given to the caucus's own Steering and Policy Committee. The caucus also took over the right to determine the number and jurisdiction of subcommittees on each committee. And it transferred to the Speaker the power to nominate Democratic members of the powerful Rules Committee. Other minor changes aimed at opening choice subcommittee chairs to junior members were also adopted.

THE EFFECTS OF THE CAUCUS'S REFORMS

The effects of all these changes are not particularly difficult to assess. Committee chairmen lost a great deal of power. They are no longer the independent barons they once were, able to defy the party, the House, their committee's members, or just about anyone else. Most of their control over the committee has been absorbed by the caucus. And the caucus retains the ultimate sanction of deposition. Committee chairmen quickly recognized this fact and have adjusted their behavior accordingly. Richard P. Conlan, staff director of the DSG, summed up the consequences:

> The power of committee chairmen to punish members who oppose them has been sharply curtailed. Even if a chairman does have such power, he is less likely to use it because members can now retaliate when the chairman stands for reelection by secret ballot. . . . Thus chairmen who a few years ago expected members to be solicitous of them are solicitous of the members.[3]

The power lost by committee chairmen has been picked up by subcommittee chairmen, the Speaker, and the caucus. The effects on party authority have been contradictory. The Speaker's hand has been strengthened. He or she now controls the Rules Committee, which stands astride the flow of legislation coming out of committee to the floor of the House and also can now set up ad hoc committees to handle specific bills and choose their members. He or she also appoints eight of the twenty-three members of the caucus's Steering and Policy Committee which, among other powers, makes committee assignments. Plainly, the image of the Speaker dealing as the first among equals with the refractory committee barons is out of date. The Speaker's power has grown while theirs has waned.

---

[3] Michael J. Malbin, "House Reforms — The Emphasis is on Productivity, Not Power," *National Journal* 8 (December 4, 1976): 1733. Reprinted with permission.

The invigoration of the caucus might also be interpreted as strengthening the congressional party. But if so, it must also be acknowledged that the caucus and the party leaders may frequently pull in opposite directions. The caucus is not easily led. One recent observer concluded,

> No one seems to control the caucus, or is able to lead all factions of the party. A majority, egalitarian body, the caucus is subject to direction by shifting factions and coalitions. Whether the Speaker or the Steering and Policy Committee has enough power to organize it and lead it over a sustained period of time is doubtful.[4]

A lingering source of conflict between the caucus and the senior party leaders is the question of what power the caucus ought to have over substantive policy. Its authority to decide procedural matters is not questioned. But its proper influence on legislation is a subject of much dispute. Both party and committee leaders reject the notion that they should bow to the wishes of the caucus majority on matters of substantive policy. Other members feel that the caucus should be heard on occasional important issues. And some younger members dream of the caucus taking a major legislative role as the voice of the majority party in the House.

The last is not a likely possibility, but the caucus has intervened in substantive matters on infrequent occasions. In 1975, heady after having ousted four committee chairmen, the caucus ordered the Rules Committee to let the House vote on a bill repealing the oil depletion allowance and passed a resolution opposing military aid to Vietnam and Cambodia. But, according to Representative Pete Stark, "that was about as much as some of the old fogeys could digest," and the protests of alarmed senior members put a temporary end to caucus votes on policy.[5]

Not until 1978 did the caucus again attempt to tell a committee what to do. Members worried about the upcoming election wanted to roll back a planned increase in the Social Security tax. They were resisted by the Ways and Means Committee, which would have sent such a bill to the floor, and were opposed by Speaker O'Neill, who supported the Carter Administration's position against the rollback. But on April 5 the caucus voted 150 to 57 a

[4] *Ibid.*, p. 1735.
[5] *Congressional Quarterly Weekly Report* 36 (April 15, 1978): 874.

nonbinding resolution urging the Ways and Means Committee to act on rollback legislation.

The question of how much authority the caucus may legitimately exercise remains in doubt. Ironically, many of the strongest advocates of a policymaking caucus are junior members most prone to independence and least impressed by appeals to party loyalty. They want it both ways: independence plus effective policy control. The combination is not likely to come about. At present the caucus seems likely to avoid policy stances except on rare occasions. Were this to change, it would be a major alteration in the role of the congressional party. In any case, it is clear that the caucus is as willing to resist party leaders as to follow them, and so if the congressional parties have been strengthened by the reforms of the 1970s, they have been strengthened in potentially conflicting directions.

SUBCOMMITTEE CHAIRMEN: THE NEW BARONETS

A third consequence of the reforms, the enhanced power of subcommittees and subcommittee chairmen, has manifestly weakened the party and added to the difficulty of building party and House majorities. Subcommittee fiefdoms have replaced committee fiefdoms; at last count there were 158 standing subcommittees. Once fragmented to the committee level, the House is now fragmented to the subcommittee level. Many more little bastions of power are distributed among many more individuals. This naturally pleases them, but it makes organizing the House for coherent policy making a more formidable chore than ever.

The devolution of power to subcommittees has the aspect of a revolt of youth against age. Younger members used the caucus, where their swollen numbers gave them the most strength, to wrest power from senior committee leaders. The powers absorbed by the caucus over the formation, appointment, and operation of subcommittees ensured the widest possible distribution of good subcommittee assignments and, most importantly, chairmanships.

So it is little wonder that junior members like the new system. It gives them an early opportunity to exercise real authority over legislation. Like other Americans of their generation, they are typically better educated, more independent of party, less awed by age and authority than were their predecessors. They seem to share the conviction that they were elected to lead, not follow. It is not surprising that they refused to wait around docilely until time, electoral security, and the seniority system elevated them to positions of power in the House. The new system they have fostered gives them a solid piece of the legislative turf early in their careers.

The wider distribution of subcommittee chairmanships also serves the electoral needs of junior members. Like full committees, subcommittees are frequently chosen for the opportunities they provide to serve district interests. Subcommittee chairmen are free to push legislation, pursue pet projects, or conduct investigations that generate favorable publicity back home.

Control of a subcommittee confers another valuable resource: subcommittee staff. Members have learned to rely on committee and subcommittee staffs to take over the legislative work that is slighted when personal staffs concentrate on serving constituents either in Washington or in district offices. "Right now," complained one member, "people want committees just so they can hire staff."[6]

The inevitable result of the demand for subcommittee chairmanships has been an increase in the supply, requiring, naturally, more subcommittees. The total number of subcommittees of all kinds grew, by one count, from 148 to 181 between 1974 and 1976. While serving the needs of individual members, the proliferation of subcommittees works against the collective policymaking effectiveness of the House as an institution. And it most clearly adds to the difficulty of exercising party leadership.

LEADING THE CONTEMPORARY HOUSE

The reforms of the 1970s have created an even more decentralized and fragmented power structure than existed in the heyday of the despotic chairmen. And this spells problems for anyone, party leader or president, who tries to lead the Congress. Coalition

[6] Quoted in Thomas E. Cavanagh, "The Two Arenas of Congress: Electoral and Institutional Incentives for Performance." Paper presented at the 1978 Annual Meeting of the American Political Science Association, New York, N.Y., August 31–September 3, 1978, p. 32.

building is harder because there are so many more centers of power to deal with; it is no longer enough to win the support of a handful of prominent leaders. With more subcommittees, members face more meetings, more work with less time for it, more reasons to be away from the floor. Planning, scheduling, and coordinating the flow of legislation are therefore increasingly complicated and difficult tasks. And with junior members more assertive, independent, sensitive to constituency interests, and insistent on having a say in all manner of policy, leading Congress is a formidable job indeed.

Under the circumstances, the current Speaker, Thomas P. O'Neill, has been remarkably effective. Part of the reason is his own personal political style. "If the times demand a Speaker whose strong suits are persuasion and an ability to mediate disputes among warring factions of the House, O'Neill may be ideally suited."[7] One congressman "likened O'Neill to a good parent with a lot of precocious but disagreeable children. 'He monitors the conflict until the parties work it out.' "[8]

O'Neill has also enlarged and extended the party's organizational apparatus to cope with the greater demands it now faces. The Democratic whip organization has been augmented. Party whips — the name comes from Britain, where the "whipper-in" keeps the hounds together during a fox hunt — form the essential information network that links party leaders and followers. They carry messages between leaders and party members, take straw polls, get members to the floor when their votes are needed, and help in the overall planning and execution of legislative strategy. A majority whip can now have a chief deputy whip, three deputy whips, ten at-large whips, twenty-two zone whips, and a budget of one-half million dollars (roughly triple that of a decade earlier). And there is little question that the larger whip operation is now necessary.[9]

The Speaker has also increasingly resorted to using special "task forces" to shepherd important bills through the House. Ad hoc groups of twenty-five or so Democratic members, frequently led by relatively junior Democrats, are put together to help the lead-

[7] Richard E. Cohen, "Tip O'Neill — He Gets By With a Little Help From His Friends," *National Journal* 10 (September 2, 1978): 1385.

[8] *Ibid.*, p. 1385.

[9] *Congressional Quarterly Weekly Report* 36 (May 27, 1978): 1302.

ers carry out legislative plans. They count votes, persuade reluctant or wavering members to vote with the party, and let the Speaker know where his personal intervention would be effective. Task forces work closely with the whip organization, but "O'Neill has found the task forces to be useful supplements to the whip system because not all the assistant whips can be expected to support the leadership on each bill or be sufficiently familiar with all bills to lobby their colleagues."[10]

For especially important and sensitive legislative jobs, O'Neill sometimes exercises his right to appoint special legislative committees to supplement the work of the regular committees. They are most useful when important legislation falls under the jurisdiction of several standing committees. They also allow the Speaker to put bills in the hands of a committee whose members are chosen for their willingness to cooperate with the leadership.[11]

The measure of success for all of these party instruments is in their ability to persuade members to cooperate with the leaders. "Persuade" is the key term; leaders control few sanctions, and pleas for party or presidential loyalty are insufficient by themselves. O'Neill has often been persuasive. The Speaker is a staunch party loyalist. He regards the party's programs as his programs, and the victories in the House are largely traceable to his efforts. Party leadership in Congress is highly *personal*; it depends on the character and skills of individual leaders. O'Neill's abilities have prevented the full consequences of the changes in House rules and House membership from being felt.

MAJORITY PARTY LEADERSHIP IN THE SENATE

Although the most dramatic changes have taken place in the House, the Senate has not been immune to the same forces working there. Traditionally, party leaders in the Senate have been less powerful than their counterparts in the House. Individual Senate leaders — Lyndon Johnson is the best example — might accumulate a great deal of influence over the Senate, but it arises from

[10] Cohen, "Tip O'Neill," p. 1386.
[11] *Ibid.*, pp. 1386–88.

personal rather than institutional characteristics. The Senate is a much smaller body than the House. The organizational impera- tives that make the party's role so important in the House are much less compelling. Senators have a stronger tradition of inde- pendence and have always enjoyed greater opportunities for indi- vidual participation, influence, and obstruction. The difference now is that more members are taking advantage of them.

> Newer Senate members share the independent mood of young House members. But there, the tools available for exerting that independence are considerably more powerful.
> Senate leaders must rely on custom and courtesy to keep debate restrained. But the informal checks have broken down in the last three years, and some more militant members have tied the Senate in procedural knots for days at a time.[12]

And not only newer members have freed themselves from pro- cedural restraints. The late Senator James Allen, one of the most senior Democrats in the Senate, developed a variety of new obstructive tactics late in his career. Senate minorities have always enjoyed the right to filibuster — to talk legislation to death — because debate in the Senate is normally unlimited. Until the Ninety-fourth Congress, it took a two-thirds vote to invoke *clo- ture,* which shut off debate and allowed a vote to be taken. Filibus- ters became so common in the 1970s (more than half the cloture votes taken in the Senate's history have occurred since 1971[13]) that the rule was amended to require a three-fifths vote to pass a cloture motion. Former Senate Majority Leader Robert C. Byrd has lamented that "it used to be that it was resorted to only in- frequently and on great national issues, mostly on civil rights. But anymore, it's just resorted to promiscuously, I think."[14]

Easier cloture has not solved the problem. Senator Allen pioneered the tactic of offering dozens of amendments to bills — each requiring some debate and a vote — after cloture has been invoked. And other obstructive techniques, such as withholding unanimous consent when it is needed to bypass time-consuming routines, have been exploited by single individuals seeking to kill or amend legislation. Senator Mike Gravel "went so far as to in-

[12] *Congressional Quarterly Weekly Report* 36 (September 2, 1978): 2306.

[13] *Congressional Quarterly Weekly Report* 36 (March 1, 1978): 452.

[14] *Congressional Quarterly Weekly Report* 36 (September 2, 1978): 2307.

clude the text of former President Nixon's memoirs within an amendment he offered and then invoke his right to require the reading of the entire amendment."[15]

Byrd has proposed changes in the rules which would allow the leadership to restrict postcloture filibuster-by-amendment and to limit other dilatory tactics. One or two members can, when time is running out, resort to obstructionist tactics and endanger any bill they're opposed to," Byrd complained. "And while they're doing that they're also endangering passage of other measures which will be caught in the backlog."[16] Senators across a spectrum from liberal Democrats to conservative Republicans have been guilty, but few show signs of any remorse. They argue that they are simply using the rules to protect their interests and have a perfect right to do so. A consequence has been very tough going on controversial proposals backed by the administration and Senate party leaders. President Carter's energy package, which took two years to get through the Senate and emerged bearing very little resemblance to what he had asked for, is the most conspicuous example.

SENATE COMMITTEES

The Senate has been slower in redistributing power downward to more junior members through the committee system. One reason is that junior Senators already enjoyed the kind of legislative influence coveted by young House members. A major reform of the Senate committee structure (reducing the number of standing committees, altering the jurisdictions of many) was carried out in 1977. A rule increasing the number of subcommittee chairmanships open to junior members, which took effect in 1979, was also passed. A senator who chairs a full committee may chair only one subcommittee of any major Senate committee plus one of a minor committee. Senators who are not committee chairmen may chair one subcommittee of every committee on which they sit. The effect is to reduce the number of subcommittees chaired by senior

[15] Richard E. Cohen, "The 96th Congress Is in for an Overhaul," *National Journal* 10 (November 25, 1978): 1910.

[16] *Congressional Quarterly Weekly Report* 36 (September 2, 1978): 2307.

members, opening more positions to junior members.[17] Most senior Democrats voted against the proposal, but to no avail. Junior senators have the advantage of numbers and so are able, like their counterparts in the House, to force a redistribution of power in their favor. If results in the Senate match those in the House, more members will control a piece of the legislative action, fostering more fragmentation and more headaches for the leadership.

THE MINORITY PARTY IN CONGRESS

Up until 1980, the Democratic party has controlled both houses of Congress for more than twenty years. Any study of the congressional parties and their impact on policy making therefore naturally focuses on Democrats and slights Republicans. But the Republican minority does merit some attention, if only because Republican votes are often essential to Democratic (and presidential) victories, and coalitions of Republicans and dissident Democrats are often fatal to them.

Minority members share equally in the abundant official resources useful for pleasing constituents and winning reelection. In that they are protected by what Mayhew calls "powerful norms of institutional universalism." The result, he says, is that "in a good many ways the interesting division in congressional politics is not between Democrats and Republicans, but between politicians in and out of office. Looked at from one angle, the cult of universalism has the appearance of a cross-party conspiracy among incumbents to keep their jobs."[18]

But universalism does not necessarily extend to universal participation in policy making. Democrats have controlled the committees, their staffs, the schedule, and the agenda. Opportunities for the minority to have a creative impact on legislation depend on the good will of the majority. The Democrats, at least in the House, have not been particularly gracious. "As far as interplay between the minority and the majority, there is very little because that is

---

[17] Richard E. Cohen, "Take Your Pick," *National Journal* 9 (September 17, 1977): 1457.

[18] Mayhew, *Congress*, p. 105.

the way the majority wants it," said House Minority Leader John J. Rhodes in 1977. "Tip O'Neill used to say to me when he was majority leader, 'If you Republicans think you are going to have anything to do with legislation, forget it.' "[19]

Minority leadership in the House is normally a rather thankless task. With so few votes the party cannot hope to enact any programs of its own. Any good ideas are adopted by the Democrats, who then take the credit. The leader may be hard pressed just to keep up the morale of his troops. And their frustrations are often taken out on the leader. Twice in the last twenty years House Republicans have deposed their leader. Charles Halleck unseated incumbent Minority Leader Joseph Martin in 1958, only to be defeated himself six years later by Gerald Ford. Each defeat followed drastic election setbacks. Republicans lost forty-seven House seats in 1958 and forty-eight in 1964. During the same period, the Democratic Speaker has rarely been challenged and never seriously threatened.[20]

During the Ninety-fifth Congress, House Republicans were again grumbling about their leaders. Congressman Mickey Edwards complained in a speech that "the Republican Party in Congress is nothing more than a custom, an old relative hanging around the party, with no purpose, no influence, and no power." His party, he said, was one

> without leadership, with a caucus that never meets, with no official party positions on any major piece of legislation before Congress, with few real alternatives on anything, with no regular spokesman on the House floor, with floor managers who look like, sound like, and vote like the floor managers for the Democrats.[21]

Complaints are heard mainly from junior Republican members who want their party to take stands on policy clearly distinct from those of the Democrats. They tend to be more conservative and more firmly attached to their ideological moorings than their seniors. As the Democratic party has extended its appeal to cover a broader spectrum of opinion, the shrinking Republican party has become increasingly narrow, and more conservative, in its range of

[19] Richard E. Cohen, "House Republicans Under Rhodes — Divided They Stand and Fret," *National Journal* 9 (October 29, 1977): 1686.

[20] Barbara Hinckley, *Stability and Change in Congress*, 2nd ed. (New York: Harper and Row, 1978), pp. 121–26.

[21] Cohen, "House Republicans," p. 1686.

views. This has made the party a more cohesive, if smaller, force in congressional politics. But it has troubled leaders like Rhodes who doubt that doctrinaire conservatism will lead to majority status for the party.

Despite criticisms directed at Rhodes during the Ninety-fifth Congress, he was not challenged for the minority leadership of the Ninety-sixth. He retired and was replaced by Robert H. Michel of Illinois in 1980. And the Republican record for the Ninety-fifth Congress was not without significant legislative successes. Republicans can manage to frustrate the House Democratic leadership on occasions when the Democrats split and the Republicans stick together. One of the most notable examples of this was in 1977 when House Republicans voted 129 to 14 against the common situs picketing bill, which would have changed the labor laws to permit unions fighting one subcontractor at a construction site to picket all of them. Enough Democrats deserted their party to kill the bill. Democratic divisions give a united Republican party the opportunity at least to stop legislation they oppose even if they cannot initiate their own proposals.

As a minority in the pre-1980 period, Republicans did this even more effectively in the Senate, where their numbers were proportionately greater and where the rules allow minorities a great deal more room for maneuver. Republican Senate leadership is very loose; a minority leader is not even permitted to chair the conference or its Policy Committee. Once in the majority (after 1980), however, the Republican leadership, under Senator Howard Baker of Tennessee, proved forceful in getting the Reagan program through the Senate.

Effective opposition in the Senate does not depend much on organization. Republican senators — and representatives, for that matter — have a long history of cooperation with conservative members of the Democratic party. The Democrats have been divided on ideological lines for years. The divisions are also usually, though not invariably, regional. Conservative southern Democrats regularly find they have things in common with their conservative Republican colleagues. The so-called "conservative coalition" that results has been a familiar element in congressional politics since the 1940s. And when the coalition is formed, it usually wins. *Congressional Quarterly* has kept track of all recorded House and Senate votes since the early 1950s. Its figures on the conservative coalition's frequency of appearance in recorded votes and its fre-

TABLE 10.2
The Conservative Coalition in Congress, 1961–77

Year	Appearances[a]	Total	Victories	
			Senate	House
1961	28%	55%	48%	74%
1962	14	62	71	44
1963	17	50	44	67
1964	15	51	47	67
1965	24	33	39	25
1966	25	45	51	32
1967	20	63	54	73
1968	24	73	80	63
1969	27	68	67	71
1970	22	66	64	70
1971	30	83	86	79
1972	27	69	63	79
1973	23	61	54	67
1974	24	59	54	67
1975	28	50	48	52
1976	24	58	58	59
1977	26	68	74	60

[a] Percentage of recorded votes in which conservative coalition appeared.
Source: From 1977 Congressional Quarterly Almanac, p. 16-B. Reprinted by permission of Congressional Quarterly, Inc.

quency of victory when it did appear from 1961 through 1977 are given in Table 10.2. These data show the coalition to be generally successful in both houses. And it was particularly successful in the Senate during President Jimmy Carter's first year in office. Conservatives won ten of thirteen votes in the Senate when they opposed Carter. In the House, President Carter won twelve of twenty-two of the votes that pitted him against the coalition.[22] The Reagan Administration was to make repeated, and successful, use of this coalition to pass its programs.

The conservative coalition is of course another problem for Democratic party leaders. It should not be overlooked simply because it is a familiar, rather than new, source of aggravation. It also splits the Republican party to some degree. In one Congress (1977), for example, House Republicans supported the coalition 76 per-

[22] 1977 Congressional Quarterly Almanac, p. 16–B.

cent of the time, southern Democrats 63 percent of the time, and northern Democrats 23 percent of the time. The corresponding figures for the Senate were 72 percent, 64 percent, and 23 percent. Some members have suggested making the coalition permanent and using it to organize the Congress. Representative Joe Waggoner made the following comment in 1973: "Don't be too surprised if eventually some efforts are made to take control of the majority in the House through a coalition that wouldn't require change in party registration." To conservative Democrats he said, "You wouldn't have left your old Democratic friends back home, you'd have brought them some more influence, instead."[23] The idea may have seemed less farfetched right after the 1972 or 1980 election (and, to an extent, this happened in Reagan's first two years); that it could be suggested by a member of Congress is an indication of the forces that divide the congressional parties, especially the Democrats.

THE PERILS OF OPENNESS

The trend toward fragmentation and independence that challenges party leaders in Congress has been reinforced by other changes in congressional rules. Measures intended to open congressional activities to closer public scrutiny have had the unanticipated consequence of making it harder for Congress to get its work done and for leaders to lead. A rule adopted in 1970 requires recorded teller votes when the House acts as a Committee of the Whole, which it often does to free itself from some of the constraints of its own rules. The changes in the number of House teller votes and of comparable Senate votes since then is apparent in Table 10.3. The number of House teller votes increased from 266 to 834 and then dropped to 353 in 1981, a reflection of the Reagan Administration's control over the legislative calendar in its early years. Recorded Senate votes were fewer in 1981 after peaking in 1976.

Recorded teller votes take time, about fifteen minutes each. The old unrecorded votes took about five minutes. Hence the time that members must spend on the floor has increased without any matching increase in legislative productivity. The 834 teller votes

[23] Hinckley, *Stability and Change*, p. 137.

TABLE 10.3
Roll Call Votes in Congress, 1971–81

Year	House	Senate	Total
1971	320	423	743
1972	329	532	861
1973	541	594	1135
1974	537	544	1081
1975	612	602	1214
1976	661	688	1349
1977	706	635	1341
1978	834	516	1350
1979	672	497	1169
1980	604	531	1135
1981	353	483	836

Source: Congressional Quarterly Almanacs for each year. Reprinted with permission.

in 1978 took over 200 hours of House floor time. Any twenty members could request a teller vote be taken, and the demand for recorded votes was sometimes used to obstruct action by using up the House's time.

Recorded votes have another effect. They make members' actions more visible, exposing them to more pressure from interest and constituency groups. Lobbyists have been quick to take advantage of this. A number of observers have remarked on the notable increase in the sophistication and effectiveness of lobbyists working in Washington. For example, in the Ninety-fifth Congress:

> Business organizations, taking their cue from public affairs activists such as Common Cause and Ralph Nader, organized highly effective grass-roots lobbying campaigns and were able, for example, to block enactment of legislation establishing a consumer protection agency.
>
> The anti-abortion lobby was responsible for enactment of strict language prohibiting the government from paying for most abortions with Medicaid funds or military appropriations.
>
> The women's lobby was surprisingly successful in persuading Congress to extend for 39 months the deadline for ratification of the Equal Rights Amendment.

The Health industry took on the administration on the question of mandatory ceilings on hospital rates and prevented one of the president's most significant bills from being enacted.[24]

Responsiveness to pressure groups is, of course, a natural companion of the electoral environment members confront. Politicians closely attuned to their constituencies are especially sensitive to interests that can work through the grass roots. And the system of campaign finance also encourages them to take the views of potential donors — to their own or their opponents' campaigns — into account when they cast their votes.

A growing number of committee and subcommittee meetings have also been opened to the public, and with similar results. Members recognize that what they do in committee will be monitored by interested pressure groups and constituents; their maneuverability is therefore constrained. In the past, party leaders were sometimes able to trade for crucial *secret* votes in committee from members who could not publicly support particular bills — southern Democrats with civil rights legislation, for example. Opening the process to public view makes such deals impossible.

PARTY UNITY IN CONGRESS

Many Congresses have been stubbornly resistant to party and presidential leadership. Data on congressional voting lend empirical support to this view, but they probably underestimate the extent of disagreement within, particularly, the Democratic party. The *Congressional Quarterly* classifies any vote in which a majority of one party votes one way and a majority of the other party votes the other way as a party vote. Party unity scores for individuals and groups in Congress are then computed as the percentage of party votes in which they vote with their party's majority.

The proportion of votes classified as party votes fell from 46 percent in the 1950s to 43 percent in the 1960s and to 39 percent in the 1970s. Fewer votes now find majorities of both parties on

---

[24] *Congressional Quarterly Weekly Report* 36 (October 21, 1978): 3000.

opposite sides. Party unity has fallen, too. Among Democrats, it has gone from 69 percent to 66 percent to 64 percent across these decades. Among Republicans, it fell from 71 percent to 68 percent to 66 percent. The trend in these general figures has not been uniformly downward, however. These figures plainly do not tell the whole story. They do not indicate how important a vote was, nor do they measure how much effort leaders had to put into rounding up members' votes. And they do not take into account the times when party leaders, after counting heads, decide against bringing a bill to the floor because they are likely to lose.

More detailed studies of voting provide a clearer picture of what has been happening. The generation gap that develops on procedural issues also appears on substantive matters, but in a much more complicated way. *Northern* freshman and sophomore Democrats are significantly less supportive of the Democrat's traditional ally, organized labor. Ironically, these younger Democrats have received much more campaign money from labor groups than have their seniors. But votes are even more important than money. Their reluctance to support labor's proposals is directly connected to their electoral circumstances. A large proportion of them — almost half — were elected to seats that had previously been held by Republicans. And it is this group that diverges most strikingly from other Democrats in voting on labor-related issues.[25]

Generational differences appear on some other issues as well. The "Watergate" generation of House Democrats are more supportive of defense spending than are members with slightly more seniority. Indeed, they are more "conservative" in this regard than even the most senior group. Those members who entered the House while Vietnam was the dominant issue are still the most skeptical of defense spending and the most reluctant to commit American troops abroad. But on environmental issues, the class of 1974 remains more "liberal" than any other group of Democrats. Sixty percent of the northern Democrats in the class of 1976 voted to relax auto emissions standards, whereas only 41 percent of their colleagues from the previous class did so, for example. Members

[25] William Schneider and Gregory Schell, "The New Democrats," *Public Opinion* 1 (November/December, 1978): 7–13.

seem to carry the scars of whatever major issues predominated at the time they were first elected to Congress.[26]

Still, the most formidable barrier to party and presidential influence in Congress lies in the electoral connection. The extension of the Democratic party into districts once held by Republicans brought swollen Democratic majorities into Congress. But at the same time it broadened the ideological base of the party to include many views once represented by Republicans. Greater internal strain has been the inevitable consequence. The interests of old and new components of the Democratic coalition are not easily reconciled. And individual members find it prudent to work out their own separate solutions. Representative Floyd J. Fithian, first elected in 1974 to a district that had been held by a Republican as long as anyone could remember, put it this way:

> Subconsciously, I began to realize that being a Democrat from the 2nd District of Indiana is a high-risk game politically and that the Democratic leadership in the House and the president didn't elect me. If the 535,000 people of my district perceive me as standing up to the president on one vote and the Chamber of Commerce on the other, they react positively.[27]

Herein lies the principal source of a president's problems with Congress. But there are others, too, and they are the subject of the next chapter.

[26] Michael J. Malbin, "New Democrats Don't See Eye to Eye With Their Senior Colleagues," *National Journal* 9 (July 9, 1977): 1080–81. Used by permission.

[27] Quoted in Richard E. Cohen, "The Big Issue for November is the Voter's Pocketbook," *National Journal* 10 (August 12, 1978): 1275. Used by permission.

11

Congress and the President

EXPECTATIONS AND REALITY

Relations between presidents and Congress have been anything but easy. One reason is that the congressional party leaders' troubles are usually the president's troubles also. The aggressive independence of the current crop of congressmen works against the president as well as the party. Bare appeals for loyalty to a president are no more effective than bare appeals for party loyalty.

But the problem has been magnified by both recent historical experiences and the performance of recent administrations. Either would be a source of real difficulties; their combination has aggravated matters considerably.

THE BATTERED PRESIDENCY

Recent presidents have had the singular misfortune to assume the presidency at a time when it had been seriously damaged by the actions of their predecessors — and by congressional responses to them. The almost automatic bipartisan support postwar presidents had enjoyed in foreign affairs had disappeared under the impact of the Vietnam War. First President Johnson, then President Nixon faced growing resistance to their war policies in Congress. Congress never took decisive action hindering the war effort until nearly all of the American forces were out of Vietnam. But after the issue of "protecting our boys overseas" was eliminated, Congress enacted a number of measures designed to restrict the president's freedom of action beyond the United States borders.

The most prominent measure, the 1973 War Powers Act, is largely symbolic. It requires congressional review and, if military actions ordered by the president are to continue, congressional approval. Congress is not likely to withdraw support while Americans are fighting (as in Grenada or "peacekeeping" in Lebanon) and the president is rallying people behind the "national interest," so it is not clear how much this act actually restricts presidential initiatives. More effective have been laws that forbid the president to use money appropriated by Congress to intervene in foreign conflicts. Congress forbade money to be spent on bombing Cambodia in 1973; other military operations in Vietnam were banned in 1975. In 1976, Congress effectively prohibited military aid to Angola by requiring that it first be approved by Congress. Congress seems most successful when it restricts presidential actions *before* they take place.

As an example, the dispatching of American troops to Honduras in 1983 to participate in an elaborate and prolonged series of training operations along the border with neighboring Nicaragua, at a time when the United States was attempting to influence the fate of the revolutionary Sandinista government in Nicaragua, was handled, and defended, as a routine military exercise. The Congress was not consulted, and although the actions of the military could result in serious incidents between the two nations, individual members of Congress could only voice their displeasure and caution against actions already taken. The House did vote a ban on covert American aid to the "contras," primarily Nicaraguan exiles and followers of the deposed dictator Anastasias Somoza, who, with American backing, were conducting guerilla raids into Nicaragua. The action too was mostly symbolic. The Republican-dominated Senate would not support such a measure, and even if it had passed both houses of the Congress, they could not have overriden a presidential veto. Yet, it is indicative of the new mood of the Congress, that the House was willing to go on record as opposing a foreign policy action of the White House. The area previously had been considered nonpartisan and not open to discussion.

Other specific problems for the president arise from the widening connection between foreign and domestic affairs. The Arab oil boycott of 1973 and the consequent shortages of gasoline and heating oil forcefully focused public attention on the domestic ramifications of what went on overseas. Members of Congress recognize that the United States's economic interdependence with the rest of the world means that foreign events can have immediate and drastic domestic effects. They are therefore less inclined to follow any president's lead automatically without assessing the consequences for their own concerns.

Congressional assertiveness on foreign affairs is not confined to any single partisan or ideological faction. Conservatives as well as liberals have become accustomed to opposing the president's foreign policies when they see fit. The collective result is a Congress no longer willing simply to follow the administration's foreign policy lead. Support must be solicited by the usual means of political persuasion. And it is by no means certain that the administration will always win. The fragmenting of power in Congress and the stubborn independence of its members make the problem worse. Representative Lee H. Hamilton remarked,

> It used to be that the Secretary of State could call up Arthur Vandenburg [a senior Republican senator in the 1940s] and that was consultation enough. No more. Now there is no single individual who can say what the mood of Congress is on a range of foreign policy issues. It is very hard, especially because many foreign policy issues don't come out of the Foreign Relations and International Relations Committees at all.[1]

BUDGET REFORM

It was in the area of domestic policy, however, that congressional habits of resistance rather than deference to presidential

---

[1] Quoted in William J. Lanouette, "Who's Setting Foreign Policy — Carter or Congress?" *National Journal* 10 (July 15, 1978): 1121.

policy initiatives developed most fully. The lessons learned in the struggles between Democratic congressional majorities and Republican presidents have not been quickly forgotten. And institutional innovations designed to strengthen Congress's ability to make policy in confrontation with presidents has not fallen into disuse.

The foundation of Congress's power as a political institution is its control of the budget. Money to do any and all of the things the federal government undertakes must be raised, authorized, and appropriated by acts of Congress. During the postwar years prior to the Nixon Administration, Congress had been content to watch much of its budget-making authority slip away to the administration. This was partly a consequence of the way Congress operates. The decentralized committee/subcommittee system promotes fragmented decision making on financial as well as other matters. The aggregate fiscal effects of the balance of authorized expenditures and federal revenues raised by the mix of taxes imposed were systematically overlooked before Congress established its own budget office and budgetary process. Presidents do concern themselves with such comprehensive fiscal questions, and wisely so; the health of the economy is closely linked to their political fortunes. The Office of Management and Budget is the institutional embodiment of the president's intense interest in the federal budget.

Congress's instinct is to make citizens happy by (1) authorizing and funding as many programs as possible and (2) cutting taxes. The separate interest of each member of the Congress is in providing programs that please constituents. Less attention is given to the collective impact of each of these programs on the national budget. But the aggregate result is too much spending. That means either raising taxes or having too large a deficit, neither alternative politically desirable. For years the problem was solved by leaving it up to the president. The president, his eye on the deficit and its negative economic consequences, would "impound" — refuse to spend — some of the funds Congress authorized, saving the country (and the Congress) from the effects of congressional generosity. Members could happily claim credit for at least authorizing services without suffering the embarrassment of presenting a bill for them to the public.

This mechanism for controlling federal spending broke down during the Nixon Administration. Nixon refused to play the game.

He used impoundment to impose his own spending priorities on Congress and to subvert those of the Democratic majority. Even authorizations passed over his veto were impounded. The challenge to Congress as an institution was unmistakable, and Congress understandably responded. Language in existing laws that the Nixon Administration used to justify impoundments was removed. Procedures were set up to keep Congress informed about impoundments and to compel the release of impounded funds if Congress chose to do so. Most importantly, Congress took steps to alter its own procedures so that impoundment would not be necessary to keep the gap between revenue and spending from becoming too wide. And these were *congressional,* not partisan Democratic moves; they had the overwhelming support of both parties in both houses.

The centerpiece of the legislation restricting presidential impoundment, the 1974 Congressional Budget and Impoundment Control Act, was the establishment of a Budget Committee in each house. The task of these committees is to help Congress keep its spending and revenue-raising policies in harmony. Each spring, the budget committees must report a budget resolution setting spending and revenue targets for the fiscal year beginning the following October. Once the budget resolution is adopted, the regular committees go to work on their segments of the budget as before. But they are now expected to abide by the constraints imposed by the budget resolution.

In the fall, when work has been completed on the appropriations and tax bills, the budget committees review the result. If the targets set in the spring have not been met, the budget committees can recommend reducing spending, raising taxes, or revising the original goals. Congress is thus forced to determine the size of the deficit. It must acknowledge the fiscal consequences of the myriad separate decisions that are made during the session.

It is still too early to judge whether or not the new budget process will give Congress the kind of control over the budget it desires. So far, the results are mixed. The system has occasionally bent (the Senate budget resolution has been ignored by some committees) but not broken under the pressure to do what is individually pleasant (providing services and projects) without paying the price (raising taxes). Members have even learned to use the budget resolution to appear generous and tight-fisted at the same time. They vote for all kinds of items that add to the budget, then vote against the higher deficit they would produce. "That's the beauty of the budget process," explained one House member. "You can vote for all your favorite programs, and then vote against the deficit."[2]

Least happy with the new budget process are the senior committee chairmen, especially those heading the important financial committees (Appropriations and Ways and Means in the House, Appropriations and Finance in the Senate). The weakened House chairmen are in no position to do much about it, but the chairman of the Senate Finance Committee, Russell Long, has fought, with a fair degree of success, to keep his committee's power intact.

Having cranked up the machinery to do their own budgeting with Republicans in the White House, congressional Democrats have not seen fit to let it rust away. Congressional and presidential priorities inevitably clash, and Congress is in a much stronger position than it was a few years ago to hold its own in budgetary contests. "Congress," said Senator Henry Bellmon, "as I am hopeful the president will one day fully understand, now has its own budgetary process. It is a good budgetary process. It is working."[3] It is, but not necessarily as the occupant of the White House would like it to.

Research suggests that the conventional political wisdom is correct. Popular presidents have more success with Congress than unpopular ones.[4] The reasoning here is clear. If constituents like and support the president, then at least some voters will reward or punish their representatives according to how consistently they support the president. Local activists, campaign contributors, and potential primary and general election challengers will consider it a factor in their decisions. Close association with a popular president will help to discourage opposition before it becomes serious. Conversely, separating oneself from an unpopular president of one's own party may also be a very wise move, as many Republicans learned in 1974. President Nixon's staunchest supporters suf-

[2] Joel Havemann, "Budget Process Nearly Ambushed By Carter and By Congress," *National Journal* 9 (May 21, 1977): 787.

[3] Joel Havemann, "The Congressional Budget Committee — High Marks After the First Years," *National Journal* 8 (September 25, 1976): 1351.

[4] George C. Edwards III, "Presidential Influence in the House: Presidential Prestige as a Source of Presidential Power," *American Political Science Review* 70 (1976): 101–13.

fered the consequences at the polls.[5] There is no evidence that presidents really help their party's candidates in the off-year elections by stumping for them, but as long as members of Congress think they might, it remains a useful way for popular presidents to accumulate political credit.

The best example of this may be the Reagan election. Reagan won an unexpectedly decisive victory in 1980. He beat the incumbent, Jimmy Carter, by 10 percentage points in what was expected to be a very close race and despite his running in a three-man field (independent John Anderson being the third candidate). In addition, the Republicans managed to win control of the Senate, the first time they were able to gain control over either house of the Congress since the Eisenhower victory in 1952. The Republicans won by generally replacing liberal Democrats with far more conservative Republicans, continuing a process begun in the 1978 off-year election.

Reagan had a distinctively different and more conservative economic and social program. Few in the Congress appeared to believe in either — Reagan's "supply side" economics had been referred to as "voodoo economics" by George Bush, an opponent in the primaries who later served as Reagan's vice-president. Most in the Congress appeared to share Bush's appraisal. Nonetheless, in a stunning series of legislative victories, the administration was able to enact its economic programs over the little opposition put forth by the dispirited Democrats. The Congress was shaken and chose to interpret the 1980 election as a mandate for conservation and, more specifically, for Reagan's policies. There is evidence that this interpretation might constitute a misreading of the election returns. The perceptions of Jimmy Carter's lack of leadership, general unpopularity, and inability to handle the office may have had more to do with the outcome than anything Reagan had to offer.[6] Perception of reality is more important than reality itself in poli-

[5] See Gerald C. Wright, Jr., "Constituency Response to Congressional Behavior: The Impact of the House Judiciary Committee Impeachment Votes," *Western Political Quarterly* 30 (1977): 401–10.

[6] Gerald Pomper, ed., *The Election of 1980* (New Jersey: Chatham House, 1981); Paul R. Abramson, John H. Aldrich, and David W. Rhode, *Change and Continuity in the 1980 Elections* (Washington, D.C.: Congressional Quarterly Press, 1982); and Thomas Ferguson and Joel Rogers, eds., *The Hidden Election* (New York: Pantheon Books, 1981).

tics, and the perception was that Reagan had won a mandate. Under these conditions, the Congress can be most compliant.

CONGRESSIONAL SUPPORT FOR THE PRESIDENT

President Reagan's initial success with the Congress is borne out by empirical data (Table 11.1). Not only was the substance of what Reagan proposed a marked change from previous administrations, but his rate of success — 82 percent — beat the best rates of presidents Carter, Ford, and Nixon. Not since the Johnson Administration, acting in the wake of John Kennedy's assassination and the build-up for the Vietnam War (1964–1965), are higher figures of legislative accomplishment found. As a consequence of

TABLE 11.1
Proportion of Presidential Victories in Congress, 1953–81

Eisenhower		Nixon	
1953	89.0%	1969	74.0%
1954	82.8	1970	77.0
1955	75.0	1971	75.0
1956	70.0	1972	66.0
1957	68.0	1973	50.6
1958	76.0	1974	59.6
1959	52.0	Ford	
1960	65.0	1974	58.2%
Kennedy		1975	61.0
1961	81.0%	1976	53.8
1962	85.4	Carter	
1963	87.1	1977	75.4%
Johnson		1978	78.3
1964	88.0%	1979	76.8
1965	93.0	1980	75.1
1966	79.0	Reagan	
1967	79.0	1981	82.4%
1968	75.0		

Source: Congressional Quarterly Almanac, 1981, p. 18-C. Reprinted by permission of Congressional Quarterly, Inc.

both the substance of the Reagan program and its high rate of passage in the Congress, observers declared the early years of the Reagan Administration as the most significant since Johnson's "Great Society" or even possibly Franklin Roosevelt's "New Deal." Whatever the lasting impact of the Reagan policies, he was unusually successful for a modern president in getting his programs passed.

The same was not true for President Jimmy Carter. The widespread opinion in Washington was that Carter had an unusually difficult time with Congress. This opinion is borne out by the data. Carter's rate of success, measured against those of his predecessors going back to Eisenhower, is also shown in Table 11.1. His victory frequencies — 75.4 percent and 78.3 percent for his first two years in office — are the lowest of any Democratic president in any year but one. That was 1968, Lyndon Johnson's last year in office, when he was taking the full brunt of criticism for Vietnam and was no longer a candidate for reelection. Even John F. Kennedy, who had well-publicized difficulties with Congress, enjoyed a distinctly higher rate of success. Carter did little better than Richard Nixon during his first three years in office. Nixon of course faced a Congress dominated by the opposing party. And these figures may even underestimate Carter's weakness, since many of his proposals never reached the floor for a vote.

The *Congressional Quarterly* computes how frequently individuals and groups in Congress vote in support of the president's positions. The data on Reagan are quite interesting. They show, not surprisingly, that he drew more support from Republicans than Democrats; comparison with previous years indicates that this is a common pattern. Support scores since 1961 for House and Senate Democrats and Republicans are listed in Table 11.2. Notice the differences in presidential support by party depending on the party of the president. Reagan's support in 1981 among Republicans in the Senate was the highest recorded since 1961 for any president in either party. The fact that 1978 and 1980 saw the election of an increasing number of conservative Republicans and, in fact, the Republicans' capturing control of the Senate after the 1980 election, undoubtedly helped. Still, the achievement is impressive. Reagan proved to have the most support among his party members of any president in recent years. He also managed to capture one-half of the Democratic votes.

Reagan also did well in the House. His 68 percent support score among Republicans ranked among the better efforts of recent administrations, and 42 percent support score from the Democrats was generally better than that for presidents Carter and Ford, although not as good as for President Nixon.

Reagan's immediate predecessor, Jimmy Carter, had unusually low support among House Democrats; his first-year figures are much lower than Kennedy's or Johnson's. His support among Senate Democrats was unusually high by historical standards — higher than anything Kennedy or Johnson could muster. So was his support from Senate Republicans in his first year in office. Indeed, the *Congressional Quarterly* points out that Carter's "biggest legislative victories were, in large part, the result of Republican support and were achieved despite prominent Democratic defections. Controversial proposals that did not have much Republican backing — the bill designed to control hospital costs, for example — were defeated."[7]

The House-Senate differences in Democratic support for Carter are intriguing. What accounts for them? One answer is found in the regional breakdowns in the presidential support figures, examining the levels of support for Kennedy, Johnson, and Carter in their first year in office, by region, in the House and Senate. Carter's support in the House is lower everywhere; the smallest drop-off is in the south. Southern senators support him much more frequently than they did Kennedy or Johnson; his support elsewhere is similar to theirs. Thus the higher level of Democratic support Carter enjoyed in the Senate can be attributed in large part to his fellow southerners.

Even with very large Democratic majorities in both houses, Carter could not rely on his own partisans to enact his major programs. Despite consistent support from party leaders, the many forces working against individual loyalty to the party and the president were simply too strong. And so any hopes that, after eight years of divided rule, Democratic control of Congress and the presidency would bring a new era of cooperation and the enactment of an ambitious new legislative agenda were disappointed. The data in Table 11.2 suggest that they were vain in the first place. No postwar president can count solely on the support of

[7] *Congressional Quarterly Weekly Report* 36 (October 21, 1978): 3000.

TABLE 11.2
Congressional Support for the President's Programs, 1961–81

Year	Party of President	House Democrats	House Republicans	Senate Democrats	Senate Republicans
1961	Democrat	73%	37%	65%	36%
1962	Democrat	72	42	63	39
1963	Democrat	72	32	63	32
1964	Democrat	74	38	61	45
1965	Democrat	74	41	64	48
1966	Democrat	63	37	57	43
1967	Democrat	69	46	61	35
1968	Democrat	64	51	48	47
1969	Republican	46	58	40	64
1970	Republican	53	66	45	60
1971	Republican	47	72	40	64
1972	Republican	47	64	44	66
1973	Republican	35	62	37	61
1974	Republican	41	51	39	55
1975	Republican	38	63	47	68
1976	Republican	32	63	39	62
1977	Democrat	63	42	70	52
1978	Democrat	60	36	66	41
1979	Democrat	64	34	68	47
1980	Democrat	63	40	62	45
1981	Republican	42	68	49	80

Source: Congressional Quarterly Almanacs for each year. Reprinted with permission.

his party to pass his legislative programs; all have had to pick up votes from both sides of the aisle. Some presidents' problems are more acute than, although not fundamentally different from, others'.

THE ISSUES

"It used to be that a central piece of information on a vote was the president's position. Now the central information is the issue," said a State Department congressional liaison official.

"With the breakdown of party discipline, it is clear that voters expect members to exercise independent judgment. That means voting on the issue, not just to agree with the president."[8]

If true, this means that the president — and congressional party leaders — must make a greater effort than ever before to convince members of Congress of the intrinsic rightness of their proposals. And given the kind of issues the federal government now faces and the surly mood of the American public, it is no wonder that success has so far been modest. The president and Congress confront a host of particularly tough issues, many of which directly affect how millions of people live and many of which do not conform to traditional party divisions.

Consider energy policy. It splits Congress — and the parties — by region and state. Oil- and gas-producing states have interests contrary to energy-consuming states. On this and other economic issues, states of the so-called "snow belt," the northeast and midwest, oppose states of the so-called "sun belt" of the south, southwest, and west. Snow-belt congressmen have even formed a northeast-midwest Congressional Coalition, a bipartisan group with 213 members from eighteen states, to protect their regional interests.[9]

Or consider environmental questions. They divide the educated, middle-class Democratic environmentalists from traditional labor-oriented Democrats who would give priority to economic growth. The distinctive voting patterns of junior, "new politics" Democrats is a visible result. Older Democratic divisions have been crosscut by a newer one, according to political scientists William Schneider and Gregory Schell. Northern Democrats are divided between traditional prolabor Democrats and "new politics" social liberals. The latter group is thoroughly liberal on race, environmental, and foreign policy issues, but that liberalism is not associated with support for the claims of organized labor. And the prolabor Democrats are hardly social liberals.[10]

Economic issues no longer conform to the familiar New Deal categories. A tax system that a Democratic president (Carter)

[8] Congressional Quarterly Weekly Report 36 (March 4, 1978): 596.
[9] Congressional Quarterly Weekly Report 36 (November 18, 1978): 3330.
[10] Schneider and Schell, "New Democrats."

called "a disgrace to the human race" because, he argued, it unfairly burdened middle- and lower-income taxpayers was "reformed" by a heavily Democratic Congress — acting on a Republican proposal — to give tax relief to upper-income groups. This emphasis, whatever its moral value, of Democrats voting in favor of Republican-sponsored relief for upper income individuals and businesses continued in the Reagan years. In recent elections, many Democrats were campaigning for Congress on the traditional Republican promises of lower spending, lower taxes, less regulation, and balanced budgets. This is not an anomaly but rather a logical consequence of all the trends discussed in this chapter. If members are as sensitive and responsive to district opinion as they seem now to be, it is scarcely surprising that they adjust their campaign appeals to the popular mood. Discarding old party chestnuts when they become stale hardly requires a second thought. The party and its symbols are no longer the primary political guideposts.

12

Congressional Parties: The Future

The sources of conflict that fragment the congressional parties and hamper presidential and party leadership lie outside Congress. In a sense, Congress is too representative. American citizens are plainly divided themselves on many important political questions. But their divisions do not compose coherent patterns. Clear political battle lines have yet to form across a range of issues. There is little consensus on what issues are important, let alone on what alternative solutions are preferable. Parties, politicians, and governmental institutions are viewed with suspicion if not hostility. Insofar as people are represented by organized groups, the pressures on political decision makers will be as diverse as they are intense. Members of Congress who seek to "represent" their constituencies do not find it easy; no wonder they find it hard to cooperate on partisan or any other consistent basis.

CONGRESSIONAL ELECTIONS AND PUBLIC POLICY

Like the members of Congress whom they elect, Americans like to have it both ways. They enjoy the programs and benefits the federal government provides, but they dislike paying the price in the form of higher taxes, more inflation, and greater government regulation. Public opinion polls find solid majorities for national health insurance, wage and price controls, government guarantees of jobs, and current or greater levels of spending on the environment, education, the cities, and health care. They find equally solid majorities believing that the federal government is too large, spends too much money, and is too intrusive into people's lives.[1] Senator Lowell Weicker put it succinctly: "Everybody wants to go to heaven, but nobody wants to die."

Even the publicized "tax-revolt" of recent years has generated few demands that government services be curtailed. Many Republicans (including Ronald Reagan) campaigned as supporters of a 30 percent across-the-board cut in federal income taxes that was *not* wedded to any cuts in federal spending. (An economist's theory supported the happy notion that the economic stimulus the cut produced would keep total revenue from actually falling.)

Conflicting signals from the districts provide a ticklish problem for members of Congress. The problem for congressmen is obvious. Members are expected to bring home the usual projects and benefits while holding down spending and taxes — which means rejecting the special projects of *other* members. The old solution of everyone backing everyone else's district pork will not work. If there is a clear popular mandate to cut spending *somewhere*, reduce inflation, and lower (or at least not raise) taxes, the president has a clearly specified set of popular objectives to pursue. This could help him in several ways. An administration policy that members think their constituents favor finds readier support; witness the public works veto. He can also take full blame for killing individual programs and projects — in return for general credit for holding down spending, taxes, and inflation. Members can still claim credit for pursuing district benefits while blaming the presi-

---

[1] From a study by Everett C. Ladd, Jr., cited by George F. Will, "Slash 'Waste,' Cure Everything," *Hartford Courant*, December 14, 1978, p. 30.

dent for their failure to provide them (their use of the budget resolution is instructive here). Congressional Democrats may also legitimately suspect that the administration's success on these issues will affect how hard they have to campaign to retain their seats.

As president, Ronald Reagan has been able to dramatize many of these issues and to take advantage of the tensions between legislator and district, party and party, and one congressman's needs as against another's. Working within a system that appeared to stymie his predecessor, and constantly using television and the media to go over the heads of the Congress to the people back home, he has proven to be a skilled legislative tactician.

ORGANIZING THE CONGRESS

"I've voted for every reform — to open committee meetings, to reduce the power of seniority, to do a number of things which reduce the power of a few in Congress — and somehow the end product is worse than it used to be," lamented Representative Charles W. Whalen.[2] Members complain of too much work, too many subcommittees producing too many bills, and too much time wasted taking too many recorded votes. Some of these problems were addressed by new reforms passed by the House Democratic caucus in 1978. Others are likely to prove more intractable, since they are a consequence of the redistribution of power to younger members, a trend not likely to be reversed by its beneficiaries.

Roll call votes were made more difficult. Provision was made for clustering some votes and eliminating other procedural votes entirely. Republicans were not pleased with these changes, since they had been using demands for roll call votes to delay legislation they opposed. But the Democratic majority makes the rules.

The Democrats also voted to limit the number of subcommittee assignments any member may hold to five. The immediate effect is to open eighty-four subcommittee slots to new members, and in this sense it continues the devolution of power in the House. The long-term intent, however, is to cut down the number of subcom-

---

[2] *Hartford Courant,* November 28, 1978, p. 32.

mittees. The issue is a sensitive one. It took years to wrest power from twenty committee chairmen; imagine the potential for resistance of more than 150 independent subcommittee chairmen.

Some of the "young Turks," from the classes of 1974 and 1976 are not yet satisfied with their work in limiting the power of the committee chairmen. One proposal would have prohibited full committee chairmen from chairing any subcommittee, a crucial blow at a time when subcommittees hold the power. It was defeated easily, but chairmen of standing committees were prevented from chairing ad hoc, joint, special, or select committees. And other minor changes opening subcommittee assignments to new members by limiting committee seniority rights were adopted.

Even the Republicans moved toward redistributing the small amount of institutional power they hold in the House. The conference voted to allow each member to be the ranking Republican (who would become chairman if Republicans won a majority in the House) of only one committee. Back in 1971 the House Republicans, like their Democratic colleagues, had opened the way to modification of the seniority system. Ranking minority members must now be officially ratified by secret ballot in the conference. So far, no senior member has been denied the post on any committee. But these are clear signs that the Republicans have not remained untouched by the forces that have affected their rivals.

Assaults on the seniority principle show no signs of abating. Junior members are elected to subcommittee chairmanships over senior members. Ideological and policy views — "voting on whether one candidate's views are closer to theirs than others' "[3] — have become more important in such decisions. At the same time, convicted, indicted, or reprimanded party members have retained influential committee chairmanships. And party leaders have been hard pressed to find anyone at all willing to sit on the Committee on Standards of Official Conduct.

And so the process of adjustment continues. Members of Congress maintain ambivalent attitudes toward their party because electoral and policy-making incentives remain in conflict. Reluctance to follow party — or presidential — leadership grows out of

[3] *Congressional Quarterly Weekly Report* 37 (February 3, 1979): 183.

the desire to stay in office. But its deeper roots must therefore lie in American society, in the moods and expectations of the diverse constituencies they represent. The parties remain, however, essential to effective collective action by Congress. They provide the machinery through which members cooperate to make national policy. Strong congressional leadership — strong party leadership — enhances the collective power of Congress. Changes in rules that simultaneously give members more independent authority and leaders more tools to manage congressional business are not really so strange. They simply reflect the conflicting needs and motives of members of Congress.

Epilogue:
A Concluding Note on Political Parties and the Future

We end this book on a speculative note. The picture of political parties presented in the preceding chapters is not a pleasant one. The American political parties do appear to be in decline, and the consequences for our democratic system are enormous. The argument made to this point can be summarized.

THE DECLINE

Concerning the Electorate

The number of voters participating in elections continues to (1) decline to levels low enough for us to begin to question the relevance, and should the trend continue, the stability and representatives of American political institutions. The picture is bleak. The electorate has become polarized between the higher socio- (2) economic-status adults who remain in the 30 to 50 percent of the eligible population that continues to participate in elections and the lower socioeconomic-status groups who have dropped out. How representative is a governing system that does not include in its decision making in any meaningful way those most in need of effective political representation? You will have to answer this question for yourself.

Within the evolving electorate, political parties are becoming less relevant. The number of people identifying with the major parties is decreasing, to the point where the proportion of independents equal those identifying with the larger of the two parties, the Democrats. As the number of independents increases — as it will with the entry of new voters into the electorate, a group for whom the parties have the least appeal — independents will become the dominant group in the electorate. Within the American political system an independent identification has been associated with a lack of political interest and involvement. There is evidence that this depiction is no longer totally accurate — independents are a disparate group — but the development of such a large pool of unattached voters is not a hopeful sign for a party system that has depended on a continual stream of new adherents to replenish its ranks.

The weakening of party ties has led to a volatile electorate, one capable of swinging from overwhelming majorities in favor of one party to, in the space of one election to the next, competitive outcomes or equally decisive margins in favor of the other party. The stability, predictability, and, if you will, mooring mechanisms of the American electorate have been seriously undermined. The future suggests the evolution of a basically partyless electorate, with little of the placidity of, say, the 1950s. The normal ties of identification with the parties continue to be eroded.

To make matters worse, the voters' perceptions of the political parties and of the government continues to be negative. The turn-around in indicators of public trust, efficacy, and faith in government in less than two decades has been remarkable. However one defines it, Americans are alienated from their own government and its leaders. It is unlikely that anything that has happened in recent years has renewed the voters' faith in the government.

As the electoral impact of the parties has declined, issues have increased in significance as an influence on voter decision making. Without party identification to provide a powerful (and simplifying) cue to the voter, issues decisions demand more of a voter's time and mental energy that most are willing to give. An issue-oriented electorate is one likely to increase the dominance of the better-educated and upper-income groups over electoral decisions. Lower socioeconomic groups face enormous difficulties in reincorporating themselves into the electorate without the political parties to encourage, organize, and guide their efforts. One of the strengths of the two-party system has been its ability to include large elements of the less well-off in their coalitions. The weaknesses of the parties in the electorate have already indicated that there will be future difficulties in mobilizing and attracting this vote. Specific candidates may be able to appeal enough on occasion to nonidentified, nonvoting adults to stimulate them to turn out and vote. Whether this will move, as the parties have done in the past, to incorporate these lower socioeconomic groups into the electorate in any meaningful, long-term manner and to allow them a vehicle through which to exercise a consequential influence on political decision making is doubtful. There is no evidence that the trends depicted in this book in regard to these concerns will change to any significant degree in the forseeable future.

Concerning Campaigns, the Rise of PACs, the New Technologies, and the Increasing Costs of Politics

The campaign functions of the parties have been seriously undercut. Parties are no longer the principal funders of campaigns. PACs are. Television has replaced the party as the dominant communicator of political information and, as a consequence, the preeminent influence on voter attitudes. Parties are no longer the major organizers of campaigns. Media consultants, public relations and professional experts can create "instant" parties for candidates with the funds to pay for them. As the campaign function of parties has decreased, the role of money — and hence of those who can supply it — has increased dramatically. The new politics is an expensive one.

The response of the parties to these developments has been uneven. The movement for party reform was an effort to produce a more participant-oriented party structure responsive to, and in line with, contemporary political concerns. The movement has experienced a varied success. The presidential nominating system has been remodeled. More voters are involved, and the decision over the nomination is now in the hands of those who take the trouble to participate in the process. This is a pronounced change from the closed, elitist nominating politics of the old (pre-1972) party system.

The reform movement may have many commendable qualities, but it has created problems. It could be argued with justification that reform resulted from the inability of the parties, and especially the larger of the two, the Democrats, to adequately represent the major concerns of the parties' constituencies. Nevertheless, in many respects, reform has also contributed to the continued erosion of the party system by weakening the parties' control over their most vital function, the nominating process.

Reformers and party regulars both recognize the problem. Many states, in order to meet the reform guidelines and (not incidentally) to benefit from the exposure television can provide, adopted primaries. In a dozen years the number of primaries has better than doubled (from sixteen to thirty-five), and the number of delegates selected through primary elections has increased from an average of less than 40 percent for the two parties to over 70 percent. Since primaries neutralize the role and influence of the party, they have contributed to its demise. The void has been filled by the media (particularly television) and by the groups with the financial resources needed to mount serious candidacies in a media-oriented age.

Reform has had little impact, good or bad, in other areas. The national party structures have shown little evidence of change. The parties also have failed to take command of the new technologies of politics and to use these to their own advantage. In this regard, Republican efforts have been more substantial and impressive than those of the Democrats.

The leaders of both parties pay lip-service to the problems the parties face. Given the chance to rebuild party coalitions and strengthen party services, they do little. From Richard Nixon to Jimmy Carter and Ronald Reagan, the chief concern of those most in a position to help revitalize the party system has been their own political survival. If the leadership of the two parties fails to recognize the fundamental seriousness of the problems confronting the parties, it is unlikely that anyone else can be of much assistance. Party regeneration will have to begin from within. At present there is no sign that party leaders truly appreciate the extent of the parties' malaise and are willing to extend themselves to do something about it. The future in these regards is bleak.

Concerning the Party in Congress and in Policy Making

The party in Congress has been subjected to an increasing dissolution of discipline and a decline in party line voting. The congressional leadership in recent years has on several occasions lined up against the president of its own party on policy issues. There has been a continuing split between the electorate of the presidential party and that of the congressional party. At the same time, the advantages of incumbency in seeking reelection have been magnified; the congressman's relation to his constituency has become more service-oriented; and PAC funds have increasingly supplied the capital needed for campaigning.

There have been reforms within the party and within the institutions of Congress. Some have helped to strengthen the party; most, however, have weakened it. Generational differences within the congressional membership have become more pronounced, with the newer members less amenable to party and presidential direction. Congressional electoral politics, the demands of legislative performance, party needs, and the will and priorities of a president, for the most part, all appear to pull in opposing directions. As a consequence, the factionalization evident in other aspects of American politics has adversely affected the national-level policy formulation and implementation and the parties' role in, and control over, them.

These changes have been in progress for at least the last several decades. To compound the difficulties and accentuate the trends, in recent years the nation has been led by presidents with weak ties to the national and congressional party and a poor understanding of party needs (at any level) or legislative demands. It may be that the worst manifestations of the debilitating forces assessed in this book have yet to be seen. If this is the case, future years will witness the continuing decline in party performance and relevance. The question remains, then, as to the consequence of these developments. What does it all mean? What will American politics be like with a progressively more ineffectual party system, one characterized by weak leadership, an increasing lack of coherence, an inability to control its own activities or members, and undue responsiveness to special interest funds and influences?

THE FUTURE

Again, we can only speculate at this point, but it would seem that a partyless politics contains both risks and opportunities. The biggest difficulty will be in the absence of the bonds that held party coalitions together and that allowed for some coherence among different levels of party concerns (the president, Congress, and the voter). These bonds — which were largely internal, personal, and attitudinal — allowed for a sense of order to prevail in American politics. Democrats, usually, stood for something; the voter did not need to know the details on every issue to reasonably assume that his party was different from the Republicans' and that it served different group needs. These are no longer safe assumptions.

A president, regardless of how liberal or conservative his program might be in contrast to that espoused by the congressional party, could count on his legislative party leaders to support his major recommendations, and therefore those of the party nationally, and to exercise their influence to have these enacted. Again, this is no longer the case. Likewise, party leaders within Congress had the tools — in consultation with the baronial committee chairpersons — to force a degree of loyalty to party-endorsed programs and therefore to deliver in some manner on policy commitments. The results were often a cautious, conservative muddle of programs; Congress was run by its most conservative interests (southerners; committee chairpersons from noncompetitive areas; interest groups with a personal stake in supporting or opposing legislation). Bold programs were hard to come by, and it took, normally, a national crisis in order to force Congress to move (Birmingham on civil rights; the Watts rioting on urban decay; Vietnam on the war powers of the president; and so on). It was not a happy situation, and it is often forgotten. A major reason for the rise of the imperial presidency, beginning with Franklin Roosevelt and the New Deal and extending through John Kennedy, Lyndon Johnson, and Richard Nixon, was the inability of Congress and the political parties to give adequate attention to the nation's needs.

More and more, voters looked to the presidency for leadership with results that in the long run (Watergate) may have been predictable.

A Congress factionalized and divided to the point that it cannot act on policy questions is an unpleasant prospect. One less under the control of the president and its own more repressive elements has some positive elements. The congressional party may be in decline, but a congressional membership more in tune with and responsive (in a service-oriented way) to its constituents may allow for a more flexible approach to policy issues and one more immediately responsive to the ongoing concerns of the nation. This may be a best case example, but it is a possibility.

Toward securing the end of a Congress more in tune with its electorate, one must check the advantages of incumbency. A limitation on PAC contributions to negate their presently overwhelming influence on elections would be welcome. Also, and more generally, the public funding of congressional (and other level) elections, with spending quotas set sufficiently high to allow challengers to compete effectively with incumbents, would be a step in the right direction.

The dissolution of the party in the electorate raises other questions. To date, political parties have been the most effective vehicle found for mobilizing an electorate and, in its highly imperfect way, representing the views and serving the needs of the outgroups. Without political parties, the less well-off have no effective, consistent representational outlet. Coupled with the decline in all forms of political participation by lower socioeconomic groups, these are disturbing developments. A discontented group — and any coalition of groups not serviced by the government and its policy rewards would increase its distance from the political system — is not a happy prospect for a democracy. It has been argued that neglected lower socioeconomic groups of this type provide fertile recruiting grounds for demagogues, from the Huey Longs and Father Coughlins to the George Wallaces of the future. The threat is real enough. Political parties incorporated these groups into the government, gave them a stake in its decision making, and educated them to the nature of their own role in the political process as well as to the limits that could reasonably be expected from government activity. The parties also acted as a restraint on the prospective candidate. To win, he had to satisfy the needs of a broad coalition. To accomplish his goal, he had to be (normally) an experienced politician (thus ensuring some skill in governing) sensitive to the wishes of a diverse, but interconnected, constituency. The party provided the coherence to this coalition, and it placed limitations on what a leader could or could not do. The checks generally worked well. The system was not foolproof — the Nixon Administration's Watergate crisis is hard to explain in this context — but it did serve the ends of responsible, reasonable government managed by experienced professionals and representative of the interests of most of the groups in the nation's electorate. These functions are unlikely to be performed by any other agency. The loss to the system in these regards is incalculable.

This is not to suggest that responsible and moderate government is less likely to occur in the future. What it does argue is that the restraining influence of the political parties on candidates, campaigns, and governmental excesses will not operate as it has in the past. Similarly, the representative qualities of parties competing in a broader and more inclusive electorate is also likely to decrease.

There is no immediate or obvious solution to these dilemmas. It may be that a higher order of electorate is evolving, one with a direct concern for policy outcomes, blinded less by habitual party loyalties and more demanding of a responsive government on the contemporary issues it considers important. In such a scenario, the decline in participation — at least as worrisome as the decline in performance of its traditional functions by the party — may be a short-term phenomenon, indicative of an electorate in flux. If so, and under the right conditions, involvement in American politics could increase over the coming decades, as the governing system becomes more directly responsive to its citizenry and their concerns.

In this last regard the role of the media, especially television, could be extremely important. The failure of television to fulfill its potential as an information-distribution and educational outlet has concerned everyone from social commentators to television critics. The problems with television as they relate to the political parties are discussed in this book. There is enormous power inherent in television to reach, educate, and involve the American citizenry more knowledgeably in its political affairs. If the concept of television constituting a public service enterprise and the belief that the airways actually do belong to the people ever gains currency, and both are heard often from representatives of the television industry and from government officials, changes of consequence could occur. The debate over the role of television and its contribution to American society is not new. The very fact that it has continued so long with little to be shown for the effort expended indicates that, realistically, little change can be anticipated.

CONCLUSION

The structure of American politics has changed in fundamental ways. These changes are likely to continue over the next several decades. A new political order is emerging with consequences yet unclear. One thing is certain. The role of the political parties within this new political arrangement will be different. More than likely, their impact will be reduced and their contributions to the governing system and the society nowhere near as substantial as they have been in the past.

It is possible to anticipate many of the changes that will come, to debate their consequences, and to move to alleviate some of the worst of the potential problems that are likely to arise. The United States has been an experiment in democratic governance, and quite clearly this experimentation will continue. Part of the debate over the emerging political order should concern the proper role and functioning a revitalized party system could play.

We end on a somber note. E. E. Schattschneider, one of the more eminent students of political parties, has claimed, "the political parties created democracy and . . . modern democracy is unthinkable save in terms of the parties."[1] Maybe so. Schattschneider was writing well over a generation ago. The contemporary era may be forced to adjust to a democratic system in which political parties no longer play a dominant role. The transformation is in progress. Future decades may see the trends developed in this book accentuated. If so, a partyless era, with implications still uncertain, may be settling on us.

[1] E. E. Schattschneider, *Party Government* (New York: Holt, Rinehart and Winston, 1942), p. 1

Index